AMBASSADORS OF
Goodwill

MARK PEEL

Touched by
Greatness
The story of Tom Graveney,
England's much-loved cricketer

21
JUL 1899
ENGLAND
ON THIS DAY
HISTORY, FACTS AND FIGURES
FROM EVERY DAY OF THE YEAR
27
MAY 1981
RICHARD MURPHY

T0294307

FLETCHER S

THE SECR
CRICKET
ENGLISH CRICKET FROM TH

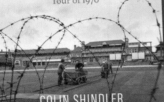
BARBED WIRE
AND CUCUMBER SANDWICHES
The Controversial South Africa
Tour of 1970

COLIN SHINDLER
FOREWORD BY SIR MICHAEL PARKINSON CBE

OVER
AND OUT
Albert Trott:
The Man Who
Cleared the
Lord's Pavilion

Steve Neal

KEEPER OF
STYLE
JOHN MURRAY, THE KING OF LORD'S

CHRISTOPHER SANDFORD

All Wick
Great and S

IN SEARCH
GRASSROO
JOHN FU

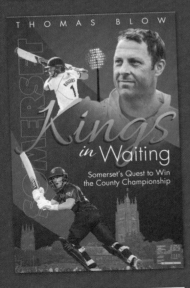
THOMAS BLOW
Kings
in **Waiting**
Somerset's Quest to Win
the County Championship

28 DAYS DATA

PETER MILLER AND DAVE TICKNER

IN THE
SHADOW
OF PACKER
1977/78
BY DAVID BATTERSBY

"One can feel nothing but admiration for the tenacity of
Gray's pursuit... it belatedly gives the losers their say."
Gideon Haigh

2020
Longlist

THE
UNFORGIVEN
Mercenaries or Missionaries?
ASHLEY GRAY

The untold stories of the rebel
West Indian cricketers who toured
apartheid South Africa

David Tossell
THE
GIRLS
OF SUMMER

"Excellent"
THE WAR

REAL INTERNATIONAL
CRICKET
A History in

Also available at all good book stores

9781785318405

9781785318191

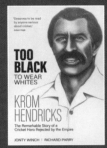

9781785318252

9781785316340

9781785319860

9781785318306

9781785317798

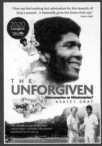

9781785315329

9781785317644

BOWLER'S NAME?

TOM HICKS

BOWLER'S NAME?

The Life of a Cricketing Also-Ran

First published by Pitch Publishing, 2021

Pitch Publishing
A2 Yeoman Gate
Yeoman Way
Worthing
Sussex
BN13 3QZ
www.pitchpublishing.co.uk
info@pitchpublishing.co.uk

ISBN 978 1 78531 841 2

Typesetting and origination by Pitch Publishing
Printed and bound in India by Replika Press Pvt. Ltd.

Contents

Acknowledgements

ALTHOUGH I never achieved my first-life ambition of captaining England, this book represents the fulfilment of a second ambition, and hopefully goes to show that not all the effort and energy put into supporting me has been wasted. And there has been a huge amount of support from so many people, not all of whom can be listed here by name, but I owe thanks to everyone I played with and against on the cricket field, and those who make cricket happen from behind the scenes – the umpires, scorers, administrators, tea-makers, groundstaff. You are all kindred spirits and custodians of this great game. Thanks for being part of my journey.

Above all, I have to thank mum and dad. For the countless hours driving me and Guy around the country (mostly to Taunton), sharing our successes and making sure we didn't take failure too hard. I'm glad that you have been able to be there for so many of the good times and I hope I've made you proud, despite the poor decisions. To my 'little' brother, Guy, for far too much to encapsulate here. I couldn't ask for a better brother. And my auntie/big sister Annie, who I know will be crying with pride reading this. In fact, I couldn't be luckier with my entire family – any family which thinks getting together as a group of 35 for a week at Christmas is normal deserves a mention. I've also been fortunate enough to marry into another remarkably large and equally warm family. Thanks to David and Susan for letting me look after Penny (or vice-versa). Penny – what can I say? You make me so proud every day: I am in awe of you as a person, a wife and amazing mother, not to mention having the most classical cover drive. I love you. And of course the little monkeys – Toby, Jessica and Oscar – who I hope all grow to love the game as much as I do. I hope sport brings you challenge, friendship, success and failure, but above all, fun. Never forget that.

Although not quite family by blood, my 'summer Mum and Dad' – John and Pug Caines – deserve acknowledgement for looking after me on many long Dorset nights, and Tom has been a central part of my life ever since the under-10s. Cricket brought me together with him, Ralph Dorey, Charlie Warren, Tim Lamb and Matt Swarbrick as kids, and gave us lifelong friendships, despite our recent diaspora (look it up, Swarbs).

Specific cricketing thanks go to all the clubs I have played for and all those associated with them. Child Okeford CC, Brook CC, South Wilts CC, Hong Kong Cricket Club and Farnham CC above all. To Oxford University CC, not least Jack Potter and Graham Charlesworth as head coaches. To Dorset County Cricket Club and Phil Lawrence as my first youth coach – still going strong at Port Regis. Amazing. And a special thought to Peter Moxam, Derek Bridge and Ken House, sadly now no longer with us, but who showed me what commitment and service to a county club is all about. The same goes for Sean Walbridge, Richard Scott, Julian Shackleton and Alan Willows as coaches. As for the players, it would be invidious to pick out too many, but Rints, DC, Parky, Lamby, Deaks, Swarbs, Rupes (and Jenny for the cricket tea chapter), Treags, Matty M, Aza – true Leopards, who made a massive impact on me. At the MCC, thanks to all those who managed games for me as Area Rep and all the tourists, not least Luke

Stoughton, Phil Wise, Darren Bicknell and Darren Cousins. I hope I haven't given away too many secrets. The Clayesmore Cormorants, and Andrew Beaton and Greg Swaby, especially for being the driving force behind the club, Blanty, the Dikes, Morgan x 2, Gav Tew, all the Lacks. And back at school, Roger Denning for extending the cow-corner boundary, doubling my wicket tally. And my surrogate big brother Graeme Owton – heroes don't come bigger than you, mate. We'll get there with being colleagues one day.

Away from cricket, I have to thank the staff and leadership teams at all the schools where I have taught: St. George's Weybridge; Lord Wandsworth College; Wellington College; Uppingham School and Harrow International School Hong Kong – thanks to those who allowed me time to indulge my hobby and to those who had to cover for me. I promise it was worth it.

Chris Radmann, Virginia MacGregor, Polly Evans (Gutteridge), Olly Derbyshire for your advice on being a teacher/author and to Andrew Murray and David and Pip Edwards for ongoing quality control. To Ian Higgins of The Grade Cricketer podcast and Farnham CC for advice and support. Also to the whole Catz crew – 'it takes me back'.

Finally to Luke Sutton, who, from our very first phone call, has understood my vision and has been instrumental in making my dreams come true. I hope there is much more to come.

Introduction

WHEN I set out to write this book, it could have taken on many different angles. For a time I wanted it to be something of a cricketing cultural history, exploring this most English of games at a time when it was undergoing seismic change. The 'flannelled fools' I grew up reading about are giving way to a game hardly recognisable to that which grew up in the green fields of Hampshire and Surrey. And my own cricket career came at a time just before this revolution: the Minor Counties no longer exist by that name, and the university game is a pale imitation of what it once was. So to be the last first-class Oxford captain to toss up at Lord's is a marginal note of which I am proud, and represents a world for which I am nostalgic. Not that I dislike the modern game at all – far from it.

The book might also have been more sharply focused on mental health, something which is rightly gaining far more exposure. I do touch on the challenges facing men in particular, which can be alleviated by sport, but which can also be horribly exacerbated by the pressures of sport. Cricket is unique in many ways: the brutal reality of only having one chance with the bat, the threat of the dreaded 'yips' and long periods of time during which to brood on loss of form or a poor decision against you. It is uniquely lonely in being a team game played out as individual battles and can be unrelenting in exposing weaknesses not only in skill, but in character. Having to walk away from the game through injury, age or selection is a hard pill to swallow. Others have suffered more than me, and have done a far better job of articulating issues of mental health in sport. I would love it, though, if this book was able to open people's eyes to the fact that mental health issues are not just a professional player's problem. If just one person reaches out for support as a result of my story, I'd be delighted.

It might have been a book about leadership. Indeed, there is a chapter devoted to captaincy, but it is more a parody of Mike Brearley's outstanding *The Art of Captaincy* than any serious treatise. Time will tell if there is a leadership book in me, and much of my leadership experience will have stemmed from the litany of mistakes I have made, many of which are captured, or at least alluded to here. My biggest failing, I think, is a common one: fear of failure. Looking back with the coolness and perspective of being long past it as a player, I can psychoanalyse the young man who dreamt of going from his Dorset county roots to becoming captain of England. I am convinced that the constant attempts at humour, playing the fool, and the far too many nights out were often a shield for failure. If I wasn't fully prepared, then I could always blame myself and imagine how good I might have been had I focused more. I rarely, if ever, gave myself the chance to be my very best, possibly because it would have been too hard to take if my best was found out to be not good enough. I learned that there is a lot of truth in the cliché that you only get one shot at life, and have had to reconcile myself to my own choices.

So in the end *Bowler's Name?* ended up being a reflection of the cricketing life I actually led. I have given much of my life to cricket, but it has given me back so much more. This book is an attempt to capture some of the richness of my own cricketing journey. Some of it is serious, some silly, some may be controversial and might even border on the distasteful. It is my own story, or at least a version of it, and I am privileged to be able to tell it. I hope many aspects will be recognisable to cricket lovers and anyone who likes a good yarn. Some anecdotes have been omitted, some may have become hazy in the memory and some names may have been changed to protect the innocent (and the guilty!) If any offence or embarrassment is caused, I offer my heartfelt apologies. Above all I hope it is fun and lends some entertainment at a time when the world sorely needs it.

'And when the one great scorer

Comes to write against your name,

He marks not that you won or lost,

But how you played the game.'

Chapter One

Early Days

THIS IS a book about cricket.

And about me.

If you picked it up, you probably know what cricket is, and there's a good chance you like it. It's highly unlikely you've ever heard of me.

If I am honest, I am a nobody. A statistic. An occupant of a very low rung on the cricketing food chain. If you Google my name you will find hundreds of articles about the multi-millionaire American former owner of Liverpool Football Club. If you are a cricket fan, you might have slipped as you were typing in the name of Zimbabwean run-machine and England Test batsman Graeme Hick and landed on my name. But if we are honest, I am really utterly anonymous.

So what on earth makes me think I'm qualified to write a book about cricket?

Well, firstly, I'm not a totally terrible cricketer. And although you've never heard of me, I managed for a good 25 years to rub shoulders with some of the game's greats, and to play on some of the world's finest grounds as I shuffled along in cricket's margins. As a former captain of Oxford University and Dorset County Cricket Club, I made a career in a world which no longer exists. After fossilising for decades, university cricket is no longer first-class and the Minor Counties Championship is also now a relic. I guess that makes me a dinosaur.

And yet I've led teams out at the Home of Cricket; I have a first-class fifty and five-wicket haul to my name; there is a Wikipedia page about me which someone must have written; I've been sworn at by Test legends; nightclubbed with the fastest bowler of his generation; showered with one of my England heroes; shared cigarettes with an Ashes winner. I even have a World Cup winner's medal on my mantelpiece. And more.

I may still be a dinosaur, but I'm a dinosaur with a tale to tell.

The Best Team in the World

I'm not entirely sure where my passion for cricket came from, but I certainly became obsessed with the game from an early age, completing mini-projects at home on the Ashes, reading Bradman's *The Art of Cricket* and *Barclays World of Cricket* cover-to-cover, as well as any other cricket literature I could get my hands on. I suspect I covered some ground which was not age-appropriate, dipping into the autobiographies of Ian Botham, Phil Edmonds and others, and many of the jokes flew above my head. But it was a world I wanted to be part of.

I was found one summer holiday with my nose deep in a book on cricket I'd found in the boot of the car, unaware that this was intended as a birthday present for me which had yet to be wrapped up. In those days, if there was cricket about, in any form, I'd sniff it out. Early photos of me on holiday show a little boy of five or six fully padded up in roasting heat in France. My parents tell of being scolded by French families who thought they had put their son into some kind of torture device, rather than him pretending to be David Gower, and forcing any relative who came close to offer endless throwdowns. Another photo shows me next to my brother, who won the fancy-dress prize at a village fete for his caveman costume. Again, there I am, dressed like a baby Gower.

There were endless tournaments of 'pencil cricket', like the dice game 'Owzthat', played between teams made up of internationals, county scorecards found in the newspaper and school teams. So you could quite easily find the Under-11 Clayesmore Prep School team thrashing England, with our *victor ludorum* Nic Hillyard scoring a double century against the likes of Gladstone Small and Phil DeFreitas. But if that was not strange enough to comprehend, the majority of the cricket my brother Guy and I conducted – on paper or in the garden – was by using our vast array of soft toys and teddy bears as the cricketing All Stars. So detailed and ingrained was our imaginary world, that I can still recite the Toys' first XI now and give you a description of their skills and characteristics. Here is the side which was undisputed in quality in the Hicks household in the late 1980s:

1. Big Ted: Captain and elder statesman. Think Graham Gooch. Had been my mother's favourite teddy and as such, fell foul in later years of being retired at the statutory age of 18. Rather like Alastair Cook, finding an adequate replacement was hard, although Big Sooty (a panda glove-puppet) and Brown Sooty (no relation) both had a go. Big Ted actually had a proper bat made for him by our lovely neighbour, Bob, which doubled up for late-night indoor games when mum and dad were out at the pub quiz.

2. Big Jumbo: As the name suggests, a big elephant. Indian heritage but England qualified. Solid foil to Big Ted. The Sutcliffe to his Hobbs.

3. Little Florri: Adam Gilchrist before he was even a thing. Little Florence was a miniature finger-

puppet frog, who combined being a stylish right-handed bat with being an extremely agile wicketkeeper. Like several of this team, he also made it into the Toys football team and rugby team (oh yes, we had these as well, as goalkeeper and scrum-half respectively). Quite literally, the greatest sportsman since C.B. Fry.

4.   Little Sooty: Another finger puppet. Little Sooty fitted into the pouch of the aforementioned Big Sooty, but outplayed his big brother (the toy designers were probably thinking more mother and baby, but what were we to care?) Dependable right-hander in the mould of Graeme Hick, with the occasional off-spin to boot. Became captain after Big Ted's retirement.

5.   Crums: The only girl to make the team, although I think this probably made us quite progressive considering the era. Crums was a tiger glove puppet bought at Longleat, who channelled Ian Botham – big hitting but without the tearaway pace of the 1981 vintage. Think that spell in Melbourne in 1986 when he strangled a five-wicket haul bowling at 'gnat's pace'. A game-changer.

6.   Goonie: Goonie was one of my brother's favourite toys. A glove-puppet gorilla and boyfriend to Crums, who bowled at the speed of light with the action of Ezra Moseley. Would usually take the new ball, although the Toys' West Indian pace barrage was as feared as even the greatest four-pronged attack the real Caribbean ever produced. Goonie probably batted too high at No.6, but offered a left-handed variation to the top order. The only issue with this being that both Guy and I are right-handed.

7. Bommer: A late addition to the squad, given to me on the eve of the Oval Test in 1989 (when Alan Igglesden and John Stephenson were about the thousandth people to get an Ashes cap that summer). Bommer was a walrus who also bowled fast with a high, chest-on action. I think I was going for something like Martin Bicknell but quicker when deciding on this one.

8. Brownie: Also fast. Bowled like Jeff Thomson, with a high front leg and slingy action – unmistakeable. Hailed from a combination of the Caribbean and County Armagh. Clearly I'd picked up some of the news stories of the time, as we came up with the tragic narrative of Brownie Bear's parents being killed by the IRA.

9. Wonkwing: So-called because he was a bird with a wonky wing. Fast-medium but like the bowler on whom he was fashioned – Terry Alderman – deadly. Always one to go for when the Gooch-like Big Ted was batting … Wonky went everywhere with me – on tour, to university. A real good-luck mascot, whose shape meant he didn't play rugby for the Toys, but acted as the ball itself.

10. Little Munk: Another finger puppet. This one was Malcolm Marshall, which was perfect as the bending run-up was required to negotiate the shape of our patio.

11. Whistle: Steady off-spinner and tortoise. Spin was not a big feature of the Toys' team, which is surprising since Guy and I both went on to bowl off-spin. A small garden does not lend itself to tweakers, though, and who wants to bowl spin anyway?

12. Little Jumbo: Recognising the need for leg-spin, Little Jumbo was our one concession to this, but as

we were both a bit rubbish at landing our leggies,
we rarely opted for L.J.

Our games followed a strict format, with each bowler only getting two overs and batsmen retiring at 25, but being able to resume the innings once the other brother had had their turn. You had to bowl and bat in the manner which was appropriate to the agreed skills of that player. That is, if you had chosen Big Ted, it was bad form to start slogging across the line, whilst if you chose Wonkwing, you were duty bound to keep the pace reasonable and not fling it down as hard as you might with Little Munk or Brownie, say. This kept us from arguing too much, and prolonged our games, as did being able to blame a dismissal on Little Sooty's poor shot selection, rather than seeing it as a personal failure. Given that my brother was prone to the most epic of 'wobblies' as we called them, this sort of preservation was in both of our best interests.

My mother remembers games of Monopoly which would end up with the board overturned, plastic hotels flying across the dining room and metal top hats and irons pinging into the furthest-flung corners of upholstery. She recalls that on one occasion he went to bed in such a fit of pique that he even woke up still angry. He had all the excuses – the pitch was too bumpy, the ball was too hard, or too soft, the shed had cheated (yes, such was my brother's sense of injustice at getting out, or letting in a goal, that he felt inanimate objects had come alive, simply to conspire against him).

So when it came to garden sport, for me it *was* about winning (when is it ever not?), but this was balanced with an understanding that cricket or football on your own is about as much fun as playing 'ball-in-a-cup'.

However, our forces were aligned when pitted against a common enemy. We had a shared nemesis in the small but menacing shape of our next-door neighbour – 'Bossy Barbara'.

Barbara was about 4ft, with wispy hair – on her chin, that is – and an even shorter fuse than my impatient younger sibling. And yet she was married to the kindest, gentlest soul: Bob, who would often fill us with chilled Robinsons Barley Water whilst helping us make wooden toys in his shed. Barbara on the other hand seemed delivered from Satan to be the scourge of any young boy who had the audacity to want to have fun in her vicinity.

If the ball happened to clear our fence and end up next door, a dark shade descended on our garden and a chill wind made our little hearts shudder. One of us would have to take our life in our hands and run the gauntlet to fetch it. It's funny how history repeats itself. Now, when my children are playing garden cricket, they face an equally intimidating foe. And do you know what? I'm just as scared to ask for their ball back as I ever was back then. I hope I never become a grumpy so-and-so like that.

School Cricket

Of course, at school, sport was more serious and you couldn't go around pretending you were some finger-puppet frog if you wanted to get into the team, although I have later had some hilarious partnerships with Guy in real cricket in which we pretended to be our toys, unbeknownst to the opposition.

It did take me a bit of time to adjust to the real game and, in my first innings at under-10 level, I walked out to bat with no gloves and continued to do so as it was more comfortable. It wasn't long before I really started to enjoy the matches and the choice to be a spinner paid off, as there were no restrictions in those days, and I could bowl spells as long as I, or the teacher/coach, liked. The choice to bowl spin, I think, came from another cricket book – Ladybird's *The Story of Cricket* – which showed a grip, and I thought I'd try it out. Once a couple of fellow pupils had made themselves look silly by running past a flighted off-break, or chipped it up in the air, I realised that there was a lot of success to be had from loopy spin, and so I never went for anything else.

And although I wasn't an amazing batsman, I was certainly better than most at school and scored my first hundred in the under-11 team against Chafyn Grove School from Salisbury, using a borrowed GM Striker – the even better version of the Maestro, which was the go-to bat of choice in the school kit bag (although the County Turbo was not far behind). Had there been a Duncan Fearnley Magnum, it would have been a really tough choice (not the Colt, which was my first real bat, left for me to find in my bed one evening by my parents, which I lovingly linseeded and sanded, and knocked in for hours, much to their displeasure).

Real cricket aficionados can tell a cricketer's era from the bats they remember being fashionable when they were growing up. If you are ever stuck for conversation with a cricketer, I promise you, they won't be able to resist this one.

Important bats of my era
- *Duncan Fearnley Magnum*
- *Gray Nicolls Dynadrive*
- *Kookaburra Ridgeback*
- *Hunts County Turbo*
- *Gunn and Moore Striker or Maestro*
- *Slazenger V12*
- *Stuart Surridge Turbo*

Of the era, but not the one you really wanted
- *Powerspot Tufcoat*
- *Duncan Fearnley Colt*
- *Gunn and Moore Skipper*
- *Hunts County Reflex*
- *Stuart Surridge Jumbo*

A tradition at my prep school was that if you scored a hundred for the school you received a bat as a reward, and so after my century, during which my dad was umpiring (surely a coincidence…), I was dropped several times, and after which I insisted on pouring a cup of orange squash on myself as I'd seen real cricketers do with champagne, the headmaster called me up in assembly to hand me … an SS Jumbo.

Proud as I was to get the award, this was certainly not the bat of choice, screaming as it did of middle-order Indian no-hoper, rather than what a GM Maestro might have done for my street-cred, making me more into a Steve Waugh-type player. And these things matter when you are 11.

Nonetheless, I did put the Jumbo into action later that season for my county team, using it to score an unbeaten (although certainly not chanceless) ton against Somerset at Taunton School. This remains the only time I scored three figures under a county banner at any age, not a record of which I am proud.

By Royal Appointment

My first representative wicket has a blue-blooded story attached. It was for the Dorset Under-10s at Port Regis School – a rather well-to-do prep school – when I was just eight. I don't know how they selected these teams, but I do know that I was entirely unprepared and felt a total fish out of water. Not least because I did not have any white trousers (at school we played in our school shorts, with a white shirt instead of the normal grey), my jumper had been knitted by my grandma and my boots were full rubbers with a rather natty frill over the laces. They were, in fact, golf shoes bought from a local charity shop, but it took meeting my team-mates, who all seemed to have the requisite gear, with sewn-on badges and no knobbly knees in sight, to make me realise it.

It is all a bit of a hazy memory, but I am pretty certain I opened the batting with an enormous, jovial lad called Andy Long, who hit the ball extremely hard and later bowled a very heavy ball – not an expression you often hear at under-10s. In fact, Andy went on to a pretty successful professional rugby career with Bath, and did actually win a cap or two for England in the front row. He was certainly a legend of the junior scene in Dorset, so I was pretty starstruck even then. I have a vague recollection of scoring six singles before being dismissed. No duck at least.

I doubt very much whether I would remember this game at all, were it not for the excitement which greeted me when I returned to the picnic blanket where my parents and my nan were sitting. Nan – or Nanny – as we called her (I have to distinguish, since at places like Port Regis, most of the pupils have actual nannies, or *au pairs*) had clocked that our next to bat, and wicketkeeper for the day was Peter Phillips. That is, Peter Phillips, son of Princess Anne. Not just cricketing royalty, actual royalty!

Now, Nanny was a feisty south London lass, who was known for her Sid James laugh and huge appetite for life. She was not going to let this opportunity go begging, and so whilst the poor lad was waiting for his turn to bat, she marched around the boundary to where he stood and promptly addressed the Queen's grandson with the question:

'I'm here to watch my grandson, where's your gran today, then?'

History does not relate whether Peter Phillips dignified this impertinence with a response, but Nanny dined out on the moment for weeks.

Again, I barely remember bowling on that day, although I do have a picture somewhere of me in my shorts, tongue out, delivering some embryonic off-spin in this game. What I do know is that somewhere there may still exist a scorecard which reads 'Stumped HRH Peter Phillips (*sic*), Bowled Hicks'. I've watched every episode of *The Crown* vainly expecting a cameo.

Young Guns go on Tour

My bowling was going great guns, and at Under-13 level, I took more than 50 wickets in a season for Dorset, including seven- and eight-wicket hauls, as well as five-fers for fun. I even took five wickets in my first 'international' match, for the West of England against the Netherlands, back at Port Regis. Playing for the region was the next step on what today would be called the 'player pathway', and I was selected to go on tour with the West of England to the Caribbean in the winter of 1993/94. There is still no feeling quite like opening a letter which has a team-sheet with your name on it, and the excitement was palpable. Not least for mum and dad, who could see a tropical holiday looming for the first time since they'd had kids.

This was when you really did start feeling like professional cricket might be a realistic future for you. Things started happening, like residential training camps where former players would come and speak to you about subjects such as the 'mental side of the game' which you'd never thought about before. I seem to remember Chris Old giving up his Christmas Eve to address the squad in the meeting room of a Travelodge somewhere near Bridgwater. There is a certain sort of modern tragedy in this, particularly considering the last I heard of Chris Old – hero of Headingley 1981 – was that he was working on the tills in a supermarket in Cornwall.

You had to keep a food diary, training plans were handed out on photocopied paper, with ideas for fitness work as well as the obvious batting, bowling and fielding drills. Some players even had sponsorship deals with bat companies and the chat was all about what sort of discount you were on (most companies were happy to give 25% as a matter of course, if it meant you spent hundreds on the whole kit and caboodle). Measurements for things like blazers and tour kit were taken, and when we made the final of many round-trips to Taunton before the tour, there laid out for us was a whole pile of official kit, all embroidered and personalised. Did we feel special, or what?

Flying out to Port-of-Spain on Christmas Day 1993 to play cricket, I couldn't have asked Santa for a better present. To say we took time to acclimatise would be a huge understatement. Up until then, my only experience of touring was the three-day Under-11 festival in Cornwall, and there's not much similarity between Truro and Trinidad.

Whilst we had been prepared for the experience in the manner of young professionals, it appeared the memo had not reached the locals, as the grounds we played at were typically ramshackle, with poorly prepared pitches and outfields of long, coarse grass. We were resplendent in our pristine new whites, fresh out of the cellophane, whilst our opponents were doing well if they had collars on their shirts and their trainers were white, not black. It was hard not to be disparaging, although we soon found ourselves chastened when play began as we were taught a lesson on and off the field. It was a great experience to show us how – clichéd though it may sound – sport levels the playing field. I believe we all grew more tolerant and understanding of different cultures as a result of that first trip.

The highlight was playing on New Year's Day at Queen's Park Oval – the famous old Test arena in Trinidad. It was a huge honour to be selected to walk out and play on a ground where England were due in a few weeks' time, and also an honour to be presented to Trinidad's greatest son, Brian Charles Lara. We had seen Lara practising in the nets as we arrived and he was hot off the back of making his name with a stunning double-hundred in Australia. When he walked down the line, shaking our hands, we were not to know that he was about to change cricketing history during that England tour. Nor was I to know that my next meeting with the world record-breaker would be in altogether different circumstances, several years later.

In the opposition that day was another future West Indies star – Daren Ganga – whom I dropped from a simple caught-and-bowled. Fair play to Daren, he went on to make more of his opportunity to play professional cricket than I did, with a smattering of Test caps and a career as a respected commentator.

After that match, we left Trinidad for the rest of the tour in Grenada and Barbados, but before we left the ground I put a message in one of the dressing room lockers for England captain Michael Atherton. I doubt if he ever received it, but I feel that act shows just how inspired I was by getting the chance to walk in the shadows of my heroes. I hope that all professional clubs in any sport do all they can to open the doors for young hopefuls to visit, train and play in their facilities, as it can fuel the imagination like nothing else. That the memory is still there for me is testament to that.

I was also excited on that tour to meet Larry Gomes – the West Indies batsman, who was well known to me from our well-worn VHS *On Top Down Under*, charting the one-day success of the England side in Australia on the 1986/87 Ashes tour. Gomes appeared one morning at our hotel, for no apparent reason, and came right up to our group with the welcome: 'Hi, I'm Larry Gomes.' I'm not sure if this is just a Caribbean thing; the next time I met Brian Lara, he did something similar, but with all respect to Gomes, he's hardly the household name Brian is.

I'm not sure if my team-mates were equally as excited by the opportunity to rub shoulders with famous players past and present, but I lapped it up. Whether it was Everton Weekes (one of the great Three Ws of Barbados legend), Dennis Breakwell (who tended the grounds at King's College, Taunton, but was also a close mucker of Joel Garner, Viv Richards and Ian Botham), or just getting the chance to see the ultimate great – Sir Garfield Sobers – across the pavilion in Bridgetown, I always felt the glow of reflected stardom and would seek it out at any opportunity. Once a cricket nut, always a cricket nut, I guess.

England Duty

The next big-ticket selection for an aspiring young player during my teenage years was to make it into the winter training camp at the National Centre for Excellence at Lilleshall. The centre no longer exists, with Loughborough now the official place for cricket development, but in those days it was a byword for elite training, in cricket and soccer. When the letter came for this one, I was really made up. This meant, for whatever reason, that I had been picked as one of the best in my region, let alone county, and in fact only two other players from the West were going, and I was the only spinner. There were only two off-spinners there for the three-day camp. Me, and a lively lad from Northamptonshire by the name of Graeme Swann. The coaches were all big names, with Micky Stewart, the former England coach leading a session on batting, and the England psychologist Steve Bull doing sessions on 'mental toughness' and 'positive mental attitude' which were the buzz-phrases of the day. The spin coach was Fred Titmus, one of England's finest off-spinners. He was so positive that even when you bowled a massive full-bunger or rank long-hop, he would say, with a sparkle in his eye, 'Ah, lad, but it's got a deadly quality; it's going to hit the stumps!'

He worked with John Barclay, another great offie, who I loved working with, too. We really were very fortunate. I don't remember much about Graeme at that stage other than his charisma and self-belief. I was probably a bit intimidated as well;

this was a guy I thought would definitely play for England, at least in our year group.

School Days

Meanwhile, my day-to-day cricket took place at school and for the age groups in Dorset. School was for the most part at Clayesmore, a small but beautiful private school, less well-known than its local counterparts, Bryanston, Canford and Sherborne. If you add Milton Abbey into this mix, you have some of the loveliest cricket grounds in the south of England. Private school pupils have no idea how lucky they are playing on manicured grounds in gorgeous settings.

I was lucky enough to have a cricket-lover for a deputy headmaster in the form of Roger Denning, a former Durham student and left-arm spinner, whose sons were also cricket-mad and lived a few doors away from us on the school site after dad took up the post of housemaster. I wouldn't underestimate the importance of having ready net partners for long afternoons and weekends of practice, as well as the free use of all the school facilities. I don't think my parents saw us during our free time for a few years, and I bet they were delighted! Denning was great: not only would he happily send anyone playing for the first team out of his geography lessons to put the boundary flags out, but he also took the unprecedented step of extending the cow-corner boundary by ten metres on one side, purely as he recognised that my flighted off-spin would draw many batsmen into holing out on the slog. How right he was – we stationed our best catcher there and even in my first year at senior school (year nine equivalent), I took 30 wickets, with at least ten caught where in previous years the ball would have gone for six.

I was also lucky enough to open the batting with a promising young player who was making waves in the school cricket world.

Matt Swarbrick scored a thousand runs in his final season at the school, including something like ten centuries in a row, on his way to bagging a contract with Hampshire after completing his A-levels. With Swarbs rattling on at around six runs an over, it was easy enough for me to tick over and keep giving him the strike. The pressure was off to such an extent that in my GCSE year I scored well over 600 runs, averaging in the sixties – a fine return in any other year – which was largely unnoticed in the shadow of his exploits. To be fair, our fixture list was not as strong as all that: we played the second teams of Millfield and Sherborne, and my two hundreds that year were against the Forty Club (members qualified by being over 40, so the Dorset branch saw a regular turnout of sawdusty, bearded folk with canvas pads and jaunty cloth caps, who couldn't chase down a single for love nor money), and the equally harmless Dorset Police (some of whom were the same chaps who played for the Forty Club). Still, you can only play what's in front of you.

We had a yearly tour with school, too, which took us to Victoria College, Jersey, Bearwood College in Berkshire and Abbotsholme School in Staffordshire. These trips allowed us to add to the season's stats, but also represented a rite of passage, as boarding alongside some of the sixth-form lads under minimal supervision might have been expected to do (nothing too sinister, but my first taste of, and suffering at the hands of, cider happened on one of these tours, and my first cigarette). Cricket was already starting to give me an education for life.

Chapter Two

Growing Up on the Village Green

Child Okeford CC

My fledgling cricket education was not confined only to school, however. During these years, my dad was captain of a village side in Dorset called Child Okeford. On weeknights, the junior side played a version of pairs cricket, in which each pair could face four overs each. I only remember these games vaguely, except for one encounter I had with a lad called Karl who was one of the only 'local' lads in the team, most of whom were my mates from the 'posh' school. On padding up, I noticed that Karl wasn't bothering with a box. Trying to help, I asked him if he thought it may be a useful thing to pop on, just in case. 'No it's all right, Tom, I've got a stiffy!' was his response. The mind still boggles when I consider what was going through young Karl's mind.

But the club came alive on Sundays. This was real grassroots stuff, and the motley crew of builders, truck drivers, sparkies and whoever could be persuaded to turn out at last orders on a Saturday night became my first real heroes. Every Sunday, the local rec became the field of dreams: men of seemingly epic scale bestrode the sward like colossi, emanating from the inner sanctum of the minuscule changing rooms, all odour of Deep Heat and Silk Cut. There was Jonah – Dave Jones – groundsman-cum-opening bowler. As he was the one who cut the pitch, his was the right to the new ball and the downhill slope. He approached the crease with legs working like pistons and a left-arm over whirlwind action which my young mind imagined was faster than Botham or Willis. Like several in the team, he sported the classic 1980s moustache and open-necked shirt combo and swore and cussed like a sailor on leave. He was also something of a local hero when it came to the annual village fete, or 'Hey-Day' as it was known, when the welly-throwing, hoopla and tug-of-war gave way to a live band in the beer tent. For Jonah was the drummer in 'The Hurricanes' (later the T-Birds), whose lead singer, Deano, gave such a performance every year that he was Elvis, Tom Jones and Danny from *Grease* rolled into one. The village wives would be aflush as Deano serenaded them from halfway up the pole of the marquee, whilst the blokes swilled pints of Badger Bitter, their teenage kids rolling around on hay bales and behind the football dugouts, drunk on White Lightning and the first flushes of young love.

Up the hill, Statham to Jones's Trueman, came Martin 'Ollie' Oliver, whose family ran the famous Great Dorset Steam Fair every August and whose old man, Michael, sticks in my mind as the caller at the Christmas village bingo. Everyone in the village knew his schtick and as children we loved the sauciness of wolf-whistling at his 'Legs Eleven', giggling at 'Two Fat Ladies', and being downright confused why we had to ask 'Was she worth it?' at 'Seven-and-six'. I still miss the thrill of walking home with a box of Danish butter cookies under one arm and a bottle of Liebfraumilch under the other. It was just a part of Christmas. Ollie – the son – was happy enough to play in a white t-shirt and although he bowled with no front arm and always from the worse end, everyone knew he was more effective than Jonah, but no one would mention it as it would mean likely fisticuffs and no pitch prepared the following week.

The seam attack was completed by Dave 'Sid' Hall, who had two false knees and played in an England rugby shirt. Lovely bloke that he was, I couldn't understand a word he said, which was awkward as he moved in next door to us and loved a chat.

The undoubted hero in my eyes was Anthony 'Lewie' Lewis, whose moustache-mullet-and-medallion combo marked him out as an Achilles. On weekdays, a run-of-the mill builder; on Sundays, and on those glorious Tuesday nights when a cup fixture meant the bonus of watching a 16 eight-ball-over smash (we were doing T20 in Dorset long before it became a thing), Lewie transformed into a Goliath of the game. To my rose-tinted view, he batted and bowled like the great I.T. Botham himself. I was just delighted to score the book and record his exploits.

The other real stalwart was Mike 'Spuddy' Murphy, a long-distance lorry driver who was the whole package: he kept wicket, bowled medium pace 'as tight as a gnat's arse' and had an effective, if idiosyncratic, technique when batting. Left-handed, his front foot would typically splay in the opposite direction to the ball whilst his keen eye and beefy forearms would launch it over point, often into the school field next door or the stinging nettles. The irony was that Spuddy was the past master when it came to finding lost balls in the stingers and would happily retrieve them and hand them back to the hapless bowler ready for more destruction. Like half the team, he also turned out for the football team in the winter, and his missus made the best teacakes and jam in the business.

Among the other key characters were Phil 'Chevy' Cheverton – a crabby, selfish batsman and local Bobby; Alec Angell – chain-smoking darting legend; Joe Cooper, who drove a car with a Status Quo banner across the windscreen; and Alistair

Underwood – umpire of dubious repute who was known to don the whites when a late drop-out occurred. I awaited the day that a drop-out would see dad turn to me and say, 'Do you fancy batting at 11 and fielding at fine leg?' But for years, it seemed, I was too young to put into harm's way, even if the alternative was a bloke sure to get a duck and drop everything that came his way. Then there was Dave Coley – my prep school PE and pottery teacher, one time Harlequin, who had warmed the bench at Twickenham and our next-door neighbour before Sid moved in. Later there was my real hero Graeme Owton, whose school batting records at Clayesmore were only eclipsed by Swarbrick; and also my Uncle Mark, who had the audacity not only to hail from Essex but also to bowl leg-spin. As far as Dorset was concerned, he may have been introducing alchemy or Ouija, so arcane was the art of spin, let alone of the wrist variety, this being before the advent of Shane Warne. Mark's first claim to fame was that he had been on the books of Wolves, and once was offered a contract ahead of Pat Jennings; his second was later playing for a social team known as the 'Two Hopes XI' with one Jofra Archer.

And there were others in this cast of legends, bit-part players in the weekly drama which enthralled my cricket-obsessed brain.

Jane Austen had it right when she wrote, 'Three or four families in a country village is the very thing to work on.' There was enough drama in our particular parochial backwater to fill the pages of several novels (and I was only a child; imagine the sorts of comings-and-goings which were going on after hours and once the Saxon Inn and the Bakers Arms had kicked out after last orders).

As skipper of this fine federation, my old man was quite the Mike Brearley figure. Indeed, his ability actually to set a field marked him out as one of the sharpest cricketing minds in the lower divisions of Dorset cricket. The fact he knew the names for all the positions was just showing off. Having a wife who was happy enough to score most weekends and would collect the match fees just sealed his position.

I'm being a little unfair. Although dad was perhaps not the most talented of cricketers, he did have genuine tactical acumen. He loved to rankle oppositions by setting unorthodox fields and his major stroke of genius was opening the bowling with a spinner, which was tantamount to the devil's own work, even within his own team, who just couldn't get their heads around it. But it certainly worked, and he took this motley crew from a nondescript village in the northern reaches of the county to the brink of the Premier League, where the likes of such big clubs as Weymouth and Dorchester awaited. Granted, the club never got beyond the second tier, but it was a rise to rival dad's (and my) beloved Wimbledon FC – latterly AFC Wimbledon. The romance of the underdog features heavily in Hicks family mythology.

I mentioned he liked to open the bowling with a spinner, and in the days before I was deemed big enough to play, this role fell to the eldest son of our neighbour Dave Coley. Lee was a tall off-spinner, who was just finishing his sixth form at Clayesmore, and another hero of mine for his knowledge of *Dungeons and Dragons*, *Highlander* and *Lord of the Rings* as much as his ability to spin the ball. He won't thank me for mentioning it, but poor old Lee had one particular drama during his time at the club when he ended up staying in the spare bed at our house, not wanting to waken his parents next door after a lengthy celebration in the boozer one Sunday. It so happened that the spare room happened to be the old master bedroom until we had an extension built. It also so happened that my dad had a penchant for sleepwalking, especially when he had been on the whisky (he had once been found starkers on a sun lounger in Gran Canaria in a drunken attempt to outdo the Germans for the best beds). On this night, my mother found herself being shaken awake by a pale and anxious Lee, who had found his old Classics teacher hopping into bed beside him, grunting and snoring away in a malty stupor. 'Kick the bugger out!' was my mum's no-nonsense response. Dad woke up none the wiser but I'm not sure Lee ever looked him in the eye again.

Eventually, my time came, and I was allowed to take my place in the pantheon. I'm sure I did OK, and I remember my younger brother even taking four-fer when he couldn't have been more than 12. Looking out for our names in the *Western Gazette* (you were mentioned if you got 20 or more, which shows the quality of the pitches) was my first sense of 'fame'. I do remember batting out to save the draw to avoid relegation for the last wicket with Lee (of the sleepwalking incident) and running off as if we had won the NatWest Trophy. As with the hero-worship, all these things really did mean that much at the time.

Sadly, like a great many small village clubs, Child Okeford CC has gone the way of the church, the post office and the pubs. I don't want to get all Prince Charles about it, but I do think something about England is lost when rural communities are forced to shut down. Occasionally, when I revisit Dorset for old boys' weeks, I will take a trip down memory lane. Everything is smaller, and Spuddy's sixes don't seem so massive after all; the scorebox has gone, as has the playground, and there is no sign of a 'square' to speak of, not even a miserly rope to cordon off a space which would offer the hope of Jonah coming back on his roller, or the sound of leather on old Duncan Fearnley.

Dorset Youth Cricket

All the while, I was now a regular with the Dorset age-group team, of whom some remain my closest friends. Tom Caines, for one, who became a proper partner-in-crime as we grew from prep school rivals into teenage tearaways, trying to live up to his father's reputation as one of the wildest men in Dorset. Old John Caines was something of a relic of what might be termed the 'days of yore'. A cattle farmer by trade, John was the type of character you imagine stepping out of a Hardy novel, or a John Bull type of national symbol. He was all grizzled chest and beard, forearms like hams and an accent which made John Arlott's sound like cut-glass crystal. Paying little heed to the drink-driving laws, he would work an honest day in the fields and then repair to one or more of the local village inns where he kept his own glass which held well more than a standard pint. He would drink it down to a couple of fingers from the bottom, then ask for it to be filled to the brim with a 'Dorset Half'. He had been a sportsman of note in his younger days, too, and would have played in the junior Wimbledon tennis championships had his father not insisted he work on the farm instead. If he could get to a game to watch his son, he would, and we loved having him there. From the under-15 season onwards, he would think of a number, keeping it to himself, and if any one of us scored that many runs, he would sidle up to us after the game and buy us one of our first pints of Boddingtons or Caffrey's (whatever the entry-level bitter was at the club. You simply did not ask for a lager.) He would also set you a target on the boundary – a fence post or bench which, if you hit it, would earn you another. Many was the summer night I spent at his home, built by his own hands out of the same Dorset soil I felt the man himself was made of.

His wife Judith – 'Pug' to all who knew her – had been something of a glamour girl in her day and spoke like Joanna Lumley. She grew up in Ceylon (never Sri Lanka) and everything about her gave off a whiff of colonial times, from the nightly gin and tonic to the cigarettes, which I would often cadge from her, knowing all the while that her son was desperate for one but didn't have the balls to admit he smoked to his parents. Pug's breakfasts were legendary and a good proportion of my Dorset fixtures, even as a grown-up, would be fuelled by her fried bread and bacon and eggs. Eventually, I had made myself so much at home that she called herself my 'summer mum'. She also often made the teas for the county age-group sides and 'Judy's melons' were very popular with the coaching staff as well as the boys.

Tom – who had been sent off to boarding school at Millfield in Somerset, where he was a contemporary of Dean Cosker, Ben Hollioake and Simon Jones – and I would bat together in the middle order and bowl off-spin at either end. Mine a classical action, his a more dubious bent-arm chuck which was never called a no-ball. Our games complemented each other, as did our characters. We loved nothing more than to play cricket and then find a way to have a few beers, before playing again the next day, or sweating out the hangover with endless games in the garden. We later joined forces again for Farnham in the Surrey Championship when he grew wordly-wise enough to leave the West Country and moved to the gold-paved streets of London.

Then there was Ralph Dorey, child prodigy. Most schools had a Ralph Dorey: six foot and shaving by the time he was 11. When the rest of us were running around pubeless and knock-kneed, Ralph was hitting sixes and kicking goals from outside the 22. He was probably the best all-round sportsman of our year group in the country. He virtually won the Rosslyn Park rugby sevens tournament single-handedly for Sherborne Prep School; he won the national high jump and was second in the sprint final; he was on that West of England cricket tour to the Caribbean with me, and was even county chess champion. If you ever needed something to happen on the field you'd throw the ball to Ralph, who despite bowling at popgun pace had the golden arm. Or he would come up with an outrageous catch or run out from nowhere. So it was no surprise that he too went off to Millfield and continued his close friendship with Tom, cemented by the fact that his father was also a Dorset farmer, great tennis player and contemporary of John's. The tales old man Dorey and old man Caines told marked them out as heroes in our young minds, and we were hell-bent on emulating them in any way we could, even if that meant getting into a few scrapes around the county.

A third mainstay of that young Dorset side was a chap called Charlie Warren, who also lived on a farm (I'm probably cementing a few stereotypes of Dorset here). His father was a Colonel, however, but another discerning gent who would often be seen casting a critical eye over events on the field. Charlie – 'Waz' – was fearless to the point of stupidity. He reckoned he had some Irish roots and played in the front row like Keith Wood on speed, actively seeking out tackles and relishing the pain inflicted. As soon as the restrictions on having a short leg were lifted around the age of 14, he got himself as close as he could to the batsman and gave me and Tom a whole new opportunity to take wickets. And if he got hit, he would take a step closer, grit his teeth and under his breath whisper 'Harder, harder' as we ran in to bowl. He loved opening the batting and whilst he had few shots in his earlier days, he was invaluable as someone who could blunt even the most potent of seam attacks, often taking blows to the body in the process. This was a guy you wanted in the trenches with you. We went on to play for our university together, as will become clear later.

This was the core of the team I grew up with, with some more motley characters thrown in alongside, marshalled by a series of somewhat odd coaches and managers. We were certainly greater than the sum of our parts and exhibited a massive underdog spirit. We loved nothing more than going to flasher counties and getting in their faces. In fact, it was rarely unpleasant, more madcap and self-deprecatory. Caines was the maddest of the lot. For an entire season, he adopted the habit of pushing his bat like a hoover after completing a run, which began to grate on fielding sides, not least when it was accompanied by calls of 'Hooooover' in an exaggerated yokel 'Darzet' accent. When standing at silly mid-off (of course observing the statutory 11-yard safety distance) he would put his head between his legs and make faces at you as you ran in. And he it was who invented (well before Robert Croft) the statue ball, and also the pirouette ball, the one-arm ball and the fall-over ball. He and Dorey came up with agricultural nicknames for all the squad. So we had 'Hayman' Hicks, 'Pitchfork' Dorey, 'Wheaty' Warren, 'Combine' Caines as well as 'Silage' Sexton, 'MadCow' Makin, 'Barnyard' Brett and so on. Strangely though, I think this did actually give us a real identity as an outfit, and by playing down our talents, we could come across as the village idiots who no one wanted to lose to. Often the pressure told and we would be giggling away as players got out either trying to whack us out of the park or too scared to play a shot. It was bonkers. It was genius.

The best season we had was undoubtedly the one before we all started to go our separate ways at sixth form. We made it through to the quarter-finals of the National NatWest knockout competition, after winning our regional group and going on to beat Worcestershire in triumphant fashion at Bromsgrove on a day when I won a pint from John Caines and almost a second as I missed the flagpole by a whisker. Although we lost in controversial fashion to Essex on home turf, we ran a team who had four England Under-16 players (all on contracts already) mighty close. We then headed off to a festival in Jersey where we and Cornwall were the only minor counties alongside six majors.

Lo and behold, at that festival the major counties were all kitted out in new tracksuits and had sponsored kit and professional coaches. We all wore our club shirts and still had the same tracksuits from the under-13s, with the sleeves getting a bit short by now. They were on strict curfews, despite this being the summer we finished our GCSEs, whilst we and the Cornish were allowed to try our luck getting served at tax-free prices. And guess what. We both ended up in the final. And we won.

But the real story was not about our cricket, although it was memorable. Nor was it really about the excitement of getting into nightclubs for the first time, pepped up on Twenty Twenty (before that became a brand of cricket), or even the fact that our opening bowler had smuggled a tin of cannabis on to the plane and could often be found puffing away behind the pavilion before racing in with his dreadlocks to rough up the pristine opening batsmen. It was like watching Worzel Gummidge off his tits being egged on by a bunch of yahoos, and it was way too much for those textbook forward defences. Opposition coaches hated it, and we didn't care.

No, the real story here was somewhat more sinister. My dad had stepped in as manager of the tour at the last minute and had inherited a coach who had represented Great Britain at water polo and who was an ace at psychology. The problem was this guy was weird. We had had a few coaches before who had been a bit eccentric, and even some about whom the rumours would go around. The word 'paedo' had been whispered in the changing rooms a few times, but no one really believed it. This was standard banter for teenage dressing rooms. And, to be fair, you do have to question the motives of some blokes who choose to spend their summers on tour with groups of young lads. These were the days before CRB or DBS checks, remember. But this guy was definitely weird. For starters, he looked weird: his glasses were as thick as the bottom of pint glasses, he walked with a limp, on account of polio apparently, and he had a shocking speech impediment. 'Megassshhtar!' he would call you, with spittle hitting you in the face if you weren't careful. But one shouldn't judge a book by its cover, and dad and I both felt we should give him the benefit of the doubt. He was certainly a great motivator, and had been instrumental in our success all season. But he was definitely weird.

I perhaps should have realised when he offered to give me some advice about treating my bad back, telling me to bend over in the shower and alternate between hot and cold water, supervising me as I did so. Perhaps we should have realised when he spent the evening knocking on Cainesy's hotel door after he'd locked himself in following four consecutive ducks. Perhaps we should have trusted the instincts of Mr Caines, who just had that uncanny knack of knowing when something, or someone, wasn't on the level. But nothing was said. And as far as I know, nothing untoward happened.

It was not until a story broke in the Bournemouth press the next summer that a convicted child sex offender had been working with clubs in the area that the awful truth, which should have been so obvious, became apparent. We'd had a paedophile for a coach for two years, and my poor parents had unwittingly welcomed him into our lives. Thankfully the law caught up with him and no one involved in this story was hurt. Makes you wonder, though.

A Man's Game – Farnham CC

By the time I reached the sixth form, my folks had left Dorset and I followed them to Lord Wandsworth College in Hampshire, where I had the choice of joining either Alton CC in the Southern League in Hampshire, or Farnham CC in the Surrey Championship. For whatever reason, I chose Farnham, and it became what I would consider 'my club', despite the odd foray elsewhere. Farnham is nothing if not historic. Perched on the top of the hill overlooking the Georgian town, the ground sits next to the walls of Farnham Castle, and traces its roots back to 1782.[1] It was one of the very first clubs in England and regularly played games against the famous Hambledon club, with such legends as 'Silver' Billy Beldham and 'Honest' John Wells gracing the 'Oval'. Wouldn't it be great if we added epithets to our players these days – definitely a game for the dressing room on a rainy day.

The Farnham club I joined was still situated in a beautiful spot, but was blighted by a very substandard pitch and some rather 'conservative' attitudes, shall we say. Being in leafy Surrey, it was a bit of a shock to the system for some when teams arrived from around the South Circular with a high percentage of West Indian or Asian players – 'you don't get many of those round here', could be heard muttered on park benches by the smattering of very Anglo-Saxon spectators, who were presumably expecting something from the pages of *Country Life*. Other comments are not suitable to be repeated. However, the cosmopolitan nature of Surrey offered a whole lot more variety than I was used to in Dorset, and was certainly a big step up in terms of the hardness of the cricket played. Getting used to being called a 'faaackin' prick', with accentuated 'Sarf Laandan' glottal stop, week in, week out took some time and made most Saturdays pretty unpleasant. This was a new world, with proper overseas players, like Ian Bishop and Brad Haddin, and Surrey professionals in every club (except ours, which was apparently too far away from the Oval to qualify, which only added to our sense of righteous indignation as we sought to make 'Fortress Farnham' a really unpleasant place to come and play).

I learnt an enormous amount from Farnham's overseas pro – a rangy Indian off-spinner by the name of Harpreet Singh, who made the ball 'drop' more than anyone I've come across, perhaps

---

1   You can learn more about the history of Farnham CC in Andrew Kieft's account at http://farnhamcc.co.uk/us/history/

Phil Tufnell aside. In the days before I could order a beer from the club bar, I would share a Coke with 'Happy', or 'Magic' as he was known, drinking in his knowledge of grips, pace, reading pitches and batsmen, setting fields and all the other arcana of the twirly arts. It saddens me hugely that these days the younger players tend not to hang around cricket clubs with the older players too much, heading back still in their tracksuits to their social media or XBoxes. It does make me sound like an 'in-my-day' merchant, but I'm sure there is as much to learn off the field as there is on it. As a school safeguarding lead in my current job, I understand the risks associated with young people sharing dressing rooms with adults, but being party to all the sorts of banter, which combined years of experience produces, offers a much richer understanding of the game, and indeed human nature, than any age-group environment could produce. You just don't get the likes of Chic Stedman and the Thorpe brothers in your under-18 group.

Having said this, I was too young to feel fully part of the set-up at Farnham, despite one or two nights out which whetted my appetite for the *après* element of weekend cricket, and I yearned for the easier times I had left behind in the West Country.

The Wheels on the Bus are Burning Down

My sixth-form cricketing years were a combination of first- and second-team club cricket and school first-eleven games for Lord Wandsworth College. Lord Wandsworth is a lovely school set in almost a thousand acres of Hampshire farmland, and established by the eponymous Lord Wandsworth (Sydney James Stern) in order to offer education to children – only boys, of course, in the early years – who had been orphaned. The LWC Foundation is still at the heart of the school[2] and is a great

---

2   https://www.lordwandsworth.org/userfiles/lwcmvcv2/Documents/01-About-Us/devthehistoryofthelordwandsworthfoundation.pdf

example of the important work independent schools do for the less fortunate in society: a fact lost on some Labour politicians. The cricket was not brilliant there, much the same strength of fixture list as Clayesmore. Although seen by local state schools as a 'toff' school, the reality was that in the grand hierarchical world of independent schooling, the schools I attended were what one teaching colleague of mine – a Harrow old boy – termed 'MPSIA', or *Minor public school, I'm afraid.*

I did manage my fair share of wickets and a couple more first-team hundreds, this time against such behemoths as the Old Boys and Winchester 2nd XI, which earned me the excitement familiar to many schoolboys of a mention in *Wisden*. But really, the highlight of my cricket at Lord Wandsworth was playing alongside one Jonny Wilkinson, more of which in due course, and touring South Africa in the winter of 1996/97.

Touring for a representative side such as a county or region was quite a professional affair: largely due to the odd official gathering, tight controls on diet, training and a sense that the holy grail of a professional contract might lie somewhere down the line. An overseas tour with your schoolmates was an altogether looser affair. Official functions tended to be no more than *braais* after a game, training was reliant on the host school offering their nets for an afternoon and, before the turn of the century, attitudes to teenagers having the odd beer were much more liberal than they are today. This tour was notable not for the cricket so much, but for some pretty average tour administration which saw us staying in downturn Durban on New Year's Eve in a hotel which doubled as a brothel, taking our lives into our hands on more than one occasion: walking the length of a 'blacks-only' beach to an Indian nightclub; seeing our coach duffed up by locals in Jeffreys Bay, where swimming near a load of box jellyfish was also on the menu, not to mention our tour bus literally burning to the ground on the Garden Route. To give you a sense of how seriously we were taking it, one of our number kept a tour photo diary entitled 'A Moon with a View', which involved him pulling a moonie (ie: showing his bare arse) at sites of specific tourist interest. I'm sure his grandchildren will be delighted to see his snaps of Table Mountain and Camps Bay. We were kids looking for a good time and to get away with as much as we could. I'm probably making it out to seem worse than it was, as my parents happened to be the teachers in charge, and in any case, this was very much the way things were done in those days. Whether this contributed to my errant behaviour or was merely coincidence I can't say. Thank goodness Wilkinson had opted not to come on this trip: the most professional sportsperson of his generation would hardly have enjoyed the approach we adopted.

So by the age of 17, the county cricket had dropped away somewhat and having turned down the chance to play for Hampshire as an under-16, my promising cricket career seemed to be drifting as my interest in more off-field pursuits – namely girls and booze – started to blur things. Were it not for the happy fact that I was doing well at school, my life might have been going seriously in the wrong direction. Academically, I was fortunate that schoolwork came easily to me, and with some excellent teachers (including my dad, who taught me Latin A-level), I was able to make a pretty reasonable application to Cambridge to study philosophy. The idea of following in dad's footsteps (he had won three hockey Blues and captained Cambridge in 1975) was enticing, and so I applied to his old college, St Catharine's.

Oxbridge at the Second Time of Asking

At St Catharine's College, Cambridge, the site of my father's youthful glories, I was put through probably the most gruelling and humiliating day of my life. I was desperately underprepared for the grilling I took at the hands of the Cambridge professors. The only saving grace was that the interviews were done and dusted in one day, unlike the three-day affairs at Oxford, which would have prolonged the purgatory. I knew I'd failed, and the letter of rejection came as no surprise, disappointing though it was. Nonetheless, I did have an offer from Nottingham University to study French and philosophy – my preferred course – and very nearly accepted it.

In his wisdom, dad was perceptive enough to realise that if I took the place at Nottingham, any chance I had of pursuing a first-class cricket career would be dead in the water. And so he sat me down for the first of a series of life-defining conversations at the bar of the local pub – The Four Horseshoes – where he persuaded me to think about a reapplication to Cambridge the following year. In those days, first-class cricket at university was still the preserve of the old Oxbridge elite, and with A grades in all four of my A-levels (the fact I took four hopefully suggested I did have a modicum of intellectual aptitude and attitude), I ought to stand a chance a second time around. Swallowing some pride, I assented, but said that having been rejected from Cambridge, I couldn't face a second rebuff, and so I sent in my application for 'the other place', Oxford.

I almost killed myself the day I received the acceptance letter from Oxford. So full of excitement and adrenaline was I that I pulled out across the main road in my trusty Citroen AX without looking, skidding almost through the front entrance of Birdworld. My future suddenly opened up ahead of me, with those letters 'MA, Oxon' after my name and, even more importantly, the chance to get my name up in that old pavilion in the Parks, and even (did I dare think it?) stepping out one day at the Home of Cricket. Many people still don't believe me, but the truth is, were it not for cricket, I would not have applied to Oxford. I tell students that if you follow your passion, other things will come along – in my case, an Oxford degree. But it was definitely that way around.

There is obviously some quite clear water, though, between the anticipation of playing first-class cricket, and the reality of actually being anywhere near good enough to be selected.

Chapter Three

First Class

Oxford 1999

There is something utterly unreal about 'going up' to Oxford as an undergraduate. It is impossible not to be aware of the weight of history attached to the place. Everywhere you turn there are echoes of intellectual and cultural legend. Strolling along Broad Street you pass the spot where the so-called Oxford Martyrs – Thomas Cranmer, Hugh Latimer and Nicholas Ridley – were burnt for their faith in 1555 and 1556 at the hands of Mary Tudor; passing by Merton College gardens you can imagine a young J.R.R. Tolkien dreaming up the Hobbit lands of Middle Earth; cycling to the Parks past the Zoology department you might well pass Professor Richard Dawkins, controversial author of *The Blind Watchmaker* and *The God Delusion*. Now, there is a man who would have gone the way of the martyrs in different times. To be in this world, and not just a tourist, is to feel part of something very special indeed. And you know you are up for an academic challenge when you receive your first reading list in the summer before you officially begin, and notice that several of the key texts have actually been written or edited by the tutors who will be teaching you. Your weekly 'tutes' (tutorials) would be with world experts in their field.

These are not people you can bullshit, as I found out within a few painful first weeks.

Those early days at Oxford were all about settling in. Getting used to the seriously demanding academic expectations was one thing (my brother followed a similar course at Durham and we reckoned what he was doing in six weeks, I was meant to do in one). And then there was the important matter of making new friends and living away from home for the first time. Cricket had to wait whilst the inevitable transition was made. You are expected to attend the 'Freshers' Fair' – a mass of exhibition stands, free gifts and colourful undergraduates who all seemed so with it, enticing you to try all manner of activities: I seem to remember signing up for the juggling society, the Gregorian chant ensemble and the badger-spotting league before I spotted a familiar figure on the one stand I was really interested in: OUCC – Oxford University Cricket Club – my ticket to dreamland.

John Claughton had been captain of the Hampshire and England Under-15 age group team and came of good cricketing stock. With a passing resemblance to Michael Atherton, Claughton was nicknamed 'Skipper Serious' at Oxford and in some quarters had been labelled with the moniker 'FEC' – Future England Captain. Fortunately for me, Claughts had been a team-mate for the West of England and we regularly came up against each other for our neighbouring counties, so he knew what I was about and was keen to get me involved, fast-tracking me through the business of being selected for winter nets. The process was not especially scientific, as one tale illustrates.

At the Freshers' Fair, you were asked to write down your previous level of experience, which would act as the first stage of the weeding-out process. I was able to claim Surrey Championship first-team cricket, as well as the representative age-group cricket. Anyone with 'county' experience and currently playing for a half-decent club would likely get a look-in, but those who just offered up a bit of private-school cricket and little else, or just wrote 'club cricket' were likely to hit the discard pile at the first hurdle.

One player whose application went straight in the bin on the basis of the 'club only' experience was an Australian named Nathan Ashley. Ashley was in Oxford for a year's postgraduate study and was already earmarked as a rugby player of distinction, who would win a Blue at Twickenham as an exciting centre. What he failed to disclose, though, was that he had also attended the famous Australian Cricket Academy in Adelaide and his so-called club cricket was actually New South Wales first grade. Not only this, he had captained the Academy who beat England during the 1994 tour of Australia under Atherton, in a team including future Aussie stars Brad Hodge and Ian Harvey. So humble was Nathan that the revelation that we had a bona fide quality first-class player to pick from only came out during a chance conversation at Vincent's – a private gentlemen's club for Oxford sportsmen (yes, these places do exist...). Thankfully, after showing up to a few nets, he made the squad (obviously!) and proved to be the class act his pedigree promised. In fact, it was a treat to have him in our side: few students give the impression of being at ease against first-class counties, but not only did he do this, he also had that ability to score runs without you even noticing – manoeuvring the field and manipulating the ball into gaps and running hard, he would be in the twenties before playing a shot in anger. He could also throw the ball equally well with either hand, which certainly caught a few sluggardly batsmen by surprise. Off the field, he also taught me a valuable lesson. Recognising that there was a good chance that I might be tempted away from the cricket by the bright lights of student life, he pulled me to one side early that season and said, 'If you're going to be last out [at night], make sure you're the first one in the next morning [for training].' I did take this on board, although probably missed the subtext that I'd have been better off not going out at all. But then again, I always felt I knew better, and there were others who were happy to have me along as a wing-man for their own escapades. Choosing the right mentor is perhaps overlooked.

'Ash' had the most amazing year: he got his Blue in rugby and cricket, and met the Queen during the 750th anniversary celebrations for University College. The only blot on his year happened at the worst possible time. Having scored a quite superb 96 in the biggest game of the year – the Varsity Match – and in his one opportunity to play at Lord's, he was then given out lbw after nicking it on to his pad. It was the only time I saw him lose his temper, and the scenes when he arrived back in the dressing room would have rivalled anything the old place had seen. It really mattered to him, and made us all realise how special our opportunities were.

We may have missed other candidates, but by the time pre-season arrived and we started our outdoor nets and fitness sessions, I had made the cut and looked likely to start in our first fixtures. It really felt exceptionally special putting my 'coffin' (the large trunk-style bags which were all the rage in the 1990s) into a free spot in the changing rooms in the dungeon underneath the pavilion, even if the older players moved me on from 'their' spots. It was even more special to look at the names which adorned the panelled walls of the Parks pavilion: Imran Khan, Colin Cowdrey, C.B. Fry, M.J.K. Smith, the Nawab of Pataudi, Douglas Jardine, B.T. Bosanquet (the man who invented the googly) and more recent additions such as Jason Gallian and, from the year before I made my debut, Mark Wagh of Warwickshire, which suggested that there was still a pathway from the Parks to the professional game. I could while away whole lunch breaks contemplating some of the composite teams that could be made from these boards. I also wanted desperately to match the three appearances my father had made on the pavilion walls of Fenner's. In short, I was not lacking for inspiration as I began my first-class career.

The 'Golden Boy' on Debut

Strangely, I don't remember a huge amount of the build-up to my first three-day game for Oxford against a county team. I do know that in the build-up, we played against Glamorgan, and I claimed the wicket of Steve James, one of the top county players and, indeed, a Test cricketer. It may have been that he gave his wicket up after scoring a hundred, but that's not what the scorecard says, and in any case, several of my later wickets came from batsmen who had got fatigued from scoring boundaries off my bowling. The trick was really just to stay on long enough and ideally be bowling in the final overs of the innings, when wickets might come cheap.

I think the exuberance of youth probably meant I went into the game against Worcestershire – the county I supported as a youngster – full of misplaced confidence and the excitement of playing against names such as Steve Rhodes, and David Leatherdale, who I recognised from the scorecards on television and the pages of *The Cricketer,* and one of England's bright young things, Vikram Solanki. I don't think I was starstruck, rather that this was what I had been dreaming of since my early days in Dorset, and here was a chance to show that I belonged in this company.

In the event, I did OK. I bowled tidily enough and didn't disgrace myself, picking up the wickets of Paul Pollard and Philip Weston, and the attractive scalp of Solanki, who made the cardinal error of playing for spin and watching the ball slide past his bat on to the off stump. That would do for game one. I had removed a potential England player and not been smashed around too much. I also felt OK batting, although there was no doubt the skill level of the professional seamers was going to take a while to get to grips with. The fact that when the match was reported in the broadsheets after day one, my name was wrongly printed as 'Hinks' didn't dampen things, although there were still several mates who failed to believe that this was actually me.

Some nicknames did stick, though. I was having such a good time in my first year as an undergraduate, and taking a decent amount of wickets as well, that one of the student newspapers labelled me as the 'Golden Boy' – something which did not escape my friends back in college who did a good job of keeping my feet on the ground, taking the mickey mercilessly any time I happened to mention I might be playing for the university. To their credit, they also were the first to celebrate my success, and in fact many of my best friends from university had no idea I was playing cricket, or even what cricket was! Friends like these are invaluable, although they would argue that my ego was still becoming inflated. Another nickname which has stood the test of time for my college friends is 'Oyster' – a great nickname born out of a raucous game of college darts (definitely the most aggressive, and un-Oxford sport played at the university, with beery undergraduates screaming in your face in greasy-walled cellar bars as you aim for double-top). The name perfectly encapsulated the fact that in my first year at Oxford, things really felt like they were going my way; the world really felt like my oyster.

It's hard not to feel that way when suddenly there are people writing about you in the press. I received positive reviews from former Oxford, and later England off-spinner Vic Marks, as well as Scyld Berry, the former editor of *Wisden*, who praised my control and flight in one of the broadsheets. There were also the doddery old cricket anoraks (or badgers, as they are often referred to), who stalk the boundaries of parochial first-class games in search of autographs. These are definitely a species in decline, but there are no doubt still dusty files in the long-forgotten corners of living rooms in the Home Counties where you can find my scribbled name alongside a raft of other wannabes.

A couple of very embarrassing autograph moments spring to mind. I'll leave aside the several times youngsters would come up to the pavilion, or catch you on the boundary for your scrawl to then utterly prick your bubble of pride by asking within your earshot, 'Who *is* that?' It was when I was named captain of the university at the end of the 1999 season that people seemed to be even more interested. This led to a red-faced moment in Bournemouth after Dorset had won the Western Division trophy for the second time in succession. During the lunchtime champagne celebrations in the dressing room, an autograph book was sent in for all the players to sign, which duly happened. Only when it was handed back was a request made for 'Mr Hicks' in person. To the predictable whoops and hollers, and attempts to pull down my trousers on the way, I went magnanimously to give this superfan some of my precious time. Again, with no sense of discretion, he asked at top volume whether I could sign a full page myself next to the team page, as I was about to be a first-class captain. Given that I was burgling my place in the team at the time as the second-, if not third-choice spinner, you can imagine how this went down with my team-mates.

And then the next season in the Parks, I was accosted on a circuit of the pitch with my dad, by another chap with little else to do with his time. However, he had waited until I was in full view of the pavilion before whipping out a full document wallet of papers, and even pictures of me that I'd never even seen before, for me to sign. The spectacle would have lasted a good couple of minutes, but it felt like a much longer ordeal as I tried to keep up the small talk, knowing I was facing down a barrage of fines later that day. At least I wasn't signed with a major county, like poor Joe Porter, a freshman at Brookes who was on Surrey's books and thus in the annual Cricketers' *Who's Who*, making him a prime target for the badgers, even though he'd not even played a first-class game. As a lad from the 'Poly on the Hill', signing autographs in front of his more conservative 'real Oxford' team-mates must have been excruciating.

Nonetheless, it was flattering to feel like a 'someone' around Oxford. I was voted in as a member of Vincent's Club, and it became apparent that there was definitely some sort of hierarchy between Blues sports. Not only were some only deemed 'Half-Blue' worthy, but the rugby and rowing clubs ruled the roost (the TV historian Dan Snow was in the Blue boat during my time and a well-respected figure in the club), with cricket not far behind. Although looking at it now, wearing your Blues blazer around town must have made you look like a proper stuck-up wotsit to the general public, there definitely felt like a sense of kudos when you entered a pub or club sporting 'The Crowns'. And in the right circles, you were likely to attract the attention of sport-loving girls, lovingly referred to as 'Blue-tack'. Times were indeed heady.

More success followed against a Hampshire side including England stars Robin Smith and Dimitri Mascarenhas, who followed Solanki by falling to another Hicks straight-break. I also scored a reasonable 42, which gave me the confidence that I might be able to score some useful runs at this level. Not only this, good performances were all being weighed up as the squad for that all-important Lord's date was being whittled down. A rained-off fixture against Nottinghamshire probably played into my hands as well (I couldn't mess up if we didn't play), although some of us almost got injured in a pretty lethal football match with the likes of Richard Stemp and ex-Blue Jason Gallian getting stuck in.

Games against Glamorgan and Warwickshire followed (notable in my mind as the game I scored four fours in an over off the future BBC cricket commentator Charlie Dagnall) and an away fixture at Essex, which was one of only two first-class fixtures I missed in my four years, having to take my first-year exams. I would have to hope I'd done enough before that to make the final Varsity eleven.

I was pretty confident, though, that my performances so far had caught the eye of whatever powers-that-be existed in the university cricket world, and I had the chance to play in my biggest fixture yet, against a fully-fledged Test nation, for the British Universities.

Taking on the Test Team – New Zealand

It seems barely believable in these days of instant communication and mass media, but on the one occasion I was lucky enough to be picked to play against a full Test-playing nation, I learnt of my selection through a hand-scrawled memo pinned to the Porters' noticeboard in my college. I had just returned from a first-year 'preliminary' exam in the Iffley Road sports centre (where Oxford trained, and Roger Bannister ran the first sub-four-minute mile). I still have it. It reads:

> *T Hicks Report tomorrow to Parks to play N.Z.*

It is one of my most treasured possessions.

The British Universities were in town to play against the Black Caps at the start of their tour of England, and the first-choice off-spinner Richard Dawson – of Exeter University, Yorkshire and later, England – had gone down injured. I don't know if it was just expediency and wanting to save on expenses that led the selectors to choose the bloke from down the road, but I hope that my early performances against counties counted for something. In any case, I quickly got myself ready to head down for training that afternoon.

Not many of our side went on to notable cricket careers, although Simon Francis had his days in the sun for Somerset. We also had a chap called Greg Loveridge, who had already played a Test as a leg-spinner for New Zealand and apparently now is one of NZ's richest men.

However, our coach was an undisputed legend. The one and only 'Arkle' – Derek Randall – who was, at the time, coach of Cambridge University. Randall needs no introduction from me, known and loved as he is and was by the nation's cricket-watching public (not least for his incredible ton in the Centenary Test in Melbourne, the cartwheel after taking the catch that regained the Ashes and *that* run-out by Geoffrey Boycott). Public personas can often mask a darker side but Arkle was everything one might have hoped for. Although I had been drafted in at late notice, he had done his homework and, with typical boundless energy, he shook my hand and said, 'You're a first slipper, right?' and moved Loveridge out of the way in the practice which had already started, installing me in prime position. I felt immediately valued and reassured. Already I knew I would do anything for this man, and I learnt a huge amount from this one simple gesture.

It was extremely sad and short-sighted of the ECB, when they appointed their head coaches of the University Centres of Excellence the following year, to relieve Randall of his duties as head coach of Cambridge because he did not have his Level 3 qualification. He had been with them for years already, knew the unique vagaries of the place and was just a top man for the players. His replacement, Chris Scott, did a fine job, but a man as committed and as decent as Randall deserved a lot more respect, in my book, anyway.

In the Parks, New Zealand were also having a bit of a warm-up and Chris Cairns was the one drawing the eye. He looked as if he could 'get it through', by which I mean he would likely be peppering me around the torso the next day. Of course, everyone looks faster side on, and my impression was not aided by the fact that the next net over was occupied by the Oxford ladies' team, which included in their number my future wife, who recalls the story pretty clearly. As she tells it, only one ball in three in her net reached the other end within reach of the batter, and the Adonis-like Cairns did the gentlemanly thing on several occasions of retrieving the ball from the overhead netting. I suspect the ladies may have had ulterior motives, although I have seen her bowl ...

The match began the following day, and the students won the toss. There is an unwritten etiquette to these unbalanced fixtures. You are students, they are professional cricketers; they are better than you – you win the toss, you bowl. But no, our skipper jauntily picked up the coin and breezily announced to Stephen Fleming (regarded then as possibly the best Test captain in the world) his intention to bat, and presumably grind the jolly foreigner into the dirt. I don't know what he was thinking. We got a few – 200-odd – including a very solid ten or so from Hicks in the lower order. I was looking odds-on for at least double that when I actually picked a hooping inswinging arm-ball from Vettori only to late-cut it straight to Nathan Astle at slip.

I was pretty buzzing after my knock, and the chance to stand at first slip, where I might even get a piece of the action in the final session (I didn't). One piece of wisdom sticks with me from that session, though, in that our left-arm seamer Jamie Lawrence bowled four decent balls in the channel outside off stump at the opener Matthew Horne. He turned to fellow left-arm seamer Dave Mather (an Oxford medic of some experience acting as twelfth man) and said: 'Four good ones, I think I'll try something different,' before seeing the next two balls disappear through midwicket for boundaries. First-class cricket is a patience game above all else, in my limited experience.

As the day drew to a close, the skipper this time did go down the traditional path and threw the ball to his spinners. Poor Matthew Bell made the same mistake as plenty of others and played for turn to one of my straight breaks and nicked it to the safe hands of Loveridge at slip, leaving New Zealand one down at stumps, honours only slightly in their favour, and me with a Test victim in my pocket. I could have jumped for joy.

As the players from both sides showered up and made ready to leave for the evening, the usual talk abounded of where might be handy for a drink and some food. Mather and I thought it would be a good opportunity to show the tourists something typically Oxfordian and invited them to Vincent's Club, just off the High Street. 'Vinnie's' is exactly the sort of establishment the layman would expect to find in Oxford: a gentlemen's club full of leather sofas, sepia prints, pipe smokers and young lads playing the Beau Brummel. You didn't have to be a Blue to get in, but if you didn't have crowns on your blazer you were rather regarded as something of a second-class citizen. Not as bad as the Bullingdon set, but a thin end of that particular wedge. Women were invited strictly only on Fridays, and ties were to be worn at all times. You get the idea.

Only Simon Doull, Stephen Fleming and Daniel Vettori pitched up, but for a keen young spinner such as myself ... Daniel Vettori pitched up! Although he was pretty taciturn, I tried to prise as much wisdom as I could from the prodigy. In hindsight, I think I must have bored him to tears as the evening was not a long one.

There was another reason for the curtailment of the evening's proceedings. It was still exam season and the following morning I was due back at Iffley Road for my next French exam. I hadn't told Randall or the management that I had exams as I was terrified I would not be selected. Luckily for me, as coach of Cambridge, he understood that my place in the university would be in jeopardy if I was absent, so I headed off the other direction from the Parks in the morning. Among its many obscure and arcane traditions, when sitting exams at Oxford, you have to wear *subfusc* – this means a black suit (I wore my DJ), white bow tie, gown and mortar board, which you had to hold, rather than wear. Even Cambridge do not observe this tradition anymore and I can tell you, it is far from comfortable, feeling like a starched penguin, sweating in all the wrong places, trying to pick apart the *passé composé* when your mind is on how to winkle out a Test top order.

As soon as the exam was over, I ran over a mile to get back to the match, even though it was the lunch break. In the space of a two-hour session, New Zealand had cruised from 56/1 to 180/1. Quentin Hughes, the captain, looked like a man in need of a plan. He had one, and I was it. 'I hope you're ready to bowl? You're on all afternoon,' he gruffly welcomed me, as the rest of my team-mates and the entire New Zealand squad looked on in bemusement at my clobber. The journos seemed entertained by me, too, and I made it into *The Times* the next day, aided perhaps by bowling a decent spell during which Matthew Horne whacked one so hard at Ryan Driver at midwicket he had to catch it, and having Stephen Fleming dropped by my mate Chris Hellings behind the wicket. Two-fer, and a decent economy rate was respectable. Three-fer would have seen me on the winter tour to South Africa, and I never let Hellings forget it.

Ultimately, though, batting first had been a mistake. Three of the Kiwis scored tons, and Vettori looked every inch the star he was destined to be in hitting an undefeated 70. As we batted again, the writing was on the wall. I remember only being amazed at how much swing Doull was able to create, at decent pace, and the immortal line of sledging I received from Dion Nash – the chap who had bowled England out at Lord's on the previous tour. For some reason, Nash seemed to take a dislike to me. Smirking at the non-striker's end (because I was out of the firing line, no doubt), Nash launched into a verbal volley:

'What are you so f***ing happy about, pal?'

'I dunno,' I lamely replied.

'You look like a f***ing accountant.'

This did make me laugh. I did not look like an accountant. I may have done later in my career, when I wore spectacles before laser eye surgery, but at 19, there was nothing about me which remotely resembled even the most stereotypical of accountants (whatever that is). I was keen to respond, though, and thinking it best not to drag the innocent Vettori into this (he *did* look like an accountant), I offered one of my best ever lines:

'I may look like an accountant, but you're meant to be a f***ing Test cricketer mate and you can't even get *me* out.'

My smugness lasted only as long as it took my partner to scamper the next single and leave me facing the music again. A couple of predictable bouncers followed, which I negotiated successfully, albeit by ducking hard and hoping. The over ended and ignoring the scowls and snarls coming my way from Nash, I arrived mid-pitch for the traditional conflab with my partner, who happened to be Francis, the No.11. Francis seemed up for it, and confidently advised me that it 'wasn't a ducking sort of pitch' and that I was best to keep my eye on it and sway out of the way when the next one came. I nodded in agreement and trotted off to watch how he dealt with the next over.

I was at the non-striker's end again when Nash ran in for his next over. 'No ducking', was the agreement once again as I settled in to watch Francis shape up. Nash went short first ball, Francis ducked straight into it, the ball cannoning off his grill into the stumps to complete Nash's five-wicket haul and the end of the match.

'You were right,' I offered to Francis as we shook hands with the Black Caps, 'It wasn't a ducking pitch...'

Nash was the perfect professional and we shook hands with good grace. I made my way back to the pavilion pretty pleased with red ink for my not out and a match average of 19 to go with my two Test victims. I passed my first-year exams, too.

Best Sledges

There are books full of the most famous sledges in cricket history and some of these may be well known to your average cricketer. Sledging is still, in my experience, part-and-parcel of the game. You just hope that it's mildly amusing and not just inane personal abuse. Following the incident with Nash, here are some others I remember from over the years.

1. 'You've got some shit on the end of your bat, mate.' When the batsman looks at the bottom of his bat, the close fielders will correct him: 'Other end, mate.' A classic humiliation that I fell for completely.

2. I must have been wet behind the ears as I fell for another one in the same vein when a slip fielder told me there was a piece of mud on my heel. As I inspected it, looking over my shoulder in a rather camp way, I got the obvious line: 'Hello, Sailor' and realised I was giving it the full Page Three model pose. It's a lonely enough place out there without being made to feel totally emasculated.

3. Arriving at the crease during a game against Wales after getting a duck in the first innings, I was met by Glamorgan wicketkeeper Will Bragg singing the tune of Bon Jovi's 'Livin' on a Prayer': 'Whoa, we're halfway there, whoa-oa, Hicksy's on a pair.' Quite clever from him.

4. Less clever was his compatriot Darren Thomas, who made the fatal error of trying to sledge the bowler, calling me a 'f***ing weapon' in full Welsh Valleys accent. He followed it up, to be fair, by smacking me for a straight six. But with only one life, you don't look so clever when you get out to the next ball and then see two of your mates go down in the same over. I enjoyed that one.

5. Talking of batsmen having a go back, Oxford batsman Graham Butcher had turned down several easy singles trying to farm the strike against MCC. It was suggested to him by Midlands legend and loose cannon David Banks that he 'might want that single later'. And so it proved when Butcher fell for 99. Banks reminded him as he trudged off, 'I bet you wish you'd taken that one, now.' Quick as a flash, Butch retorted, 'Yeah, I'd take it, and I'd stick it up your f***ing arse.' Not subtle, I'll grant you, but good on him. The knock got him selected for his Blue as well.

6. My favourite put-down of all though, is Farnham fast bowler Pete Dickinson's catchphrase of 'You know, you *can* be embarrassed out,' once he'd gone past the outside edge a dozen times. Dickinson was the dead-spit of Harry Hill without the glasses and when he accompanied the line with the old-fashioned sticking your tongue into your bottom lip mime of 'you're so dumb', it had me in stitches for overs.

7. Some others I've had to endure: 'This bloke's got more badges than Blue Peter' (when committing the sin of wearing representative kit during a club game); 'Does your husband play?'; 'Good job you've got a real job'; 'Didn't your bat come with instructions?' All of which would have been funny had they not been so apt.

The Home of Cricket

I have been immensely fortunate to have had the chance to play at Lord's on several occasions and I will try to give some sense of what it is like in due course. However, until June 1999, I had never set foot inside the grand old ground, and so the Varsity Match of that year would be my first experience of the Mecca recognised by all cricketers the world over as the home of cricket. In my mind, I was following in the footsteps of Ben Holioake, who famously had never been to Lord's before making his international debut and stunning the English cricketing public with a majestic 63 in an ODI against Australia, before his life was cut short by a tragic accident in Australia. I had actually come up against Holioake whilst at school. He was one year older than me and attended Millfield – something of a factory for first-class cricketers. Remarkably for a bloke who was not the slowest of bowlers, he didn't even open the bowling, which tells you a bit about how strong they were. Anyway, he dispatched with me pretty quickly on that occasion and I was as much in awe of his prodigious talent as the next fan, and hoped that maybe some beginner's luck would rub off on me during my first outing at HQ, even if it was a notch or two down in importance.

Nowadays, Lord's plays host to a one-day Varsity Match, but for decades, centuries even, the match had been a three-day affair. What an amazing experience! Being able to drive into the players' entrance in a beaten-up old Citroën, dropping your kit bag off in the away dressing room (for some reason, the Dark Blues of Oxford and Harrow always took up the away dressing room in their respective fixtures), having a free rein over the practice facilities, both indoor and outdoor, and getting stuck into the free soft drinks available in the dressing room all made you feel like you were the most important players in the world. I remember vividly the sensation of the pavilion floor under my studded boots – a surprisingly springy, spongy feeling – and being amazed that you didn't have to take your boots off, like in almost all club grounds. Given that we were there for three days, we could also make ourselves at home in the dressing room, which was vast enough to be able to spread yourself across a few pegs and make use of a full padded bench, although by modern standards I believe the rooms are considered quite poky. I established my own area for the duration of that match and was extremely reluctant to pack up once the game was over. Given half the chance I'd have taken up squatter's rights.

Every moment of the game felt special. A British Pathé film from 1922 shows the Varsity Match well attended by several thousands of gentlemen in hats, and although more sparsely populated in recent times, I would estimate that around a thousand people pitched up to watch us play, swelled somewhat by groups of local primary school pupils out for the day whose high-pitched cries of 'Oxford … Cambridge' grew only a little tiresome as the days wore on, especially knowing that the children had not the foggiest clue where Oxford and Cambridge were, nor why they were chanting for them, or even probably why they were there, just being happy to be away from the classroom for the day. Of course, friends and family attended and it was as much a day out for them as it was for us. My mother has wheedled her way into every corner of Lord's with a bit of charm and blagging – one minute up in the Media Centre, the next pestering the scorers in their old position in the Warner Stand. And my dad had to be dragged clear of the committee room where there was a drinks reception after the match for families and other halves; he always was a sucker for a free bar.

Batting first, we underperformed (apart from Nathan Ashley's 96) although I did get my first chance to stride to the middle.

On the one hand, the walk from dressing room to pitch is so long that the inevitable butterflies have a chance to settle down by the time you reach the crease. On the other hand, not only are you a little puffed out from the distance, you've also had to deal with not being overwhelmed by walking through what basically feels like a museum, with the famous faces of the cricketing pantheon peering down at you from their portraits, challenging you to prove that you are worthy of sharing such sacred space with them. Through the Long Room, trying not to knock over the empty high stools which would normally be full of the elder statesmen of the MCC, but most of which were conspicuously empty for the likes of us. Here you may imagine the hush when Botham returned after bagging a pair in 1981, before he turned the Ashes upside down. Imagine Gooch, weary and heavy with sweat after his marathon 333 against India, and picture Kapil Dev elated with having defied the odds to defeat Clive Lloyd's Caribbean machine to win the 1983 World Cup, and in more recent times, the throwing of decorum to the winds when Jos Buttler uprooted the stumps to take the 2019 version by the width of a cigarette paper. Down the concrete stairs – surprisingly slippy on new studs, and also just a little too long for one stride and too short for two, necessitating a little two-step as you try not to mess up your big moment by slipping arse-over-tit. Stepping aside to allow the dismissed batsman through, you reach the famous little picket-fence gate which is ceremoniously opened for you by a smiling steward in a bottle-green jacket with an uncanny resemblance to Arnold Palmer, looking like he's just won the US Masters. And then you are there, on the pristine carpet of the most famous cricket ground in the entire universe, immense pavilion at your back, the turquoise blue of the space-age Media Centre ahead of you and Old Father Time looking down paternally from his perch between the Mound and Tavern Stands. You have time enough to feel the turf beneath your feet, as echoing around the cavernous stadium comes a voice as if from one of your boyhood dreams: 'The incoming batsman … Tom (pause) Hicks.' It is a voice which has introduced legends: Bradman, Tendulkar, Root, Richards, Sobers, you name them. Well, maybe not the same voice, but when you stop to consider the journey you have just made, and whose footsteps you have just walked in, it does just give you a slight chill. Few will have passed that way without much the same chill, I'm sure. And now it was my time.

Once you are at the crease, the first thing you notice at Lord's is the slope. The ground itself drops around nine feet from Grand Stand to Mound and as you stand taking guard, the incline perceptibly takes you downhill – dangerous indeed for those prone to lbw or fencing outside the off stump. And even though the Cambridge bowlers may not have been as masterful in exploiting this as Glenn McGrath or Angus Fraser, you still had to be careful to play more at the Nursery End and leave more at the Pavilion End. Sadly, after a brief rush to eleven, I did nibble at one and edged an easy chance to the keeper. Eleven. Hmm. Not nought, but nothing to write home about either. The walk back is a less enjoyable affair, and the bloke who announced you with all the pomp of a gladiator entering the Colosseum, is now making darn sure everyone in the St John's Wood area knows you are out, discarding you like a pair of gloves tossed into a smelly kit bag as he searches for the next hopeful hero.

Fielding is a much less nervy affair. Firstly, there is safety in numbers, and even if you do make a mistake, it's not announced to all and sundry on 20 tannoys, although the big screens will identify the fielder who shamefully drops a catch or lets one through his legs. And in the course of a three-day game, the gentler pace of play allows one to take in the atmosphere in a more leisurely way. I'd be lying if I told you I didn't do a fair amount of fantasising between balls whilst standing at slip at Lord's. And for once, it was all cricket eroticism and not the normal hormonal hopes of a freshman looking to get his end away after close of play. No, this was bigger than all that. This was about soaking it all up, drinking it in and making sure that you did your best, as the chance may never come again. As a spinner, it's always nice to go and field for a spell at the end of the day, as you know the skipper will toss you the ball for a few overs before stumps, and the batsmen are normally pretty cagey, wanting to be not out overnight. Day two was less fun, as two Cambridge batsmen scored hundreds and made our efforts the previous day look pretty poor. Although I managed a wicket, it was mainly hard graft and it looked ever more likely that we would be facing down the prospect of having to bat very well in the second innings in order to save the game. This was indeed the case, and going one down in the second innings well before the close, the decision was made to throw in a nightwatchman. The nightwatchman role is controversial – some captains do not allow it at all. For me, it is one of the great quirks of the sport. It's weird enough anyway that lower-order batsmen have to bat, but the nightwatchman role defies all logic. The last thing you want to do is lose another wicket before the umpires call time, and yet teams will happily send in one of their worst players as cannon fodder in whites. For that is what the nightwatchman is: he is not there to score runs, but it is incumbent on him to face as much of the most hostile bowling as he can manage. Not only is he likely to get hit, and hurt, it is explicitly expected of him.

And so, when I was asked to act as 'lamp-man' in this crucial second innings, my self-preservation instincts all screamed no. But this was Lord's, and whilst everyone knew I'd be nightwatchman, and about seven places too high in the order, the scorecard would say I was No.3, and if I could somehow find the sort of form which I had shown in glimpses during the season, maybe, just maybe, tomorrow could be a golden day for the so-called 'Golden Boy'.

It was not pretty, and it was not chanceless, but I was still there overnight. I had done my job, and now anything the following day was a bonus. The longer I batted, the more chance we had of survival. I was actually pretty annoyed that the poor batting of day one had led to the likelihood of us not bowling again. This meant no more chances for first-class victims this season, and I had rather hoped that Cambridge would give up more than the normal county games. And so it would have to be with the bat that I would make my first Varsity Match count. And a few streaky fours and a couple of dropped catches later, I found myself pushing one into the leg side just after lunch to scamper through for a maiden first-class fifty, and a fifty at Lord's. Check your *Wisden*. It's all there, for all time. Not many people have a first-class fifty at Lord's (and there's a few guys I am happy to remind of that fact when they get a bit smart ...) I even got a headline in *The Independent* the next day. OK, rain helped us a bit, but we did save the game, and save face. And I had done enough to put myself right in the frame not only for being a shoo-in next season, but to get the vote as captain. All being well, next year I'd be leading a team out at Lord's.

Chapter Four

A Leading Role

Armed Guards and Ice Cream – Touring in Pakistan 2000

Being named captain of Oxford University Cricket Club for the 2000 season opened up some unexpected opportunities for me. Firstly, university cricket was changing: no longer would Oxford and Cambridge be the sole centres of learning who would benefit from first-class status. This move was long overdue as it was clear that it was a throwback to a class-defined system which belonged more in the 19th century than the 20th, let alone the new millennium. Also, it was quite clear that Durham University, and probably Loughborough as well, were regularly at least as strong, and more likely stronger, than the Oxbridge establishments. The big fear for us was that the ECB would decide to end once-and-for-all the first-class status of universities. In the end, the result of a significant restructuring was to create a more meritocratic system of university cricket, which would comprise six 'Centres of Excellence', seeing more traditional universities combine with local new universities (in most cases, the reformed polytechnic colleges) to allow virtually all talented cricketers leaving school the chance to continue with their studies while offering a path into the professional game. This system remained in place until 2019, and some fine cricketers have come through this route, although the first-class status of universities has now been removed, forever one expects.

For Oxford, this represented something of a sea-change. For the first time in the history of first-class cricket in the Parks, the boffins from the university would be joined by their counterparts from Oxford Brookes University – the reformed 'poly' on Headington Hill. You can perhaps imagine the way this was received in certain – more traditional – quarters of the old institution. Some of the snobbery was eye-opening. The idea of letting students of a lower academic calibre (to put it more politely than it was expressed in many cases) join the ranks of the elected elite was too much to bear for some, never mind how good they were at cricket. There were even tongue-in-cheek suggestions that there ought to be separate dressing rooms created at the Parks, or that scorecards should delineate between 'real' Oxford students and Brookes students, along the lines of that other antiquated tradition – the Gentlemen v Players fixture, in which the higher class amateur 'gentlemen' would be known as Esq. and the lower-class amateurs were not dignified with a title. This old relic had passed away in 1962.

I learnt at this stage that Douglas Jardine – captain of the Bodyline series, and erstwhile Oxford captain – had been so keen on delineations of hierarchy that he had his own dressing room as captain. Again, some comedians in our squad suggested that I might like to do something similar. Old film and pictures of Jardine are notable for his wearing the Harlequin cap whilst on England duty (the Harlequins is essentially the Oxford Blues old boys' club) – apparently the only cap other than the MCC and England caps to be worn whilst on England duty, and a deliberate affront to the Australians, for whom Jardine seemed to have little time. Sir Pelham Warner said of him, 'He's a queer fellow. When he sees a cricket ground with an Australian on it, he goes mad.' Ironically, the Aussies in our squad couldn't wait to get their hands on the 'Quins cap.

Within the new centre of excellence (not something Jardine would have been keen on, I suspect), the animosity went both ways, with some of the Brookes players bringing a degree of reverse snobbery with them, making light of and perhaps failing to respect the traditions which had underpinned university cricket for decades. What was also galling for the establishment was that this would be the last season in which Oxford and Cambridge would play six first-class games ahead of the Varsity Match. From 2001, each UCCE (University Centre of Cricketing Excellence) would play just three first-class games. The bitterness of this loss could well be used as another stick with which to beat the upstart newcomers. We would also lose the first-class fixture at Lord's, which would be replaced with a one-day match. This was the landscape I inherited as captain at the turn of the millennium and which I would have to manage as a 19-year-old. It would be an education indeed. Reflecting now, I would say that the desire, and need to bridge the perceived gap between two disparate camps has stayed with me since then, and whilst my teaching career has been in private schools, I have fought hard to challenge old-fashioned hierarchies and artificial barriers wherever I have perceived them: between genders, age, or state schools and the private sector.

Lads on Tour

The first exciting appointment I had to undertake was the pre-season first-class captains' meeting at Lord's. I felt more out of place than a Caesar salad at a David Boon barbecue. Sitting around a table at the home of cricket, discussing new rule changes and directives for the county season, I was just glad that the Oxford Blues blazer was an understated navy-blue affair with a simple badge of two silver crowns. The poor

Cambridge skipper – James Pyemont – had to try and look as unobtrusive as possible in his lurid powder-blue number. As friendly as the county captains tried to be (I remember a young Marcus Trescothick saying hello), there was no papering over the fact that we were two imposters, like a couple who had wandered into the wrong wedding and had to sit through the speeches before sloping off via the fire exit. It was, however, a thrill to get a taste of what went on in the corridors of cricketing power. I definitely wanted a bit more of that, please.

Back on less intimidating ground in Oxford, the new squad was preparing for a pre-season tour to Pakistan, sponsored by Pakistan International Airlines. Not only was this a great chance to see a new country and experience a very different culture, but we felt it would allow us to sharpen up our match fitness ahead of the first-class games, and start to work on the relationships between the old guard and some of the new lads. Although we were without one or two of our best players, who chose to stay at home to prepare for finals, we nonetheless felt we could compete with whatever came our way. The excitement of new tour kit, writing 'witty' player profiles for the tour brochure, and a couple of pre-tour socials created a real buzz around the squad before we set off.

The reality of touring in the subcontinent became apparent almost immediately. The sheer culture shock as the smells, sights and noise of Islamabad hit us was dizzying. Dirty hands jostled for our cases, the light dazzled us as it reflected off thousands of cars, tuk-tuks and multi-coloured buses jangling with beads, chains and iconic images, all tooting and hooting for a place on the highway. The stifling heat and lack of air-conditioning in our own bus meant we arrived at the Pearl Continental hotel in Rawalpindi sweaty and irritable under our starchy Blues ties and blazers, looking and feeling even more out of place than I had been in that meeting at Lord's a week before.

The reality of life in Pakistan for many was made clear to us on the way to the first ground we used for practice. Seeing people going about their daily lives living in squalid conditions was humbling; clothes hanging from corrugated-iron shacks; children drinking from trickles of dirty water, holding their hands aloft for charity as they saw white faces; older men and women, some missing limbs, some on haunches by the roadside, looking up in abject humiliation. We were a long way from the dreaming spires. By contrast to the dust, dirt and poverty we drove through, as the military-style gates of the sports complex were opened to us, a sort of Eden appeared with lush green grass fed by sprinklers of clear water and an impressive white edifice of a pavilion. The gulf between rich and poor was stark and uncomfortable.

Cricket-wise, it was amazing to see first-hand the fanatical enthusiasm of the locals for the game, with dozens of youngsters turning out to bowl in the nets and keen to show you their mystery ball. It was worrying that many of the school kids who showed up either spun it more, or bowled it quicker, than we did. Most of them wanted to run in and bowl like Shoaib Akhtar, who was clearly the local hero. The so-called 'Rawalpindi Express' had grown up on this very ground and was now synonymous the world over with lightning-bolt speed, clocking up the first televised 100mph+ delivery to England's Nick Knight. I remembered it was in nets very similar to these that Imran Khan – a former Oxford Blue himself and later Prime Minister of the country – had spotted a young Wasim Akram and elevated him almost immediately to the Test team. I just hoped there wasn't the next Wasim or Shoaib waiting in the wings for the next day's opening fixture.

As it happened, we batted first in a 40-over game (anything longer would have been suicide in the heat) and mustered a gentle but respectable 170-odd. It was when the opposition batted that we realised we might have to be a little more aggressive with our approach, as the first ball released by our opening bowler was dispatched flat for six into the wall at the edge of the ground, to the jubilation of all those watching. Our score was knocked off in quick time as the locals paid little respect to our official first-class status and taught us a lesson in limited-overs cricket.

This pattern continued. Our well-drilled and technically proficient, elbow-high-and-keep-it-on-the-ground approach was clearly not the way forward on docile pitches where you could keep your head down and swing an enormous piece of willow through the line and send the ball miles. It is worth remembering that this was in the days before the IPL, before even Twenty20 cricket, had been conceived, and so we were totally flummoxed and entirely ill-equipped to deal with what was coming at us, and which was quite natural to the Pakistani players. As such, we were on the wrong end of all but one of our seven fixtures on tour. As clever blokes, though, we did at least learn, and booked a trip to the local bat factory to ensure we went home with at least one new weapon which was twice as thick as the ones we'd brought with us. Festooned with garish stickers more appropriate for the bumper of a pick-up truck than a cricket bat, we used them in the genteel surroundings of the Parks or Fenner's.

We also learned a bit about the Pakistani attitude to gambling on sport, something for which they were developing an infamous reputation, with rumours of match-fixing, spot-betting and so on abounding. Two games were staged at the beautiful Bagh-e-Jinnah ground (or Lahore Gymkhana for those who like their colonial nomenclature) which has been likened to the Parks for its beauty. During one game, I was approached by the gentlemen watching behind me to predict what I thought would happen the next ball. I naively assumed this was just for the sake of interest, but soon realised that money was changing hands with every single ball bowled.

We learned, too, that the warnings about drinking the water were well-founded, and I spent the second Lahore match day in my darkened hotel room, losing about three stone in the process. In Karachi, Charlie Warren found himself using up his last few rupees after an emergency pit stop at the local 'conveniences' (nothing more than a hole in the ground) which were predictably devoid of toilet paper. We also learned about Pakistani administration, frequently finding that the opposition we had expected to play were now a different team entirely. In one such case, when we gratefully accepted the gifts offered at the end of the match, we learned that we had just been beaten by a team of arms dealers. Only in Pakistan …

The one exception to the run of defeats is worth describing, though. In Karachi towards the end of the tour, we were invited to play a day/night game against the team of Dr Asghar Ali Shah, at the Asghar Ali Shah Stadium. In fact, there was little about the event which was not designed to promote Dr Asghar Ali Shah, who, whilst clearly something of a local philanthropist who had set up this stadium for the benefit of the local community, was also keen to ensure that everyone knew about his generosity. Dr Shah was quite something. Having performed the toss, we were informed (by Dr Shah) that actually we would have to field first because Dr Shah – also the captain of the team – was opening the batting and would have to leave the ground once he was out. The reason? He was in the middle of a critical operation at the local hospital: apparently a patient had been hit by a bus and was stable but under anaesthetic and Dr Shah would be returning to complete the operation, but only once he'd had a knock against the English tourists!

Fortunately for the poor patient, Dr Shah was not much of a cricketer and was dismissed cheaply. Nonetheless, he insisted he would be back for the second innings. And he was, completing the surgery from the end of a mobile phone whilst standing at mid-off, setting the field all the while.

We won this game comfortably against pretty weak opposition, but the self-aggrandisement of our host did not stop with the final ball. Oh no, we were treated to a speech of a good 15 minutes in which Dr Asghar Ali Shah spoke (in the third person) about the generosity and goodwill of local surgeon, Dr Asghar Ali Shah, and how much Dr Shah had done for the community, stopping at intervals for applause. It was quite bizarre. As was the trophy ceremony. For a knockabout 40-over game, there were awards for Best Batsman, Best Bowler, Best Fielder, Best Scorer (oh, yes) and even Best Umpire. Not only that, but a trophy for the runners-up, and an enormous golden cup for the winners which would have dwarfed the oversized egg-cup that is the Champions League trophy. It was the largest trophy I'd ever picked up and it certainly drew some attention as we manhandled it back to England on the plane. Come to think of it, it was the only trophy we won that year.

The dramatic evening at Dr Shah's stadium finished on a darker note as we found our team bus flanked by three armoured vehicles for our return journey home. We were all told to turn the inside lights off and to try not to show our white faces through the windows. Purely a precaution, of course. The reality of how dangerous Karachi was for Western visitors did not become apparent until a few weeks after our tour, when the New Zealand team suffered a bomb attack in the same street as our hotel had been. Then a year or so later, the terror attacks on New York on 9/11 brought the dangers home to the whole world. For many years after, Pakistan became a no-go zone for visitors, especially cricketers, and only now is the Pakistan Super League starting to re-establish cricket in Pakistan as a safe enough place to play. All this is very sad for a country mad about the game and much more beautiful and friendly than many Westerners may believe.

The hospitality was first-rate, with everyone in Pakistan doing their utmost to make us feel welcome. We enjoyed an amazing trip to Murree, in the foothills of the Himalayas, and had drinks receptions wherever we went. It was strange to see so many grown men sipping luminous orange Fanta from bottles and getting excited over the ice cream (alcohol, of course being banned in the Islamic country). I did ruffle a few feathers at one reception by breaking with gender convention and joining the women, who had been sent to an ante-room away from the men's conversation. It was just interesting to get a female perspective on a social norm which was alien to me, and they were happy, if a little surprised, to give me a lesson in their culture.

An equally interesting, and altogether male experience was being hosted by one of the world's all-time greatest sportspeople in the imposing shape of Jahangir Khan, the titan of squash in the 1980s. Jahangir welcomed us to his squash centre in Karachi and even had a game against one of our Pakistani team-mates, Ali Sawal, which was a definite thrill for him. As captain, I was given pride of place at dinner next to the great man, who was himself something of a self-promoter (albeit not in quite the same league as Dr Asghar Ali Shah). I was learning something about masculine attitudes in a very class and gender dominated society. I also benefited directly from the in-built hierarchy of the country. As captain, I had been given my own room in most hotels, was allowed to order from the à la carte menu and was always expected to be first in any line. Our tour manager suffered from being 25 but looking about 13, and was never really taken seriously by the locals, who seemed to have more respect for my being over six foot, and our coach – the distinguished 60-year-old Australian Jack Potter.

Potter had been some player in his day and what he really thought of us was only betrayed in his lowest moments. Although described by some as 'the best batsman never to play for Australia', his party trick was bowling at us in the nets and cleaning up every member of the squad with his flipper, which was impossible to read. Prior to joining Oxford University, Potter had been in charge of the Australian Cricket Academy. He claims that this self-same flipper is the one he taught to Shane Warne when he was on the Academy books. I have no idea if this is true, but if I ever meet Warney I'll ask him.

Although the hospitality had been excellent in Pakistan, despite our finding it hard to get to grips with the different attitudes to age, class and gender, one thing we were definitely missing was alcohol. Certainly for those of us who had got used to winding down after a day's play back home with a pint or four in the King's Arms opposite the Bodleian Library, coming off a day in the dirt with nothing more than a coke and another curry was starting to drag. So much so, that I underwent a complete role-reversal in Islamabad where, sharing a room with another Pakistani team-mate Salman Khan, I found myself rudely awakened when he returned in the middle of the night after a big session on the ice cream with his friends from home. It was only on the third time of asking how his night was, that he politely replied, 'Hicksy, I'm trying to pray here, do you mind?' It was normally me disturbing room-mates at all hours, and there was not much praying, although in hindsight a bit of divine inspiration might have done me some good.

By the time we reached Karachi, we were at our wits' end and ready to head home. But Ali Sawal, who was still glowing after his squash match with Jahangir, found a way to pay us back. He had not wanted to shout about the fact, but it turned out his father was a general in the Pakistani army, which effectively ruled the country after a military coup. This, it turned out, could open some doors. And so, with a nod and a wink, Ali told all the lads to meet in a particular room of the Pearl Continental hotel in Karachi and to wait there for him. Although a little confused, with not much other entertainment available as it was too dangerous to leave the hotel, we agreed. After a while, a grinning Ali appeared, followed by a hotel porter with a trolley on which were three large cases of Murree lager and a deck of two hundred cigarettes. 'You're welcome!' he beamed, as the boys gleefully got stuck in and the first real round of tour fines commenced. The only casualty from the evening was the poor member of our party who showed off his new nipple ring, only to find himself pinned down and a padlock attached until breakfast the next day.

First-Class Captain

Although in cricketing terms not exactly a resounding success, we felt that with the Pakistan tour under our belts and with one or two key players back for selection, we could head into our opening first-class game with some confidence. Unusually, it was an away trip, to Taunton to take on a Somerset side coached by Dermot Reeve and captained by Jamie Cox, another Australian who would have walked into the England Test team at the time but was nowhere near selection for his own country. As was usual, the professionals batted first, with Cox and Marcus Trescothick opening up.

The enthusiasm and belief of the students went up a notch when, in the second over of the day, Trescothick edged a simple catch to first slip off the gentle away-swing of Ben Vonwiller (another Australian some way further down the pecking order for Test selection than Cox). I was glad to pouch that one, and to see the local hero out for a duck, and then watch Cox bowled in the next over by our veteran left-arm seamer, David Mather. Mark Lathwell – whom stattos will remember won two Test caps – followed shortly afterwards to leave the hosts implausibly reeling at 28/3. Of course we were starting to get ahead of ourselves, with talk of rolling Somerset out for under a hundred and getting a big lead. Mather, with several first-class games under his belt by this stage, offered a voice of caution, saying 'It's 20/3 now but it could easily be 300/3 by close of play.' The wet-behind-the-ears amongst us poo-pooed his negativity. More fool us, as the calm class and experience of Mike Burns and Peter Bowler set about scoring solid hundreds and teaching us a lesson about patience and application. When Somerset eventually declared with only one more wicket falling, Mather's words were ringing in our ears. And the ringing got louder as we were swept away for 144 in our first innings, the only bright spot being a dogged 72 on debut from Scott Weenink – a postgraduate Kiwi who had already won a Blue for rugby and had played first-class cricket back home for Wellington (you can even find footage of him shelling a catch as a substitute fielder for New Zealand in the 1992 World Cup if you know which dark corners of the internet to explore).

The ignominy of being finally defeated by an innings and more than 400 runs after such a good start was only briefly lightened for me by adding Trescothick to my list of first-class wickets. He was as surprised as anyone else that I managed to spin one past his bat for a stumping as he tried to deposit me over the old pavilion. He had already made a horrible mess of Joe Porter's bowling figures. Porter (on the staff at Surrey at the time) was one of two Brookes boys making their debut, and after getting neckache seeing several trademark slog sweeps land in the car park was the only player in the country with an economy rate of over ten runs per over for much of the summer. At least he could bat. My scores in the game were one and nought, and one of those was a self-inflicted run-out.

And it was even worse for poor Alan Gofton, an amiable all-rounder from Derbyshire. As if to avenge the embarrassment of being out cheaply in the first innings, Cox took an aggressive approach in the second. So aggressive in fact that he hit a straight drive so hard from whence it came that Goffy didn't have time even to look up as it pinged into his head in his follow-through. Famed for their 'mental toughness', Cox's Aussie response was simply to wave to the pavilion to summon a new bat as the poor lad was carried off to hospital. Clearly this Pommie was not up to it. It was fair to say we had been brought down to earth with a bump. Tails firmly between legs, we returned to the relative safe space of our studies for a week or so. Time to catch up on some verb tables and 16th-century French poetry. Whether the Brookes boys did any studying was a question it didn't seem fair to ask.

We only managed one day of cricket out of the next six scheduled, against Hampshire and Warwickshire. Just enough time for poor Robin Smith to be wheeled out for some light-hearted photographs with his opposing number – me – under an umbrella before we all hit the pubs of Oxford. It was a similar story against Warwickshire, albeit we had chased some leather for a day against a team of eight internationals, including Allan Donald, who was less than impressed on being charged entry to a student night when we realised that the following day would be cancelled due to snow.

Cold Comfort in the West Country

A rare away game that season came against Gloucestershire at Bristol. It will go down as one of the most boring of all time, not helped by Baltic temperatures and the most stolid of centuries by Kim Barnett, whose bizarre technique of walking into the crease from outside leg stump was an intriguing novelty for around, ooh, three overs, before becoming utterly frustrating. Matt

'Steamy' Windows (one of my favourite cricketing nicknames) also scored a ton, in much quicker time, thanks to several spilled catches with no one keen to hold on to a rock-hard missile at virtually zero degrees, and with my old umpire mate Nigel Cowley refusing to give any decision the way of the eggheads from Oxford. He even turned me down for a stonewall lbw. I know it was out because I hadn't turned one all match, so cold were my fingers. I got my own back years later on his son Darren. As his best man on his stag do in Newquay, I insisted he dress up as a blind umpire, complete with dark glasses, Dickie Bird flat cap and toy Dalmatian on a string. Not that I bear grudges at all. A brief moment of gallows humour did offer itself up when Windows launched Ross Garland for a straight six, to see the ball bounce back off the pavilion to end up back in the bowler's hands. We found it funny; whether Rossco did, well, who cares?

No wicket for 71 runs in Gloucestershire's first – and only – innings did not constitute a good return for yours truly. Nor did nicking off for one with the thinnest of edges to Jon Lewis, into the unmistakeable gloves of England's most recognisable and eccentric wicketkeeper, Jack Russell. By all accounts, Russell was one-of-a-kind, and we did manage to corroborate that he took several packs of Weetabix on tour with him, which he meticulously left to soften in milk for an exact period of time, and that he was totally paranoid about anyone knowing where he lived. Apparently, on the rare occasion when one of his team-mates needed to visit, he would meet them several miles away, blindfold them and then drive them in his car, only unmasking them when they were inside, with no obvious points of reference. An odd man, but a superb gloveman. Cricket is certainly better off for having this type of unique character, and I would argue that the nature of the game itself actually contributes to uncovering them.

In the end, we managed to dig out a draw after following on, and kept the professionals out in the field for the best part of five sessions – a taste of their own medicine, at least, even if by the end of the match everyone would have sooner been pulling their own teeth out. So we could notch up a creditable first-class draw, and I could at least resign myself to the fact that I'd been dismissed by a combination of England internationals. Cold comfort, indeed.

And then we got absolutely trounced by Glamorgan at home, after which Matthew Maynard was pretty vocal about our right to first-class status. He would have had a point: thus far in my captaincy season, we had done little since the first few overs at Somerset to suggest we were anything more than bang-average park cricketers. I remember this game as coinciding with my first date with Penny – a women's Blues cricketer who looked good in culottes, and who later took the bold move of becoming my wife. I remember it mostly for a phone interview I did with the local press after the game responding to Maynard's comments in a belligerent and no doubt vocal way, ensuring that my date knew I was something of a BNOC (Big Name on Campus). I hoped she hadn't seen the scorecard.

There was no sugar-coating it, though. We had been trounced, and the season was not looking like a resounding success. What happened next was something of a surprise, then.

Beating the 'Big Boys'

The undoubted highlight of my year as captain of Oxford was beating Northamptonshire at the Parks, in our final first-class game before we headed to Lord's for the Varsity Match. Although Northants were perhaps not at full-strength, nonetheless, they could boast two England off-spinners in their ranks, in Jason Brown and a blast from my past, Graeme Swann.

The latter who would go on to great things in an England shirt, including taking the winning wicket in the 2009 Ashes series and regaining the Ashes Down Under in 2010/11.

Day one followed a familiar pattern to usual, with the professionals batting first, although by this time in the season we were using an already-used pitch, which would hopefully give me some assistance as a spinner, even on the first day, something which I was unused to. And it paid off for me, with my best first-class figures to date of 4-63 – not quite the 'Michelle'[3] I'd hoped for, but four wickets in the first innings nonetheless. Sadly, a spinning pitch would play right into the hands of the Northamptonshire duo, and we found ourselves reduced to a paltry 87/9 in quick time and kicking ourselves at a missed opportunity.

Then – a cricketing miracle – one of those remarkable last-wicket stands which come along once in a blue moon – a Border-and-Thomson, Stokes-and-Leach moment (minus the spectacles) which turns the game on its head. For us it was Khan and Gofton. Salman – our mercurial opening bowler who would have been smarting at being No.11. He would often go AWOL after lunch on a Friday for prayers just as he was needed to bat and who occasionally, just occasionally, might come off with his idiosyncratic mixture of sweeps, glided cuts and proper cow-corner haymakers. Salman warmed up for bowling by dropping on one knee and wheeling his arm around as fast as he could ten times, whilst the professionals would have all manner of elastic bands and medicine balls to hand, and as he entered the fray to bat in this innings he was giving it the full windmill à la Botham circa 1985. At the other end, Alan Gofton – quietly spoken Chesterfield lad Goffy – now recovered from the blow to his head at Taunton. Goffy also rated his batting

3   After Michelle Pfeiffer, the Hollywood actress – rhyming slang for five-fer – a five-wicket haul.

more highly than his bowling. Well, the chance had come for both of them to prove it.

And prove it they did. With quite distinct styles, the final pair of Oxford put on an astonishing partnership of 134 and whilst we were still in arrears, the sight of the ball disappearing off the heavily stickered Kashmiri willow of Khan over fully four fielders posted on the leg-side boundary raised ever increasing cheers and laughter from the students watching, whilst the wry smiles of Swann et al were starting to turn to embarrassed scowls. Khan looked on his way to the unlikeliest of first-class tons before falling short attempting yet another village-green hoick on 87, and leaving his partner three short of a first fifty at this level.

Could we win? Did we have the momentum to capitalise? Of course, we believed this was our moment. Of course, I was the captain who had said in a scout hut during a drunken pre-season evening after orienteering around the Oxford woods that on a good day we could even beat Australia. Of course, at home, on a turning pitch, we might just manage it. So maybe.

And do you know what? It started to happen. We played really well, they made mistakes and suddenly by the close of play on day two, it was game on, with the visitors at 114/4. Bowling a county side out once was a good effort. To do it twice in a game was largely unheard of, and so when Swann junior (his brother Alec was also playing) came to the crease, we knew we were a few wickets away from something quite special. Personally, I'd be lying if I said I didn't have my eye on that elusive five-bag this time around. And with both Swanns in my pocket in each innings, I finally reached that milestone, which I am very proud of, and which sits happily on my rather sparse Wikipedia page today as one of two first-class five-fers. I was even frustrated that they declared with eight down as there was the chance of a ten-wicket match. Nonetheless, it's funny how some days when

I am teaching, that page just happens to find itself (by accident, of course!) projected on the screen in my classroom.

The chase was on. And for once, the Parks was seeing a real contest in a first-class fixture. In the year before I went up to Oxford, Mark Wagh had single-handedly won a match for the university with back-to-back hundreds against Kent, but this time, it was going to take a whole team to get us over the line.

Oh dear. 6/1 as Ross Garland was lbw. But some dogged play from ex-skipper Claughton and wicketkeeper Richard Smalley steadied the ship. Another fifty from Porter and suddenly the Brookes boy was everyone's hero. Byron Byrne – now an Oxford don, but then a nuggety Western Australian with a penchant for one-liners – took up the baton. No helmet for him, but a jaunty Harlequin cap, as if channelling the Jardine spirit. We were 143/3 into the afternoon, with just 100 left to score. Surely we could eke those out. But Porter was castled on 54, Gofton came and went, unable to match his heroics of the first innings, then Byrne was also dismissed and we were six-down still shy of 150. But Swann could not make inroads and Scott Weenink showed his experience alongside James Redmayne (brother of the Hollywood actor Eddie), who scored an unbeaten 43, to take the score to 182. And then it was Khan-time again. Salman got his way and was promoted up the order. 'Don't worry, Hicksy. I'll finish this off,' he said as he strode out to the middle, leaving me with my pads and gloves on, not believing that lightning would strike twice. But my lack of faith was shown up, as he raced to 39 from 44 balls to leave Redmayne short of a fifty. He didn't care, and nor did any of us, and we celebrated as if we'd won the Ashes.

The only disappointment about this game, and my performance, was that I was not selected for the British

Universities side against Zimbabwe, although Joe Porter deservedly was and scored 93 – he deserved three figures after the season he'd had for us. Sadly, not being at the 'proper' university, we'd have to cope without him when we took on the oldest of enemies at Lord's in our final first-class game of the season and perhaps my biggest match ever.

Last Captain at Lord's

You'd have to be at the extreme end of being a cricket 'badger' to know the answer to this one, but here's some trivia: Who was the last ever first-class captain of Oxford University at Lord's? You guessed it. This is probably one of the most niche claims-to-fame ever, but there you go. Since James Pyemont and I shook hands and then posed for some of the most cringeworthy press photos, no one has led OUCC out at Lord's in a first-class game, and I strongly suspect they never will.

It goes without saying that it was an immensely proud moment for me. Whilst it was not the dark blue England cap of my dreams on my head, walking through the Long Room, down the steps and through that little white picket gate with your team behind you is an experience few enjoy, and the great thing about cricket is that you get to do it every session you are in the field. Sadly, that was more than we'd hoped during the 2000 Varsity Match, which was really a damp squib. Literally– it was rained off from day two onwards.

The only notable memories from a match Cambridge dominated – they were 382/4 declared in the first innings – were the photos I mentioned above – the completely implausible sight of me and my counterpart walking out on to the field in jacket and tie – he with a bat over his shoulder; I with a kit bag. A scene which never happened, and would never have been likely to happen. Embarrassing, especially as it represents one of my only features in the national sporting press.

The second incident which sticks in the mind was what happened on the evening of day two, which precipitated a pretty heated row between me and Pyemont on the top tier of the pavilion. It all came down to the fact that I had agreed in principle that we would bat for a short time and then effectively forfeit the rest of our first innings, in order for them to set us a total which might mean a result was possible despite the rain predicted in the next couple of days. However, once our opening pair got off to a flyer, I – and the rest of the team – felt to withdraw would be handing over initiative, and so we changed our minds. This was not really the done thing, I know, but all's fair in love and Varsity Matches, right? So when the players came off at stumps at the end of the second day, Pyemont collared me and took me to task. It was not pleasant, but it did show just how important this contest is to those involved. That old rivalry is as bitter as any out there, and reputations were on the line. I still spare a thought for that moment when I'm in the pavilion on Test-match days, and wonder what other conversations have gone on behind closed doors in that grand old building over the years.

And to end this episode on an even more offbeat note; when I was growing up, the words 'Lords 2000' were synonymous with a particular type of cheapo cricket bat you could buy in a string bag with a set of stumps and a rubber ball. Now I had a shirt with Lord's 2000 on it for a different reason, but the joke was not lost on some of my contemporaries.

Interviewing Dilley

If the imposter syndrome from the pre-season first-class captains' meeting had worn off by the time the season was underway, it was certainly rekindled when the ECB decided to make the Centres of Excellence a permanent feature of the cricket landscape. This would require the appointment of new head coaches for all six proposed centres, which meant interviews would need to take place. The panel for interviews would include the current club captains, which is how I found myself sitting across the table grilling another one of my heroes and another bona fide England legend in the form of Graham Roy Dilley.

Dilley had always fascinated me for his curving run-up, golden flowing locks and slightly slingshot action, and he was certainly a mainstay of the England team in those important formative years when the names on the scoresheet take on mythical status in the mind of a child. He was usually first on the teamsheet when I would play one of several interminable pencil cricket tournaments. England fans will forever remember him for his role as foil to Ian Botham during *that* innings at Headingley in 1981, and the catch on the boundary to remove Rod Marsh off Bob Willis.

Now, here was this giant in my memory in front of me, having to field questions about how he would cope with the demands of managing students whose priority might not always be cricket, but rather the finer points of the PhD they might be finishing, or in the case of others, how to get away with another hangover from a night at DTM's ...[4]

As much as I would have loved to work with Dilley, it was rightly felt that his style would better suit the more professional ambitions of those at Loughborough University, and he duly went there for a successful period until his untimely death in 2011.

Another interviewee that day was Chris Scott, a former wicketkeeper from Durham, who will go down in history as the man who dropped Brian Lara on 18 before he went on to amass the world-record first-class score of 501 not out. We've all

---

4   A rather insalubrious nightclub in Oxford, DTM stands for 'Downtown Manhattan', and was anything but.

dropped a catch and thought, 'I hope that won't cost too many.' Poor Chris is probably sick to the back teeth of being reminded of that incident, rather than his 100-plus first-class matches. In any case, he seemed a nice guy, and was appointed as coach of Cambridge; the only downside to this being it meant that university cricket saw the end of Derek Randall.

In the end Oxford went for a serious, softly-spoken chap I'd never heard of, called Graham Charlesworth, a South African who had played a little bit of state cricket back home and been on the books at Worcestershire without lighting up the world. 'Charlie' couldn't have been more different from the streetwise Jack Potter. Here we had a young coach who was going to take a far more professional approach in terms of the standards he would expect from us, off the pitch as well as on. This was absolutely appropriate for the new situation in which both Oxford University and Oxford Brookes University would play an equal part, although it would be an approach which would certainly shake up some of the happy-go-lucky amateurs of the older institution (myself included). Almost immediately we were 'invited' to compulsory extra fitness sessions at hitherto unheard of hours which, anti-socially, curtailed drinking sessions at one end, and lie-ins at the other. It was clear we would be expected to front up if we wanted to make the squad. I guess the decision to employ Charlesworth was a good one in the end, since he has been the Oxford coach ever since. I'll take the credit for that!

In many ways, the 2000 season should have been one which went down as one of my best. But it was very much a tale of two halves. I loved being captain. I loved the challenge of corralling a team made up of a mixture of ages, nationalities, backgrounds and attitudes to cricket. I loved trying to bring a change to an old institution in the introduction of players from Oxford Brookes, and I loved all the bureaucracy of committee meetings and, yes, all the politics. I guess I just liked feeling important.

But it was hard work, too, alongside attempting to do enough academic work to keep the tutors from calling my place in the college into question, as well as the important matter of keeping my new girlfriend happy.

By the time term finished and the Varsity Match was over, I'd played well over 50 days of cricket and was mentally drained. I didn't realise this at the time, but my performances as professional for South Wilts CC in Salisbury were lukewarm, as described elsewhere, and I lost confidence with my bowling, most likely feeling pressure to perform. So much so that I was dropped by Dorset for the Minor Counties final which we went on to win for the first time. And so it was with a bittersweet feeling that I boarded a plane in mid-September for the little-known tropical island of La Réunion, neighbour to Mauritius, thousands of miles from the nearest set of stumps or a ludicrous little ball of cork wrapped in string and leather, ostensibly to become fluent in French. Not a bad fringe benefit from my Oxford degree.

Chapter Five

Some Real Legends

Colin Cowdrey at Arundel Castle

One of the great highlights of my young life as a cricket fan – aside from the monthly arrival of *The Cricketer*, and applying linseed oil to my Duncan Fearnley 'Colt' – was using my Bunbury Club membership to attend the traditional opening game for the season's touring side against Lavinia, Duchess of Norfolk's XI at the idyllic Arundel Castle in Sussex.

What could be more inspiring than seeing some of the world's greatest cricketers up close and personal in the flesh? I remember being dumbfounded by just how tall Walsh and Ambrose were, with my head coming up to their hips; I can remember in vivid visual detail the stitching on the badge of Paul Reiffel's Australia jumper, and I remember endlessly pacing around the boundary with my little brother to get the autographs of as many stars as I possibly could in a special book (which I still have) bought at Dean Park, Bournemouth on the occasion of the first county game I attended. Prize among these signatures is Brian Lara, the fabulous – but disgraced – Mohammad Azharuddin, Robin Smith, Chris Lewis and many more.

What was also great was being able to go on to the outfield in the intervals to play yourself. Whether I ever thought I'd get to play there for real I can't recall, but it was certainly exciting to have the chance to do so when playing for the university during one of the traditional fixtures which offered some respite from the ritual humiliation of playing the county sides. For those few uninitiated, Arundel is definitely a bucket-list ground – one of those quintessentially English venues on which any cricketer would love to play. Picket fences, a natural amphitheatre and a distant castle. Imagine, then, how an already promising day gained immeasurably in lustre when we were welcomed by Sir Colin Cowdrey. And what was more, he was attired just like us – proudly in dark blue blazer, Crowns and all. Bulletproof.

Sir Colin – what a gent – the man whose initials were MCC was born to captain England, and there is something so sturdily oaky about that Tonbridge-Kent-England heritage that Cowdrey lives in my mind as indelibly a part of 20th-century English history as Churchill. That morning, Cowdrey felt to me as if he had literally stepped out the pages of *Wisden* or one of my grandad's old annuals. Not a hair out of place, and although a touch portly, he had an avuncular bearing such that I felt he was more of a distant relation than an all-time great come to watch a side which would be a pale imitation of those he had been involved in when he was an undergraduate at the Parks.

He told us about how he would only deign to play using a 'Twort' ball – an apparently superior ball to the ubiquitous Dukes or Readers – which we indeed still used in our matches, and which was the best cricket ball I can remember using. Cowdrey was one of the last vestiges of a time before Twenty20 (which he would have found anathema), and before the great power struggles of recent years which have seen the juggernauts of the ICC and BCCI bring into question the very stewardship of the game, sidelining that other great old English institution – MCC. But before I alienate those for whom the Marylebone Cricket Club represents upper-middle-class privilege and entitlement, can I say that I love the club like I love Isambard Kingdom Brunel, the Cobb at Lyme Regis and Stonehenge. Not because they necessarily have a powerful relevance in today's society, but because they tie us to something grand and worth protecting in our heritage. In fact, exactly how I felt about Sir Colin.

Sadly, he passed away not long after, but few gentlemen have made me feel as if I were walking in the sepia pages of history.

As for the game itself, I only remember losing heavily and finding the pitch so flat to bowl on that I went away with a jaded view of the ground. Funny how our gilded memories can be tainted by a poor performance.

Lord Ted

If Colin Cowdrey is the personification of Oxford cricket, then perhaps his obvious light-blue counterpart is Ted Dexter. Dexter, too, represented the old establishment of a bygone era which was detested by the likes of Ian Botham and Mike Gatting (for whom Dexter as an administrator was like mixing oil and water). Dexter seemed a rather less amiable character and altogether more aloof and disdainful to those he deemed lesser than himself. I may be being hugely unfair, as I only really came across 'Lord' Ted on one occasion which was at the Parks during a match where a reunion lunch had been organised and he was the most well-known of the dignitaries. What was so striking about this event was watching Dexter and his old team-mates make their way from the pavilion to the marquee about a hundred metres away. These once fine athletes now hobbled their way on bowed knees and arthritic ankles and although in the flush of youth, I seem to remember thinking of this as a vision of my future. Now almost twice my life on, I wish I'd spent more time investing in my long-term flexibility and fitness. If I'm around long enough to pop in to watch a Varsity

Match in another 30 years, I have no doubt I'll be another gnarled old once-might-have-been; a cautionary reminder to another bunch of young pups who no doubt will pay as little attention as I did to the inevitable ravages of age.

Sir John Paul Getty's Ground, Wormsley

Arundel and the Parks are both beautiful grounds, as redolent of traditional English cricket as pressed flannels, linseed oil and cream teas. Another ground I was privileged to play at whilst at university was the ground at Sir John Paul Getty's estate in Wormsley, Buckinghamshire, which has since become the home for the Minor Counties one-day final. As one might expect being hosted by one of the world's wealthiest men, a day's cricket at Getty's was something quite special. The ground is fastidiously manicured, with a chocolate-box thatched pavilion atop a man-made bank which leads down steps to the billiard-table surface of the playing area. Marquees line the bank, and champagne is thrust into your hand as soon as you arrive, and doesn't stop flowing until you say stop.

Knowing this, I took the decision in 2000 to 'rest' myself for the Sunday friendly at Wormsley, after a hard week of competitive cricket. I would, however, travel as twelfth man. Of course, I had little intention of getting anywhere near the pitch, let alone donning the whites. No, I had more pressing business with the Veuve Clicquot and the captain of Oxford's women's netball team, who was my guest for the afternoon. And so it was from the sidelines that I offered moral support to the players, and from where I was able to witness Simon 'Yosser' Hughes – famed for his books *A Lot of Hard Yakka* and *Yakking around the World* as well as being known as The Analyst on Channel 4's cricket coverage. Also playing was David 'Syd' Lawrence – the burly Gloucestershire fast bowler who had played a handful of Tests before suffering a horrific knee injury. What was amusing on this occasion was that Lawrence had started by running in off a half-run, bowling well within himself in the manner of a benefit match, but found that in doing so, he could barely land the ball on the cut strip. Embarrassing for him, and mildly amusing for those watching. More amusing (in typical sadistic cricket fashion) was seeing him then decide to take his full run-up, which meant our openers suffered a ferociously quick spell of erratic fast bowling, which is always best enjoyed from 100 yards away, with a glass of something cold and fizzy in one's hand, rather than from 22 with a flimsy slice of willow.

After lunch, I was able to commit fully to what was no longer thinly disguised as anything but a date, and the netball captain and I spent a luxurious afternoon perusing the library in the house there, full of old tomes, including an original copy of Chaucer's *Canterbury Tales*. It was certainly a better first date than I managed for other girlfriends. If you ever get the chance to play at Wormsley, I can thoroughly recommend you put your hand up for twelfth man.

First Dates

The day at Getty's was notable in my memory for another reason. It turned out to be the same day which I met my future wife (not the netball captain, may I add). On returning to Oxford in a pretty well-lubricated state, the minibus dropped off the guests who had accompanied us by the Ashmolean Museum. Being a 'school night', my date politely declined my invitation to find somewhere to continue what had been a thoroughly posh and enjoyable day, and made her way home, to get ready for lectures the next morning. Being in my second year of four, and with very little interest in learning much at all at this stage, I persuaded my old mucker Charlie Warren to invite me into his college – Worcester – which was just down the road and likely to still be serving in the bar.

On arriving in the cellar bar, we found that half of the Oxford women's cricket team were already there, still in the traditional culottes which have now gone the way of button-up shirts and hobnail bowling boots and been consigned to the dustbin of historic cricket kit. It was there that I first met one Penelope Dain, happily celebrating a victory with probably too many pints of Grolsch lager. Certainly too many to be in a fit state for decision-making, as she ended up taking me to the next bar where we had a drunken kiss before she wobbled off on her bike, leaving me in a quandary the next morning about whether to pursue this cricketing maiden, or throw my lot in with the netballer.

History dictates the rest, and so we had our 'official' first date the next week, after the three-day game in which we had been soundly outplayed by Glamorgan. I was still in my Blues blazer and I hold that she was utterly starstruck. The truth is more likely that she was keen to get me into the pub and out of my ostentatious jacket as quickly as possible to see if I had more to offer than blowing my own trumpet. Twenty years on, I don't think she's yet convinced …

Chapter Six

An Englishman, Irishman and Scotsman meet on a tropical island …

IF YOU study languages at Oxford, it is expected that you spend a good part of the third year of your course living in a country which speaks the language you are meant to be learning. For most, this meant heading to work as an intern in Paris, as an au pair in the Dordogne or teaching as an *assistant* in a French school. Having given little thought to what I might do in this year, I jumped at the suggestion made by my mate from Belfast, Gareth, to join him on an island I'd barely heard of, some 5,000 miles from Paris, let alone the Parks. The next job was to persuade our tutor that this was not just a ridiculous jolly to some paradise island, but a legitimate learning trip. Yeah right. I cooked up some story about how it would benefit the linguistics side of my course, and on the promise of a paper to be delivered on my return about the development of the local creole language (still to be completed), he reluctantly agreed.

Imagine this. You are coasting over a sea of the most incredible azure, nothing for miles in any direction. In the furthest distance, land appears. An emerald speck at first, but coming closer you can start to identify an island, rimmed on one side with golden sands and a lagoon, whilst to the other, white explosions crash on to forbidding rocks. Hills of deep green forest climb from the coast, and under closer inspection, sheer ravines appear, ribboned with thin bands of silver which are waterfalls inaccessible from ground level. One side of the island is dominated by a volcano angrily spewing lava and a collapsed volcano in the centre of the island has created three natural basins fully 3,000 metres deep, where some of the inhabitants only received electricity in the 1980s. La Réunion is as bizarre and as beautiful as it sounds. It is the close neighbour to Mauritius and yet officially part of France. It was the first place in the world to use the Euro and was where I called home for three months during my third year at university. After a season which had started in Pakistan in March and ended in mid-September, I was in need of a break from cricket, and this place had never heard of the game. In fact, anyone you mentioned cricket to assumed you meant the game with long mallets, hard balls and hoops.

You get to know people pretty quickly when you are a long way from home, and Gareth and I could not have been forced into any closer proximity when it transpired that although he had told me we were registered with the university in the capital, Saint-Denis, we were anything but. My French was, and still is, pretty ropey for a bloke with an Oxford degree in the language, but I could make out some snatches of the conversation he had with the administrators:

'Monsieur Graham, we told you not to come. There is no course, and no rooms for you.'

Cue twinkling eyes and charming Belfast brogue (in French)

'Mais oui, but we are here now, so surely we can work something out?'

'Non, Monsieur. It would be better if you were to go back home.'

'Please?'

'Non, Monsieur'.

Merde. F***ing merde. My best mate had sold me an absolute dummy here, and now we were stuck like two utter lemons with backpacks on a remote island, no job, no course to study and no bed for the night. *Merci f***ing beaucoup, Gareth.*

His response?

'I knew if I told you, you'd never have come.'

He was bloody right too. I would not have had the utter temerity to arrive in a foreign land on a wing and a prayer, hoping that it would be all right on the night. I was all for heading straight back to the airport and calling it quits.

But he was not giving up that easily, and managed to persuade me to go with him and throw ourselves at the mercy of the English students who had actually got themselves together to find a course and a room. And so, for two nights, we were fortunate to be allowed to doss on the floor of a chap called Andy from Sheffield.

It is to my total discredit that I have no idea where Andy from Sheffield is now and even what his surname is, but he saved our bacon for that 48 hours. We owe him more than one.

And then a remarkable thing happened. We had been continuing to pester the administration office, who were not changing their tune, but who were beginning to realise that my Irish friend was a stubborn beggar and was not going away. And on the third day, just as they had said there was no room for us at the inn, the wearied lady offered a lifeline:

'There is something, perhaps ...' she offered.

A chink of light. An olive branch perhaps. We needed it. Andy's floor was rock hard and his patience was ebbing.

'There is a cleaning lady on the sixth floor of the halls of residence. Go there and ask for Madame Rosette.'

OK. That was enough. We raced over there and found the woman: a short, roundy Madagascan lady with gleaming eyes and a beaming smile. She told us (from what I could make out with my limited French) that God had come to her in a dream and told her about these two British lads who needed a bit of help. So far, so weird. But she was willing to take us to stay at her place until we could sort a job and a roof over our heads. It was as close as I have come to a miracle. And consider that this was a single woman who had escaped an unhappy relationship, and was living with three children in a two-bedroom apartment on a council estate. It was the most generous and kind act I have ever witnessed, and one I will never forget. Never mind that Gareth and I would have to share a bed for a fortnight, this was only possible with her having given up her own bed and having asked her 16-year-old daughter to share with her little sister. It was quite remarkable.

It did take us a couple of weeks but we eventually found jobs as teaching assistants down the coast towards the more touristy areas of the island and could give her her bed back. Sadly, the only place we could find a room was the tiniest box-room (the old laundry) of a hotel in the tourist resort of St-Gilles-Les-Bains, where we spent yet another four weeks sharing a double. By the time we moved out of those digs, Gareth and I knew each other better than our own mothers, but we were starting to have a ball.

Life in Réunion consisted of 12 hours' work a week, teaching in a school which knocked off at 1pm and overlooked the most amazing surfing beaches. Aside from the work, which was hardly onerous, we spent our time lazing on the golden sands or drinking local rum-based cocktails and smoking Gauloises in one of the many bars along the strip which was dubbed the 'St

Tropez' of the island. This was far better than studying. Gareth and I moved in with a short, tubby, pasty-white Glaswegian ex-chef called George, which meant that we were, literally, an Englishman, Irishman and Scotsman on a tropical island. You could make your own jokes.

And we quite quickly became part of the cast of characters around this eclectic beach resort, supporting such protagonists as Tony, the topless drunk who serenaded anyone and everyone with his harmonica, and another local vagrant by the name of 'Sinon', who moped around wearing fully four layers of clothing despite the 40 degree heat, and who had apparently been a pop star back home before his jealous brother made him eat a local white flower which gave him short-term memory loss. It was a town ripe for a sitcom.

Réunion was the only place I have ever experienced being on the receiving end of racism. The local population hate the French mainlanders for historical and economic reasons (a bit like the Welsh, Scots, Irish, Australians, and well, basically everyone hates the English). So when people came across our white faces for the first time, the feeling was frosty at best. But as soon as we opened our mouths, it was painfully apparent that we were not French at all, and suddenly we were welcomed with open arms as 'Les Britanniques'. People would stop to say '*bonjour*' as we went about our business and we were able to rack up tabs in various bars.

Probably the best illustration of how well we were received was when George found himself teaching a class of 18- to 19-year-olds, among whom was one particularly attractive local girl. All caramel skin, dark hair and blue eyes, he would describe how he found himself hot under the collar as she smiled sweetly at him and tried to speak English with a faltering accent. Worse for him, his lunch break would usually consist of a walk along the beach, where he soon found that she and her classmates had the habit of sunbathing topless. Night after night, he would come home from work flustered and anxious, asking us how he should deal with this. Eventually, the final straw came, as this tropical beauty stopped to talk to him after class. Gulp. This could have been the end for George and his teaching career. As he relates, the conversation went something like this:

'Monsieur, you are very handsome.'

'Och, that's kind, but I'm not sure that's true. I'm five foot five, overweight and balding.'

'Oui, but you are so different from other men.'

'Oh aye, how's that?'

'You are, how do you say, *exotique.*'

Exotique! George was about as exotic as a deep-fried Mars Bar. In any case, as she fluttered her eyelids at him, he knew it was time to get a new job before he got himself in trouble. I was glad my pupils were all much younger.

We had a fabulous time. I learnt to surf (sort of), flew in a helicopter over the volcano, learnt some of the language, had too many amazing nights out sleeping under the stars and waking up by the ocean to remember and made some fabulous friends and memories. We also finished the trip with Penny and Gareth's girlfriend coming to join us for a week in Mauritius, just a short hop away for us, but a pretty lavish first holiday as a couple in their third year at university. But cricket was still calling me, and by Christmas I was itching to get back. Although I was meant to do six months' immersion in French, I decided that more first-class wickets, the chance of another Blue and even maybe some county trials was more important. So I headed home.

Chapter Seven

On Trial

2001 Season

The 'Intruder'

During my second 'gap year', when I was meant to be 6,000 miles away on a tropical island learning French, I returned at Christmas to get properly stuck into pre-season training without the inconveniences of lectures and tutorials. I had reasoned that as long as I stayed the other side of town from my college, swore a few people to secrecy and just kept my head down, I could sustain the illusion that I was dutifully immersing myself in a foreign culture whilst actually girding my loins for another season in the Parks. So I moved into Penny's room in Merton College, overlooking the mulberry tree under which, allegedly (and probably apocryphally), J.R.R. Tolkien conceived the universe of Middle Earth for his *Lord of the Rings* trilogy. Unfortunately, she happened to be studying hard for her finals, so whilst I was splitting my time between the nets, the gym and various coffee shops and pubs of Oxford, she was needing more and more focus on her Classics degree – seen by some as the hardest degree going, with more than 20 hours of exams to face after a four-year slog. So once the initial romantic glow of 'living together' had worn off, with me returning late and not in great shape from a weekday nightclub excursion, the decision was made (unilaterally, may I add) that I should move out for the crucial 'Finals' term, which meant begging a bed for the cricket season from some college mates in the year below, up in the student area of Cowley, a stone's throw from the indoor nets at Iffley Road, where Roger Bannister famously broke the four-minute mile. I can't imagine what poor old Roger would have made of the likes of me puffing and wheezing our way around the track during training sprints.

So it was that I took up residence in the smallest box-room in Christendom for what was to be an unhindered 2001 season, which would end in glorious victories over the 'filthy Tabs'[5] both at Lord's in the new one-day Varsity Match and on their home turf at Fenner's. But all that was to come, and much fun was to be had between times in that house on Hurst Street.

One particular incident has become legend in our circle of friends, and was even wheeled out in a best man's speech several years later, despite neither me, or Penny – the real protagonist of the story – being there. It happened on a night when Penny had deigned to grace me with her presence overnight in the box-room. In the next-door bedroom was my housemate Dom, who had once made the obliquest of comments about a top which Penny was wearing, which led to incessant ribbing about how he was ogling her and fancied her rotten. In the middle of this particular night, we were woken abruptly by the sound of windows and doors crashing, and before we knew it Dom had appeared at the door in his underwear with a golf club in hand shouting at us to wake up as an intruder had scaled the flat roof at the back of the house and was trying to get into his

---

5   The Oxford nickname for those from 'The Other Place'. 'Tab' derives from *Cantab* – the word you put after your degree from Cambridge (e.g.: Michael Atherton, MA (Cantab)). The Oxford equivalent is Oxon (e.g.: Sir Colin Cowdrey, MA (Oxon)). Our sole aim every year was to 'Shoe the filthy Tabs'.

room. However, as he entered our room, he also instinctively switched on the light. In true chivalrous fashion, and to cover my compromised modesty, I grabbed the (single) duvet, leaving Penny with not a scrap to cover herself, and Dom now not knowing where to look.

Of course, blokes being blokes, we were all totally sympathetic and recognised this was just an unfortunate accident. Or did we? Well, of course not. The story, even after all this time, is that Dom had cooked up the idea of the intruder just to cop a gander at Penny in the buff.

Centres of 'Excellence'

The start of the 2001 season was a time of change for the university. A new coach – Graham Charlesworth – came in to replace Jack Potter and their styles could not have been more different. Jack was old-school and happy for us to rely on raw talent, team spirit and what you might call an 'enlightened amateur' approach. Charlesworth was more plastic cones, throw-downs and shuttle runs. What he may have lacked in character in comparison to the old Australian, he made up for in time spent with players, throwing balls, hitting catches, analysing videos. He brought some much-needed professionalism, not that this was welcomed by all the players of course. Nor were his new, higher expectations immediately adopted in all quarters.

One of the first things we were asked to do in pre-season was to keep a food diary. Anything which passed our lips was to be recorded on a sheet – standard issue I'm sure for any pro sportsman these days, but when you are a student, you may not want to be totally honest about all your lifestyle choices. When it came to declaring the first week's calorific intake, one naïve new boy worked out that 66% of his week's intake had come in alcoholic form. Not exactly the way to prove your dedication to your sport. We also had weekly fitness sessions on the track which were vomit-inducing, although our attitude to recovery left a lot to be desired. After one of these sessions, we felt he had 'earned' a night out, and I found myself in one of those debauched university 'dining' societies (which was just code for putting on a bow tie and drinking yourself silly). At this one, the expectation was that you would bring a bottle of sherry or Madeira, which would have to be finished single-handedly before the main course arrived. Although Oxford largely avoided too many of the sporting initiations which, sadly, still run rife through university sport, and actually put young people off joining clubs these days, still some of the unsavoury stereotypes of posh lads misbehaving definitely took place on a regular basis.

The landscape of university cricket had changed, with now six 'Centres of Excellence' (Bradford/Leeds; Cardiff; Durham and Loughborough plus Oxford and Cambridge) enjoying the chance to play official first-class matches against counties. Of course this made sense, but for Oxford and Cambridge it represented a backward step. Now we would play three matches, not six, and all in the early weeks of the season, when professional seamers would lick their lips at the prospect of some easy early wickets to get them up the averages table, and the students would not have the luxury of acclimatising as we had the previous year. We did, however, manage to persuade the authorities that the Varsity Match should remain first-class, so we would have four bites at the first-class cherry. Also, this was the year that university cricket became a meritocracy, and our new coach was very keen to tap into the resource of Oxford Brookes. We even changed our logo from our treasured crowns to a more generic ECB logo. The times were indeed a-changing.

Our three matches would be against Middlesex, Hampshire and Warwickshire.

Three 'Test' Wickets in an Innings

I once won a quiz at a dinner party where several ex-cricketers
were present, and at which the answers all referred to one of the
guests. One of the questions was an easy one for me to answer.
'Which person around the table took the wickets of three Test
players in one first-class innings?' I was immediately taken
back to the opening day of the 2001 season when we took on
Middlesex, and which marked the debut of a fast bowler from
Warwickshire whom we thought would go far in the game. Tom
Mees had joined Oxford Brookes, was on a summer contract
at Warwickshire, and bowled as fast as any student we'd seen
in the past three years. So much so, that we started putting
plans together which involved such hitherto unseen weapons as
bouncers, and getting players caught 'on the hook'. There was
even some excitable talk about being able to employ a short-leg
fielder, rather than adopting our usual ring-field-with-sweepers-
once-the-shine-has-gone approach, armed only with a small
battery of military medium dobbers. A little like Joe Root's
over-enthusiasm when given the chance to play Jofra Archer, I
was keen to see Mees used as much as possible, especially having
had to endure a painful morning in some pre-season nets at
Radley College when Mees made clear, through a barrage of
bouncers aimed at my posh, hungover, Oxford bonce, that he
was not respecter of reputation.

Mees made an instant impact in his first innings with ball in
hand, removing two Test captains, no less, in a hostile opening
spell, which saw Andrew Strauss clean bowled and Stephen
Fleming plumb in front on his way to a deserved six-wicket
haul. It gave us a chance to compete and once again stoked some
hope that we might challenge the pros this season.

It was in this innings that I managed the feat of dismissing
three Test players, at least one of which is worth being proud
of! Owais Shah was a mercurial player for England – at times

he seemed to have the Pietersen magic about him, being able to conjure up shots beyond the dreams of the average Test batsman, yet at others he would throw his wicket away, or more closely resemble Inzamam-ul-Haq, as he got involved in yet another hare-brained run-out. I had once caught Owais during the Bunbury Under-14 regional festival (when he was playing alongside Rob Key, whom I later saw take West Indies for a double-ton at Lord's), and my hands stung for days afterwards. Now, years on, I managed to bag his wicket twice in the match, once with a trusty non-spinning 'straight-break', and then again caught-and-bowled. The fact that neither time did he have a century makes me feel like I did deserve these ones, unlike some of the late giveaways which accounted for a number of my first-class and Minor County victims.

Joining Shah in my pocket that day were two England bowling legends: Angus Fraser and Phil Tufnell. Whilst no one will give me any prizes for taking the wickets of two gents whose reputation with the willow was not renowned, the bagging of 'Test' wickets is good fodder for a few minutes of changing- and bar-room chat on slow days, and Gus and Tuffers themselves will tell you that they all look the same in the 'W' column. As ever, it was a rare treat for a cricket fan such as myself to have the chance to share a beer at the King's Arms on an equal footing, if only for a day or so, with heroes you'd seen for years on television. Fraser held court talking about 'finger-control' – the subtle variations in finger and wrist position which allowed him to move the ball just enough to take the edge or jag back into the pads. This was also Tufnell pre-media career, but you always knew he'd be a firm favourite with the public, and he was good company with his endless fags and London drawl, commenting on the posh totty passing by the pub of an early summer's evening among the dreaming spires. Sometimes you got the feeling these visitors were as interested in our esoteric world as we were of theirs. I guess you become blasé about the rarefied academic atmosphere if you're in it day-to-day, much like the 'grind' of county cricket seems impossible to someone for whom it's been a lifelong dream.

The match itself petered out into a draw in which we more than held our own. Only four visiting batsmen made double figures in the first innings, but then our highest score in the first innings was a frustratingly measly 32 by Jamie Dalrymple, and we ended still around 80 behind. And although we managed to remove Strauss for a sum total of three runs in the whole game, we ended up having to chase 289 in not much time on the last day. Realistically we had to bat for a draw, which we did, but not without losing three quick ones to stare ignominy in the face. Crisis averted, we remained unbeaten, unlike Durham University, much to our delight.

The Hampshire game was a dead loss, raining for three days. That was a possible 20 wickets down the pan in my ambitious estimation (more like two days of chasing leather avoided). My memory of those damp days is hazy, but my hunch is that I did not use the time making up for missed lectures.

The Warwickshire game did indeed involve a lot of chasing leather. It was Jamie Dalrymple's second game, and his figures were not pretty. Michael Powell scored an almost run-a-ball 236, with four sixes. Those came off the first four balls of one of Jamie's overs, and whilst feeling for a team-mate, I don't think I was alone in secretly hoping to be part of a game in which six sixes were hit in an over. I actually felt more for the poor bloke at long-off who had to keep fetching the ball from half a county away.

This was also the game in which Ian Bell scored his maiden first-class ton. Few will know, but Bell himself will, that he actually feathered one to the keeper early on and didn't walk. It was a windy day and Test umpire Peter Willey kept his finger in his coat, never one to do the toffs a favour, let alone crack a smile during three days. My only wicket was Dougie Brown as I went for more than a gallon – 122 precisely. And although I caught Ashley Giles, the 'King of Spain' had me stumped for a blob in the first innings. I was starting to doubt my ability with bat and ball, and wondered whether giving up life on a tropical island for this had been such a good idea after all.

Warwickshire were in no mood to do anything other than grind us into the dirt as they had batting practice. David Hemp was the primary beneficiary this time around with one of the most beautiful hundreds I've seen. I'd put him in the category of one of the best players I've come up against. We were set an enormous 526 to win, and I suspect they felt they would blow us away easily. Neil Carter ran in hard and aggressively, but this time we showed some real steel, and Neil Millar – a self-confessed James Bond lookalike – batted for 97 balls, taking several nasty blows to the body through the baggiest sweater ever seen in the Parks to see us home after Dalrymple had again showed his class (70 and 41 in the match). Only five down at the close, we were happy to head to the King's Arms honours even. With this game in June, we were treated to some of the exam-season spectacles which come with the territory of playing in the middle of a wide open space. We had had the odd streaker before; the one this match came with a surfboard which he took to the middle of the pitch and gave his best Keanu Reeves impression before scarpering off the other side of the ground. So university town, so what? But where the hell do you get a surfboard from straight after an exam?

Two draws and one rain-off ahead of the Varsity Match – we had an opportunity to go through an unbeaten first-class season here. Just don't look too closely at the scorecards.

Before that match, we had the unbridled pleasure of watching our arch-rivals play Birmingham University at the neutral venue of the Parks. Not only did they lose to a much weaker outfit, it happened as a result of rain and a bowl-out which saw Birmingham win 1-0 after ten bowls each. The 'Filthy Tabs' had come on to our turf and not even hit the stumps once. See you at Lord's, losers!

Playing with the Missus at Lord's (so to speak)

Although the Varsity Match was not being played at Lord's for the first time since 1827, we did play a one-day game against Cambridge on the same day that the women's Blues teams were playing simultaneously on the Nursery Ground. The atmosphere was helped by the fact that several hundred students headed down, Pimm's at the ready, to support their mates, and create a more partisan atmosphere. I was still of the mind that with a bit more creative and aggressive marketing, the universities could have made a case for televising the match, and encouraging crowds closer to the numbers which flocked to Putney for the Boat Race, or to Twickenham for the rugby event. Nonetheless, it was to be a special day for me and Penny, as she had been selected to play. There can't be too many couples who can boast having played at Lord's on the same day.

The confidence at having been unbeaten in our first-class games, and having watched our rivals limp home from the Parks after a bowl-out, was boosted by the huge good fortune of winning the toss on one of those overcast Lord's mornings, when the ball swings around prodigiously. Our seamers made the absolute most of it, and reduced Cambridge to 24/4, a situation from which they barely recovered, scratching around for 177/8 from their 50 overs. A niggardly 1-26 from my nine overs would do nicely. And despite losing our talisman Jamie Dalrymple for not many, Richard Smalley scored 75 and South African Steve Hawinkels 50 to see us romp home with time to spare. Time enough to pick up the C.B. Fry Trophy and a gin and tonic and head across the ground to swell the crowd watching the ladies, which was fully two or three people deep as unfortunately the Tabs got their own back. There was little time for a big celebration though, since the four-day match – still with first-class status – began at Fenner's two days later.

Matt Floyd Drops Anchor

Another positive spin-off from the switch away from a three-day match at Lord's was that the big game of the season between the arch-rival universities would now offer home advantage and, being played over four days, the likelihood of a draw was diminished. Few of the lads had played at Fenner's before and, whilst I had played a one-day game in 1999, I was excited to spend an extended period of time at the ground where my father had won three Blues for hockey. Seeing his name on the pavilion wall gave this match a nice sense of history for me (and for him, I am sure). The pitch was pretty slow and low, however, which meant that this match was a slow-burner. Even the most enthusiastic spectators could have been forgiven for falling asleep into their Scotch eggs as the run-rate for the first three days was painfully slow.

Many cricket watchers and Sky Sports subscribers will recognise Matt Floyd as the bald-pated ex-presenter of *Cricket AM*, and for his role as anchor of some of the more obscure international Test series of the last decade or so – a poor man's Ian Ward, if you will. While Sky sent their A-team of Atherton, Hussain, Botham, Willis, Gower *et al* off to the Caribbean, Australia or Sri Lanka, Floydy would be sat in a draughty studio in west London picking over matches which always seemed to be between Bangladesh and Zimbabwe. But back in 2001, Floyd could be recognised by his full head of carefully coiffed and gelled jet black hair, open-necked shirt and gym-sculpted body. He looked like a cross between Johnny Cash and a stereotypical

Greek waiter. But the rock-star good looks belied the fact that Floyd would also block the living daylights out of the cricket ball. He was so Tavaré-esque that we used to joke that rather than hitting the ball down the ground past the bowler through the so-called 'V', he was more likely to score his runs off inside or outside edge between fine leg and third man, through the 'A'.

Following Cambridge's stolid first innings, Floydy made the game his own. He batted nearly eight hours and faced 373 balls, carrying his bat for 128 (given that in his entire five-game first-class career, he made only 184 runs, this must constitute some form of run/career total ratio record, although I'll let some other statto look into that one). If anyone were to dust off their *Wisden*, they would also see that this was the innings which saw my highest first-class score of 58, to go past my fifty as a fresher at Lord's and which helped us gain a first-innings lead. My old Dorset team-mate Charlie Warren also won his first Blue in this game and added a gritty 30. He was up to his old tricks at short-leg, too, catching our under-11 county captain Chris Sayers out for a golden duck, which we saw as retribution for his knock in the one-day Varsity Match the year before and for having defected to Somerset when we were 13. Don't ever tell me cricketers don't have long memories.

But despite the superhuman vigil from Floyd, our lead was only 29, and by the end of day three, the game was poised, with both teams feeling they might win it. The home team were 184/4 but would need to score quickly to have a chance to bowl us out, whilst with quick wickets, we might be able to chase a gettable target. And there was plenty of needle, too. Umpire Barry Dudleston, who had stood in two Test matches, told me over a beer that this was one of the worst-tempered games he had officiated. I don't think he could believe the things which were being said between 22 well-educated young men. As we went to bed before that final day, we knew someone was going to have to perform well.

A wiser and far better cricketer than I once said, 'It's not how much you average, or how many wickets you take; it's about how many matches you win for your side.' Looking back on 2001, I'd have to mark it down as one of my best performances. Certainly by that measure. On the final morning, we took six Cambridge wickets for just 49 runs, and I bagged my second first-class five-wicket haul. In enemy territory, this was sweet. It also proved a triumph of selection. We had gone in with three spinners: me and Jamie Dalrymple were no-brainers, and he took four in the first innings. We also had the little-known Tom Wortley, who was picked for his debut with the single job of removing the Cambridge No.3 Vikram Kumar, who had scored a ton against a county side earlier in the year. Worters – a hit-and-miss leggie – came up trumps to get his man in both innings, which must have been sweet for the selection committee.

Of course, chasing any total is fraught with nerves, but 205 on the fourth day against your bitter enemies adds some spice. The stickability of Floyd, which had proved so useful in setting up the game, now looked as if it might be our downfall as he chewed up overs without scoring, our collective heart rates rising with the asking rate. And on a pitch which was now going underground and a ring of fielders as impenetrable as May Ball without a ticket, the top order fell to 120/5 in a bid to keep momentum. Thank goodness for Warren's fighting spirit. Warren was the most popular man in the side; I've mentioned his toughness and, as a junior doctor, he could be relied upon to hook himself up to a saline drip after a big night out. His changing room wit centred around his ability to create sculptures with his genitalia, and he had started to make a habit of riding statues of horses after a few post-match beers (he had the famous horse in Jesus College quad in his sights if he could win this game for us). He certainly hadn't come this far for us to f*** it up, as he reminded me in no uncertain terms when I joined him at six-down. I'd actually been promoted up the order after my half-century on day two, which led Essex boy Ben Collins shouting in earshot of everyone as I walked on:

'It's Manhattan or bust, lads, it's all on this bloke now.'

Waz and I carved and scurried our way towards the finish line, not without the odd scare, and it was looking like the Dorset boys would walk off with the spoils. But I managed to give it away, getting giddy, leaving Alan Gofton the horrible job of seeing it through. We had 'shoed the Tabs' on their own doorstep, and at Lord's, and we could boast an unbeaten first-class season. To quote Neil Diamond in what has become the unofficial cricket anthem, 'Good times never seemed so good'.

On Trial – Worcestershire

Whether it was my performances in the Varsity Match, or whether a good word was put in for me somewhere along the line, I have no idea, but after the euphoria of a great end to a university season which had seen me return from my supposed immersive language-learning to pick up a fifty and five-fer at Fenner's, I got a call from Damian D'Oliveira at Worcestershire. Dolly (another original nickname) was coach of the second team and invited me to come and trial in a couple of matches. This was the call that all young cricketers wanted. Anyone with ambitions wanted a contract, or failing that, a summer contract, or failing that, some game time with a professional county. For me, this was a chance to prove I could hack it as a pro. This had been my dream ever since I first pinned up a poster of Graeme Hick at the age of eight. And Worcestershire. This was my team. I'd supported them as a kid during the era of Botham, Dilley, Tim Curtis, Phil Newport and Neal Radford.

Even the slightly lesser lights of Steve O'Shaughnessy and David Leatherdale were heroes to me. And I'd made my debut against them. The stars seemed to be aligning.

However, on arriving at Kidderminster Cricket Club after a night in a hostel which did not give me the impression that the life of pro cricket was all five-star hotels and six-figure salaries, I was forced to take stock of my preparation. Sure, I'd had a good season and was in good form, but I'd also been a student with no work to do, and my turnover of cash in the King's Arms had topped three grand. I had even taken to using it as a bank, withdrawing cashback on a regular basis to cover nightclub costs. As such, I was hardly the picture of fitness. I was also using the cartoonish cricket bat I'd bought in Karachi, and my boots had broken, so I was forced to play in my dad's – a bottom-of-the-range pair of Pony boots from the Morrant catalogue which were about as comfortable as a pair of brogues. And being a trialist, you were not given the county branded kit, so rather than looking the part and feeling the pride of pulling on the famous pears, I wore my Blues kit, which of course drew unwanted attention from the sledgers of our opponents Gloucestershire. Despite having recently notched up some pretty good first-class stats, I was definitely coming across more Dorset villager. You can't hide your roots.

I didn't quite make the splash I'd hoped for. Scoring only one run in a total of more than 400 hardly marks you out as special, and even though I reeled off six consecutive maidens on the first evening, I looked steady at best. Far from picking up any wickets, the only thing I picked up was a new nickname to add to the collection. Wicketkeeper Jamie Pipe christened me 'Jo' after Page 3 girl Jo Hicks. It helped to settle me into the team, but was hardly likely to get me a recall. Neither was the fact that I chose to head out for some beers with skipper Paul Pollard (incidentally my second first-class victim), almost certainly a test of character which would be passed back to the management. It's one thing going out on the town when you are established, a different proposition altogether if you are attempting to gain employment as a sportsman. Not my best choice, on reflection.

My second game was meant to be a one-dayer against Somerset, but this one was rained off, and so my one-game stint ended and I didn't receive another phone call. I had reconciled myself to the fact that I hadn't really done enough to earn even the chance of some winter nets, and so it was a surprise to get a call the next year asking if I was available. They say that getting a break in sport is as much about timing and luck as innate ability, and this timing could not have been worse, coming slap-bang in the middle of my final exams. It was the hardest 'No' I've ever had to say. And it was the last time I was ever approached by a county.

Down to Earth

It was pretty surprising to get a call from Worcestershire in my finals year. In 2001 I was in great form with bat and ball and, had I been given more than that one game at Kidderminster, I reckon I'd have gone OK. Now, in my final year at university, things had got serious. I was living back in college and actually attending lectures (it turned out they were pretty useful – who knew?). Penny had left and now had a job. It was all starting to feel a bit grown-up. The team was a lot younger then as well, with the influx of Oxford Brookes players, which also changed the dynamic. It certainly felt more like the county second team I'd experienced than the old boys' club I'd first walked into in the Parks.

I was still making the side, though, and with Northants coming up first, misty-eyed memories were evoked of that win in 2000. Normal service resumed, I'm afraid, and whilst I added my old adversary Graeme Swann to my wickets tally for the third time, he bagged me in the second innings and we were soundly beaten.

I was absolutely gutted to miss the second game of the season (only the second one missed in my four years at Oxford). This was because it was against Worcestershire. How I wished I could have played against my favourite county again, and perhaps even shown them that I was worth another punt when my exams were over. But even more so because it would have meant the chance to play against Graeme Hick. He was one of my biggest heroes growing up and just to have had the chance to bowl at him would be its own story to tell, just like Robin Smith had been. There's nothing like rubbing shoulders with the best. As it was, of course he scored another ton. It was nice just to watch a bit from the pavilion. Kabir Ali – another who might have played more for England than he did – took seven second-innings wickets, of which five were bowled and two lbw. Full and straight was often enough for us students, especially if you bowled north of 80mph.

On the other hand, I wish I had missed the last county game that year which just saw a lot of leather-chasing as Mark Hardinges (whom I dropped early on) and Matt Windows scored big hundreds for Gloucestershire. The one shining light for us was seeing Jamie Dalrymple come of age with 148, followed by 54. It was then that we knew he was destined for greatness. Well, some England one-day caps at least, which we all would have given our left arm for. But the season had been dire really, and a massive comedown from the relative success of the previous year. Surely the Varsity Match would prove the turning point?

Once again we won the one-day game at Lord's. Steve Hawinkels scored three figures this time around, but the highlight for me was my 14 from five balls, including a six into the Edrich Stand, and walking off gleefully with Warren (he always seemed to show up when it counted) – what a way to finish our last game together. It was made all the sweeter by having several dozen of my mates from St Catherine's College in the Tavern Stand. They were especially vocal as, not only was the Tavern Stand only about 40 metres away from the pitch right on the edge of the square, but they had got well-and-truly tanked up in the Tavern watching the World Cup football. So, I was serenaded all the way to the pitch and all the way back again to the strains of:

'We love you, Oyster, because you're 16 stone, We love you Oyster, you should be on the throne …'

We felt we were unassailable after setting 323 to win, and I felt like a rock star (albeit a rather tubby one at that stage). But when the Tabs reached 185/0 at the halfway point of their reply, we were not feeling so smug. Thankfully, having the likes of Dalrymple in your ranks helps, and he took four wickets to add to 78 with the bat, and Hawinkels somehow burgled four himself, despite barely being a passable net-bowler.

Pride comes before a fall, though, and my last outing against the light Blues almost ended in ignominy. Two pitches had been prepared at the Parks – both very flat, and we chose the flatter of the two, gambling that we would win the toss and that JD and I would repeat the trick from last year and roll them over twice. But the coin had other ideas and came down wrong, sentencing us to yet more time in the field. Cambridge racked up over 600, with a big hundred from a lad we'd never heard of called Stuart Moffat.

If Floyd's innings had been remarkable in 2001, this was something else. This was Moffat's only first-class cricket appearance. He brought up a century off just 103 balls and had amassed 169 by the time Ben Vonwiller trapped him leg-before. It was the highest score by a cricketer playing their first match for Cambridge University since Test batsman Hubert Doggart made a double hundred in 1948.[6]

As Moffat did not bat again, either in that match or at first-class level, his career average remained 169. It's one thing to have to face a big hundred from a cricketer, difficult to swallow if it's from a rugby player. Moffat went on to win four caps for Scotland. Dalrymple sent down over 50 overs in that innings alone, and I churned through 35 of our mammoth 157.4. One wicket was all I had to show for the effort.

In reply we made 224. Oh dear. We were not getting a win this year, nor was I adding to my first-class wicket haul, which has remained steadfastly at 41 ever since. I did bat well, as seemed to be my happy habit in the Varsity Match, but then an umpire made a massive blunder, giving me out off my thigh pad for 38 when I felt set. I remember setting off for a long walk around the Parks after that, with random picnickers and joggers no doubt wondering what this poor bloke with Tourette's syndrome was doing out and about on a lovely afternoon, the air turning blue wherever I went. At least we chewed up 109 overs as the follow-on began. Luckily, the pitch was just so true that, once we'd gathered ourselves together, we made a much better fist of things in the second innings. This time Dalrymple did not miss out, and scored a ton, which he would eclipse with a stunning double the following year. James Redmayne was the other star of the show, seeing us to a draw with only five down. The only shot I remember though is Redders – who was also a football Blue – performing a textbook 'flick-on' from a bouncer, off his forehead as if from a corner, over the wicketkeeper for four leg-byes. A conundrum for the umpire: can it be evasive action if the bloke gets up and nods it like Alan Shearer?

---

6   https://en.wikipedia.org/wiki/Stuart_Moffat

Although it was largely a disappointing season to end my time 'up' at university, we did get another go at Lord's, having made the final of the inter-university BUSA competition. No one was surprised that Loughborough turned us over, but any day at Lord's is a good day in my book.

And do you know what? I got a half-decent degree. I didn't get a Geoff (Hurst = a first (class degree)), but I avoided a Desmond (Tutu = a second-class, second degree, or 2:2) and worse, a Douglas (Hurd = a third). I was awarded a very creditable 2:1 (known unpleasantly as a 'clitoris': 'because every c***'s got one'). Add to that four Blues, I'd call it a success. What next, though?

Chapter Eight

Switching Codes – Some Rugby-Related Tales

The Perfect Ten – At School With Jonny Wilkinson

Not everyone goes to school with a bona fide legend of sport. Sure, a lot of people have stories about the boy or girl who stood out at school, and maybe had a bit of a career in sport, maybe making it to international level. I was lucky enough to witness first-hand the national treasure that is Jonny Wilkinson as a schoolmate in sixth form at Lord Wandsworth College.

There have been many greats over the years in many sports – people who have dominated, won serial trophies and awards, yet very few sportsmen and women can claim to have actually changed their sport in a meaningful way. Michael Jordan, Babe Ruth, Ronnie O'Sullivan maybe, and the likes of Nadia Comaneci and Dick Fosbury could all stake a claim. I believe Jonny is one of those people, and I think this grants him genuinely legendary status.

As so often in sport, timing is important, and Jonny's arrival on the rugby scene coincided with the game turning professional. He had been dominating the school scene for a few years and in his Lower Sixth year (Year Twelve in non-public-school speak), he formed a partnership with Peter Richards – later of Harlequins, London Irish and England – as half-backs, and with a well-drilled team around him, took the small school of Lord Wandsworth College to the semi-finals of the Daily Mail Cup – the national schools trophy. It was such a big day that we were all given the Saturday off to go to Coventry for the match.

Jonny was amazing at school. Where his opposite No.10 would clear his lines for touch, Wilko would launch the ball clear of the trees lining the pitch and into the staff houses beyond. Visiting schools would give 'safe' innocuous penalties away on the halfway line only to see the ball fly between the sticks from impossible distances in a way which became so familiar to the nation's rugby-loving public as he cemented his place as a regular in the white shirt of England. Chants of 'Wilko would have had it' rang out as rival fly-halves failed to convert points (until we were banned from wearing our football shirts and acting like yobs, which in hindsight was probably a fair call).

As also became legend, Jonny's tackling was ferocious – one reason why I feel he changed his sport. No.10s in the past were there to be protected. Rob Andrew – later a mentor for Jonny – was a superb kicker but not renowned for wanting to get his knees too muddy, yet here was a lad putting forwards on their backside. Turning defence into attack changed the world view on what was possible. And most rugby pundits agree that you wouldn't have Dan Carter or Owen Farrell without Jonny Wilkinson.

Clearly his work ethic also was transformational, and although I do think that the evolution of the game to one played by athletes of superhuman sizes was probably inevitable in the long run, it was Jonny who made this the norm and accelerated the process. In truth, he set the template for what training to be a professional rugby player looked like. His relationship with Steve Black at Newcastle became synonymous with the modern game and now all professional teams have a strength and conditioning team as standard.

And that metronomic kicking only came from that same work ethic. He would always finish training sessions by landing six kicks from difficult angles. If he failed with any, he went back to zero and started again. Obsessive? Yes. The cause of some later, well-documented, anxiety issues? Yes. The key to being a world-beater? Oh, yes.

That work ethic was never more in evidence for me than one Christmas morning, when around 11am my family were just popping the first of several champagne corks in the boarding house my dad was running at the time. Our living-room overlooked the first XV rugby pitch, and as I was taking the edge off my Christmas Eve hangover, who should roll up but Jonny and his dad for a two-hour session of goal-kicking. It was quite remarkable, really –a 17-year-old lad having the determination and drive to drag his old man out to train when everyone else in the country was over-indulging. I guess it is the Floyd Mayweather philosophy of 'if I can be training when my opponents are not, I'll have the edge', and you know how good *he* ended up being.

It was probably at this moment that I also realised that I didn't really have what it took to make it as a top international athlete. I do believe that skill-for-skill, I was not far off being as good a cricketer as Jonny was a rugby player at that point. But when he was in the gym, I was in the pub; when he was kicking and I should have been hitting balls in the nets, I was out chasing girls, and when his chance came, he was ready, he took it and headed off to Newcastle Falcons, earned his first cap the next winter and the rest is history of his own creation. When my chance came in the form of trials for Worcestershire,

I was over 16 stone, smoking and wearing my dad's strapped-up boots. Attitude and preparation are all. Benjamin Franklin had it right when he said that, 'the key to success is being ready to take your chance when it comes along'. Jonny was not only ready to take it, but he changed the game.

This is not to say that he was totally squeaky clean. I remember one occasion where a food fight broke out in the school dining room when Jonny landed an impeccable direct hit with a well-directed muffin on the head of one boy lining up for his sausage and mash. The majority of the sixth form joined in and were 'invited' to see the deputy head (who also happened to be the rugby coach) in his office. Already sniggering at the sight of 30 blokes trying to fit into the room for a bollocking, we all glanced at Jonny when we were asked who started it. This was one moment Wilko failed to take the hit for the team, and a bunch of us ended up doing a week's scullery duty as penance.

I also remember the first time Jonny had a beer, which was the evening after the Daily Mail semi-final. The whole school seemed to have descended on a pub in the local village and when the team arrived, they were treated like conquering heroes. Jonny was usually absent during our Saturday night escapades, and so caused quite a stir when he walked in. Beers were thrust his way as we all clamoured for some reflected glory, and he ended up back with me and my brother at our place in the school grounds, doing his patented impression of Mark Knopfler from Dire Straits.

In truth, JW was actually a total legend – a dry wit and decent company, as well as being a bright spark, too. He would have got straight As at A-level had rugby not intervened, and I am sure *I* remember copying *his* work in French (on the way to my Oxford French degree).

So there is not much dirt on the lad, but my favourite story, and to bring it back to cricket, happened in a game at

Winchester College when he and I were sharing a pretty good partnership. Jonny came in at No.3 (he actually captained the side and bowled decent wheels, too) and used to hit the ball as hard as you'd expect from a man with cast-iron forearms. We were both well past fifty and really enjoying ourselves when he picked up a short ball and deposited it over the little pavilion for a six into a massive patch of nettles. Chatting mid-pitch, I congratulated him and was surprised to see him looking like someone had just pinched his favourite kicking tee.

'What's up, mate? You properly smashed that.'

'Yeah, I know, but it's probably lost.'

'That's OK. They'll just use a spare, which is good for us anyway.'

'It would be, but do you know where the spare from our innings is?'

'No. Do you?'

'Yep, in my bag with all the spares from the whole season.'

It turned out that England's finest fly-half had been half-inching the match balls for his own practice and was about to be rumbled.

'Don't worry mate,' I offered. 'Keep schtum and no one will find out.'

As I was proffering these words of sheer schoolboy integrity, my old man appeared on the pavilion steps (he was coach at the time), waving a ball and shouting, 'Here you are, Umps, and I'll see you after the game, Wilkinson.'

Putting off the inevitable as long as possible, Jonny knocked off the runs and returned not out to the applause of his team-mates and double detention the next morning.

As much as Jonny became the housewives' favourite during that incredible Clive Woodward era, I don't remember him being enormously successful with the fairer sex at school (probably partly on account of the fact his mum still packed his schoolbag), although one anecdote does bear retelling.

Due to a quirk of familial poor planning on the part of my grandparents, I was in the same school year as one of my aunties, who did have a brief dalliance with Jonny, and for whom he perhaps held a bit of a torch for a while. Nothing much came of their brief relationship, as is often the case with schoolyard romances, but as his fame grew more and more people would stop my auntie and ask her about the one who got away.

This came to a head at her hen party. There she was, with friends and sisters, merrily quaffing cocktails on a roof bar in London, when her phone rang. It was Jonny on the line; he had had an issue with his then girlfriend and wanted to get the train down to meet up with Annie. My auntie, flustered, returned to the table, to the inevitable barrage of questions:

'Who was that? You shouldn't answer your phone on your hen do.'

'Oh. Only a boy.'

'A boy!' (Whoops and hollers followed).

'Yeah, he wants to come and join us.'

'What?'

'No way!'

'You can't have boys at your hen do!'

To which my auntie uttered words which are now infamous in our family.

'Well, it's not really a boy. It's just Jonny.'

At that time, these words would have been seen as pure heresy. Pinned on the wall of a million teenage girls' (and boys') bedrooms; lusted after by the majority of England's middle-aged mums and revered by men the country over after *that kick*, my auntie had reduced this titan, this Warrior, this DEMI-GOD, to the status of a fawning fool.

'Just Jonny, indeed ...'

Some Six Nations Stalwarts

Closer to home, one of my first proper overseas tours was in 1993/94 when I was selected to go with the West of England Under-15 squad to the West Indies, leaving on Christmas Day. This really felt like proper cricket – all the lads on the flight would have harboured ambitions of 'making it' as professionals in a few years' time. Our year threw up no stars of the future, although Ryan Driver did play a bit for Worcestershire and Lancashire and John Claughton and I both went on to captain Oxford University. The biggest sporting successes from that group were probably Joey Barrington – son of squash legend, Jonah Barrington – who himself went on to play at a decent level and now commentates on the world tour; and Simon Danielli, who, despite having an Italian name and coming squarely from Gloucester, ended up winning 32 caps for Scotland at rugby.

Danielli was one of those kids that exist in every school – 6ft and 14st by year nine, with a beard to match (he was perhaps even the match for Ralph Dorey, who I mentioned earlier). You could imagine scrawny, pigeon-toed prep schoolers being pinged hither and thither as they attempted to tackle this man-mountain. Of course, he was also our quickest bowler, despite being a year young for the tour, and tended to wallop sixes for fun.

He was a bit wet behind the ears, though, and he and his room-mates fell foul of one of the classic tour gags on the night before we left Grenada for the final leg in Barbados.

Fun was quite sparse in the hotel on this tour, given that we were all too young to drink, the sun went down early, and it had been deemed too dangerous for us to go to the mall, or even KFC. In hindsight, it was probably good training for what professional cricket is really like – lots of long, lonely nights in hotel rooms with your workmates. We mostly whiled away our time either playing versions of cricket in our rooms, or throwing ice cubes at the circulating ceiling fans, desperately trying to avoid the shards which resulted when the blades hit. I can recommend this if you are ever at a loose end in a two-star.

I can't remember who came up with the idea, but some practical joker thought it would be funny if we were to trick Danielli and his room-mates by pretending that they had overslept and were about to miss their flight. All the other players were in on it, and so the word went round and we all said goodnight before surreptitiously packing our bags, and arranging to meet around midnight. Midnight came, and we met in a designated room, dressed in our travelling kit. We all synchronised watches for 6.45am, with a planned leave time of 7am. The agreed line was that we would all go to the room, pretending that we were on the bus and had just noticed they were not there, but that they had five minutes to get up and go or we would miss the flight.

Hook, line and sinker. The looks on the faces of the giant sporting prodigy and his sleepy companion were just priceless. The lads just about held it together long enough to see shirts flying, boxes and socks being stuffed into any old pocket of cricket bags as the panic took hold. Oh, how we laughed for the rest of the trip. It was definitely one trick which has stood me in good stead on other tours, and I've learnt that it is better to be in the know than to be the one with egg on your face.

When Good Sponsors Go Bad

Welsh rugby fanatics (which is just about everyone in Wales) will remember Aaron Shingler as a promising flanker for Llanelli, Scarlets and Wales, but not all will know that Shingler once represented England Under-19s as a fast-medium bowler, and was lucky enough to turn out at the 'home of cricket' – yes, Dean Park, Bournemouth – for the Wales Minor Counties team.

Cricket in Wales is a bit of an oddity: essentially it boils down to one first-class county – Glamorgan – based at Sophia Gardens, Cardiff, which is now a recognised Test venue, probably best remembered for the heroic rearguard action of Monty Panesar and Jimmy Anderson in the 2009 Ashes series. Most young Welsh cricketers, when they have given up the dream of representing their country at rugby, will aspire to getting on the books at Glamorgan and following in the footsteps of the likes of Simon Jones, Matthew Maynard and Robert Croft. But if you don't quite make the grade, or are on the way up (or down), you can find yourself plucked from club cricket – and there are some beautiful club grounds in Wales – to be part of the Wales Minor Counties team and spend your summer across the lesser western counties of England, plying your trade from Trowbridge to Tewkesbury, probably wishing all the time you were back in the land of your fathers with an oval ball.

That was certainly the feeling we got when Shingler turned up for a dead rubber in the last game of a drab season in 2007. One suspects that he was doing the team a favour and was looking forward to pre-season rugby training rather than urging his body to get anything out of a placid August pitch against a bunch of amateurs. In one of those awful *wrong place, wrong time* moments, Shingler bowled a spell reminiscent of Mitchell Johnson's infamously wayward offering at Lord's in 2009, when Strauss and Cook took him to the cleaners and even the usually stuffy MCC crowd could be heard mumbling along to the tune: *'He bowls to the left, he bowls to the right; that Mitchell Johnson, his bowling is …'*

It so happened that this was also the day which saw our sponsors – a small-time local contracting business – having their annual corporate 'jolly'. Do not be deceived: this amounted to little more than a couple of bottles of Echo Falls and a tab behind the bar. However, in the after-tea session, the handful of 'executives' were starting to get increasingly vocal on the seats on the pavilion concourse. With the big flanker hurling down faster and faster balls which were disappearing faster and faster into the hedges behind the parked cars beyond the boundary, the first lines of the song started to drift across the field. Nothing will stir a Welshman like song, and Shingler gave this small section of the crowd what it wanted, cupping his ear and issuing some less than professional gestures from his station several hundred yards away on the furthest boundary.

The pantomime continued for another over with the regulation 'Oooooooh' as he ran in and the cheers as the ball was once again dispatched whence it came. This time, at the end of the over, Shingler chose not to trudge back to his fielding position, but headed the opposite direction towards the baying sponsors, and, in what I believe is the correct parlance, 'offered them out' after the match had finished. As soon it did. And true to his word, after the handshakes between the teams, we had to witness quite an unpleasant stand-off as both sides had to recognise that the assumed roles of pantomime villain and baying mob no longer existed and what you were left with was an uncomfortable and embarrassing spectacle befitting of the outside of a Neath nightclub, rather than a cricket ground.

Happily, common sense prevailed and the Welsh players bundled their team-mate into the dressing room whilst the sponsors were quietly asked to head home. It did get me thinking about the sort of pressures top sportspeople are under when tens of thousands may be chanting obscenities at you, and not just criticising your ability, but often your heritage, race, sexuality and even your nearest and dearest. If there is a lesson, then it is for people both sides of the white line to recognise that we are all human beings and to behave in a way which does not dehumanise, but shows respect for people who are just trying to do a job.

I have to admit being called out on this by one of Shingler's erstwhile team-mates – Michael O'Shea – whom I think I had called a 'lucky c***' after a particularly poor shot. Having run to the bowler's end, O'Shea stopped me and said: 'Would you call me that off the field?' Narrowly avoiding the temptation to cheekily answer in the affirmative, I agreed that I probably wouldn't. 'Why do it on the field, then?' he continued. The conversation ended there, but I never forgot it and I don't think I ever used that sort of language on the field again.

The Rebuilding of Neath

I mention Neath as it goes down in Dorset CCC legend as one of the roughest spots for an away weekend many of us had experienced. Arriving early having not played on the Saturday, I went to meet a team-mate in one of the pubs near to the Castle Hotel, which was right in the middle of town. My first impression was not overwhelmingly positive as I brushed past at least one hen-do with a bride tastefully decked out in a veil with plastic phalluses, condoms and learner driver plates attached on my way to the bar where all the beer was being served in cans – not a tap in sight – and all the prices advertised on those luminous star-shaped labels which are the hallmark of a certified dive.

After a couple to wet the whistle, we moved outside to see where else might be worth exploring, to be met with a sight straight from Dante's *Inferno*. A man lay apparently dying in his own vomit, sprawled on the steps of our hotel, kebab meat strewn by his outstretched arm. Down the road, a couple were clearly up to no good down an alleyway lined with dustbins, whilst another amorous duo were making good use of the bonnet of a nearby car. At least two fights were in progress outside other pubs, while loud music and the sound of boy racers screeching up and down the streets added an intimidating soundtrack to this vision of hell on earth. And apparently Saturdays were not as bad as Fridays! We attempted to escape to the relative safety of our hotel, but we were soon to learn that nowhere was safe in Neath, with an over-40s nightclub thumping away in the basement which some of the lads infiltrated as residents of the hotel, with some interesting encounters ensuing between lads barely out of school and women who were old enough to be their mothers, but patently not acting like it.

The big joke was that, since the mines had closed across the valleys, the population of Neath had come up with the novel idea of demolishing the town on a weekend, so that there were jobs available rebuilding it during the week.

The second night saw us decide to remain in the hotel, but to light the blue touchpaper, we had made short work of a very poor Wales side to leave ourselves just a couple of wickets away the next morning from an innings victory, so the lads were understandably thirsty. What ensued was one of the craziest 'lock-ins' I have experienced, with some of our number pretending to be Chinese dragons with a toilet seat around their necks and duvets over their heads, roaming from room to room, whilst some of the successful players from the day attempted to woo a couple of local lasses by pointing to the scorecard which was on a loop on Ceefax (I know – Ceefax!). Others had made use of the Victorian-themed décor of the hotel. I have vague memories of wearing a top hat for the majority of the evening whilst a mate mimed smoking a stove pipe. Whilst we were warned away from the very friendly barmaids, on account of their still being school-age, we did manage to persuade them to join us for what was left of the game the following day and they joined our celebration in the dressing room afterwards, with the committee unsure where to look as we all bundled together for a team photo (which I sincerely hope has been since destroyed, and thank god that the advent of social media was still some years off, for everyone's sake!)

That Wales were so poor was down to the fact that, apparently, whilst we were witnessing the Sodom and Gomorrah of Saturday night in Neath, the manager and captain of the opposition had had to scour the pubs and clubs of South Wales for anyone who was eligible, free and owned a pair of whites, after a couple of late withdrawals from their team. Wales tended to be whipping boys in the era before Glamorgan started using the Minor Counties team as a breeding ground for the professional unit, but this was so bad, and conditions so good for our seamers, that we had seven slips for the whole first innings, and even our non-bowling skipper took a couple of wickets. I enjoyed the catching practice but hated not bowling. It was rightly decided that with a boundary as small as I have seen at that level that spinners would be easy meat (a point proven when we batted as our big hitters battered the houses behind the sightscreen).

There had been a game in Wales before my time when Dorset had had their own selection issues, and had to borrow a local player for their twelfth man. At the time, the captain was John (J.J.) Hardy, formerly of Somerset and Hampshire and owner of the Chase bat company, who had a no-nonsense, abrupt and quite plummy manner about his team talks. After his talk on this occasion, Hardy uncharacteristically finished with, 'Anybody else got anything to add?' At which there was the expected silence of assent, until, in a thick Welsh accent redolent of daffodils, leeks and male voice choirs, a voice broke the hush, *'I don't know about you boys, but you've come a long way, and you haven't come here to lose. So let's go out and donkey-f**k 'em!'*

And with that he strode out in front of the hysterical team, and Hardy, who was struck dumb for the first recorded time.

Chapter Nine

The Leopards – Dorset CCC

Walking in the Footsteps of W.G.: Dean Park, Bournemouth

If you ask any cricket lover around the world where the home of cricket is, I'd wager over 95% would tell you it was Lord's. Of course, as the balance of power in world cricket shifts inexorably away from St John's Wood to the subcontinent and the vast wealth of the Emirates, some might begin to contend this fact. Few, however, would identify Dean Park, Bournemouth as being the epicentre of the cricketing universe. For me, however, this oasis of green which nestled like an emerald gem amongst the residential suburbia of a south coast resort played host to some of the most significant moments of my life – cricketing and otherwise.

Let's take a seminal moment from childhood: the first professional match I went to watch with my dad. It was Hampshire against Kent in 1990, with the big draw of Robin Smith (and his brother Chris), David Gower and Mark Nicholas (now known as one of the smoothest pundits in world cricket). I loved it. It was where I bought that first autograph book and spent most of the day pestering anyone in whites for their signature until the intervals, when we were allowed on the outfield to play our own games. I marvelled at how fast they bowled, and how hard the ball was hit, and I marvelled at the sponsored cars and the mobile phones (unfathomably large, with extendable aerials) which were the status symbol of sporting starts in those halcyon days.

What also became apparent during the day was that the ground had history as one of Hampshire's outgrounds which would traditionally host one or two games during the championship season; taking the game to the people, so to speak. It turned out that 'The Doctor' himself – W.G. Grace – probably the most iconic player ever to play the game, had once stepped on to the Bournemouth turf, instantly making it consecrated ground. In later years, modern legends such as Andy Roberts, Gordon Greenidge, Malcolm Marshall and Barry Richards had all graced the arena.

So when Bournemouth was returned to Dorset from Hampshire (in a gesture every bit as politically significant as the UK handing back Hong Kong to China, or the formation of the nation state of Israel), it was with no little sense of history that I first stepped on to the hallowed turf of Dean Park as a player. Whether anyone else shared my sense of spiritual transcendence is doubtful, but then, it's not their story. What follows are some memories of 18 years playing for the so-called 'Leopards', which is possibly the least appropriate emblem for a county ever, and must always be pronounced as if to rhyme with leotards. They come in no particular order and, if the details are hazy, I can only apologise and thank the lord for lack of video evidence.

Glamorgan Knockout

One of the great things about playing Minor Counties cricket which has sadly lapsed was the chance to qualify for the domestic one-day trophy by finishing in the top four of one of the two divisions (the Minor Counties Championship was split into a Western and Eastern division, with a grand final between the respective winners). This would guarantee a home draw into what in 2000 was known as the NatWest Trophy – English cricket's equivalent of the FA Cup.

Dorset had won the Western Division in 1999 and had been drawn at home to Glamorgan, which was good news for me, as I had just started dating my future wife and she was still smitten enough to be impressed by the fact the general public would have to pay good money to watch me play. In those days, Dean Park even had a couple of ramshackle stands – not quite a stadium as such, but bypassing the turnstiles and having a distinctive, cordoned-off players' area offered some mystique around what was normally something of a free-for-all.

It was rare for the minnows of the Minor Counties to run the professionals close, although Dorset had, some years previously, reduced Hampshire to 0/3 before normal service resumed. This time we were up against stiff opponents as Matthew Elliott – the elegant left-handed Australian Test batsman – opened up for the Welsh side. There is some brilliant footage from BBC South, which we would all avidly tune into, or record for posterity, of our opening bowler – Toby Sharpe – head in hands, looking as if the world had ended when a feathered edge down the leg side was shelled by the wicketkeeper. Elliott went on to an unflustered century, effectively putting the game out of our reach.

Of course, the next time I took Penny down to watch a game, she was surprised (and visibly deflated) by the fact there was no ticket office and the cider-fuelled locals had been replaced by the 'regulars', which amounted to around a dozen hardy souls who had the time, and more surprisingly, the inclination to come and support us in our normal round of county matches. I could name most of them, which gives you an idea. It is to Penny's great credit that she continued to come and support, probably out of a sense of loyalty, sympathy or a combination of both, swelling the attendance at least 5% by her presence.

'You Should've Done it on the Tannoy'

Although crowds were generally very paltry, aside from those rare occasions when professional teams were in town, one of the features which marked out the rarefied level of Minor County cricket from Saturday Premier League cricket was the use of a loudspeaker to announce the names of incoming batsmen, bowling changes and from time to time when obscure records were broken. *'Tim Lamb now has more leg-side stumpings against Herefordshire on a Sunday than any other wicketkeeper born in Bolton ...'* and so on.

There was always a *frisson* of excitement and pride as you were announced to the crease – *'The incoming batsman is ...'* – which was far too often accompanied not long after with the details of your demise: *'Tom Hicks, lbw, no score.'* I tried to bribe Pat, the announcer, to keep quiet if I scored below double figures, but such was his professionalism on the mic I remained subjected to the regular, resigned tone of disappointment in his voice as I nicked off for four, or padded up to a straight one from a left-armer for a streaky seven. Of course, all these failures would have been preceded by some determined and lofty chat as I awaited my turn to bat. Anything is possible while you've still got your pads on, and the game is far easier from the dressing room than from 22 yards.

The summer of 2006 was special for Dorset; the year in which we reached the final of the knockout competition which was to be played at Lord's. For many of our squad (and supporters – a lot more than the usual suspects came out of the woodwork for that little trip, I can tell you) this would be the one and only opportunity to play at HQ, and even for those of us who had been lucky enough to play there already, getting there on merit, rather than tradition, meant something a bit more special.

So there was a real buzz around our home ground during that hot summer. Arguably the heady excitement had made me giddy, but I had decided that the time was right to pop the question, and being the incurable romantic that I am, I decided that Dean Park would be the most appropriate place to get down on bended knee. Every girl's dream, right? I had a ring from Burrells jewellers – the same place Kevin Pietersen had purchased his – just to keep the cricket theme running, and was going to leave it until the last day to do the deed.

It was normal custom at tea time during home games for my best mate on the team – Darren Cowley – to take a doughnut to Penny, but on this occasion I phoned her at her usual spot across the ground to ask her to come over as I had procured some sugary snacks for her this time. Like all good sportsmen, I let some of the lads in on the plan, and so when I headed out of the pavilion with cakes in hand and diamond sparkler in my pocket, they knew what was up, and by the time we met on the outfield, two sets of players, coaches and umpires were peering out the windows, eager to see if she'd say yes, and maybe hoping in some quarters that I would end up with egg on my face.

Happily, I got the right decision from this particular appeal and I returned to the dressing room with a tear in the eye and heart racing, to applause from everyone there.

The evening session is not the clearest in my mind, funnily enough, but I do remember some pretty lame sledging from the Berkshire boys about adding another ring (a nought) to the scorecard and more lewd hoop-based puns which I'll leave to your imagination. The Berkshire wives were all very excited and suggested that the more romantic gesture would have been to propose over the Tannoy, or indeed, wait until we were at

Lord's and do it over the loudspeakers there. As far as Penny was concerned, this had been enough exposure already.

Where's the Umpire Gone?

Aside from the romantic interlude in this match, it was also notable for a bizarre and somewhat unsavoury incident which made the national press the next morning. During Berkshire's first innings, we made serious inroads, taking five early wickets and looked about to take a sixth when Julian Wood was struck on the pads, stuck in his crease, on the stroke of the lunch interval. Wood is now one of the world's leading experts in power hitting, working with England's limited-overs cricketers on improving hand speed and using such novel methods as heavier balls and hurling mallets as the game becomes more about bludgeoning boundaries than finesse. Wood himself was a renowned hitter of the ball in his pro career with Hampshire and I remember one extra cover drive on the up off Toby Sharpe which flew flat for six through the window of the scorers' box. So, his was a wicket we wanted.

As well as a powerful hitter, Wood was also a powerful personality and was actually captain at the time, so when the finger went up and he was standing rooted to the spot, pointing at the edge of his bat and insinuating that the ball was heading over the stumps anyway, we realised the fuse was getting mightily close to the flame. What ensued does not reflect well on anyone involved – words were exchanged during which it was reported that Woody called into question the umpire's ability as well as integrity, mostly in four-letter terms.

During the break, word went round that the umpire in question had asked the Berkshire management for a formal apology from the captain, who was still seething in the dressing room and hadn't emerged for lunch. Wood was not in conciliatory mood, to say the least, and refused, suggesting that perhaps the umpire himself ought to be apologising. All of which we found mildly amusing, especially given that they were six down for less than a hundred.

When we took the field for the afternoon session, only one umpire emerged, and he informed us that his colleague would not be joining him until he received an apology, which left us with the rather 'village' situation of one proper umpire doing both ends of the match (not an easy task in itself) and a rotation of dismissed batsmen, twelfth men and coaches standing at square leg in shorts and a long white coat. It was all pretty amateur. Not to mention that the aggrieved arbitrator had not just packed up his kit and left, but had actually had a shower and was now watching the match on his own from a bench in the pavilion, and remained for the rest of the day. And there he stayed until stumps, when, with no apology emanating from the Berkshire changing room, he shook hands with our skipper and drove home, not to be seen again. A substitute umpire was found for the next day, which ended up being the last as we routed them. It also turned out to be Woody's last game at that level; I think he had just had enough by then, but it was a sad way for such a good player to finish.

Twenty-Two Fielders and no Batsmen

If the Berkshire game with the disappearing umpire was shambolic, let me take you to the Minor Counties final of 1999, at Netherfield CC in Cumbria. A beautiful traditional ground, nestled in the lee of Netherfield castle in Kendal, right in the heart of the Lake District, and flanked by a bowling green. Picture perfect, but what is known in cricketing terms as a 'postage stamp', i.e., a ground with a very small boundary – one imagines that the host county chose this venue specifically to counter the threat posed by Dorset's spin attack. Not me, I must add, but our leg-spinner Vyv Pike, who had already taken

65 wickets in the season and who was the scourge of batsmen across the country at this level.

We thought Vyv was something really special. Approaching the crease at pace from an oblique angle, he fizzed the ball out and spun it sharply, with the added weapons of at least two different googlies and a vicious top-spinner. His googlies were a joy to behold; if you were standing at slip, that is. Often, he would bowl a really wide, obvious, back-of-the-hand wrong 'un which the batsman would read and feel a sense of relief that he could 'pick'. This would then normally be followed a ball or two later by a completely disguised googly which the smug batsman would leave, or pad up to, looking foolish as it spun not safely away towards the slips but back into his stumps, to the accompaniment of knowing sniggers from the fielders. So good was this disguised googly that Vyv had to develop a signal for it, as our keeper Tim Lamb could not pick it either and had got into the unhelpful habit of conceding four byes on a regular basis as he shifted to the off stump to gather a ball which disappeared two foot to his left, rather defeating the object of the surprise.

So integral was Pikey to our chances of winning that our captain Stuart Rintoul was christened 'No Plan B' and usually if Vyv did not take at least ten wickets in the match, we would be half the side. So much so that in one match we bowled our entire 90 allotted first-innings overs with just three bowlers; Vyv bowled all 45 from one end and I bowled 29 overs of off-spin from the other. On that day, he left the field more beetroot red and beading all over in sweat than ever, and celebrated his eight wickets with his customary beverage – the 'Muddy Puddle', a teeth-rotting combination of orange juice and Coca-Cola, which I never saw drunk by anyone else.

Dorset had never won the Minor Counties Championship, let alone the Western Division, in its history, and then won three divisions in a row from 1998 to 2000, coinciding with Vyv's heyday. Coincidence it was not. We used to joke that VJ would become the first player since the legendary Staffordshire bowler Sydney Barnes to make the jump from Minor Counties straight to Test cricket. I honestly don't think there was a better leg-spinner in the country at that time.

He did play for Gloucestershire, but ankle injuries, family responsibility and a lack of opportunity stood in his way (these were the bad old days of English seamers being produced for English conditions, with spinners playing a bit-part as medium-pacers benefited from green-topped pitches and the helpful Dukes ball). Professional cricket's loss was our gain, and we certainly backed him to do a job against a Cumberland side with its fair share of old pros: Ashley Metcalfe from Yorkshire and another of my boyhood heroes Steve O'Shaughnessy from Worcestershire, to name a couple. And having lost the final to Staffordshire the previous year, we were keen to go one better this time.

Frustratingly, we failed to win the toss, which would have given us the huge advantage of bowling last, making full use of our spin attack. But, with the aggressive Cumberland side racking up an imposing 315/7 having been three down for 12, we were very much behind the eight-ball. So much so that, after a lacklustre batting display on our part (from 86/0 we ended 130 all out), we were well over 150 runs in arrears, short of the follow-on mark when our tail-enders trudged off. I was rapidly going off O'Shaughnessy, who scored a battling hundred in that first innings.

Now, of course we knew that we would be expected to bat again, but it had not been a good-natured game and so we took it upon ourselves to play to the very letter of the law (if not the spirit). It is customary for the bowling captain to 'invite' the other team to follow-on (there's a cricketing euphemism for you), but the Cumberland captain Simon Dutton had not formally approached our skipper with such an invitation and so we decided to do the childish thing and got dressed in our whites ready to field and waited for the umpires' bell to ring before emerging at the same time as the Cumberland side also came out to field again. Twenty-two players, no batsmen, two umpires and the temperature rising. The joke was on us in the end as the umpires failed to see any humour in this and ordered our batsmen to pad up and face one solitary over before the tea break. You could sense now that everyone in the ground was against us. Despite a quite magnificent 196 from Andy Sexton – enough to get us a lead we could bowl at, and to earn him a contract with Hampshire the following season – the only other real memory I have of the game is Lamb's dismissal in the first innings. A diabolical decision by the umpire to give him run out was met with mutters and shakes of the head by the knowledgeable and fair Kendal crowd, which turned to fierce reproval of Lamb when he put his bat through the door of the pavilion in anger, precipitating a disciplinary visit to Lord's.

Pike was largely anonymous and Cumberland's other big-gun Metcalfe scored a ton in the chase. I was actually Dorset's top wicket-taker in that final, with four in total, but I'm not sure you can count 4-195 as any sort of success. I also know now that it is a hell of a long way from Kendal to Dorset when you've just lost a final. Happily, revenge would be ours 12 months later.

County Cap and the Jumper Challenge

One of my favourite places to play Minor Counties cricket was Shropshire. I don't know if it is something to do with the fact that nine out of ten people in the UK probably don't know it exists, let alone could identify it on a map, or whether it's because it's the only county which feels it needs a nickname (what the hell is Salop, anyway). Or maybe it's because their logo was something known as a 'loggerhead' – a sort of mythical cat-like beast, or whether – more likely – it's because my first experience was taking one of my best hauls on one of the early 'northern tours' at Shifnal, when we were all footloose and fancy-free, or because my first visit to Whitchurch included a night out at one of the very worst nightclubs I've experienced (the 'Caddyshack'). Whatever it was, I developed something of an affection for the Shropshire fixture, even though they were usually hard to beat and generally humourless, being made up of a largely Birmingham League core.

I especially enjoyed playing at Whitchurch. Again, a place which few will have ever heard of, and I think the tourist board would have a tough time bringing the punters in, unless they happen to like golf in the rain, average cricket or sticky-floored nightspots. It was Whitchurch where I actually won my county cap in 2004, although I still am unsure whether this was more down to scoring my then highest score – a paltry 44, if you must know – or to my off-field antics. For it was during the evening session of the first day at Whitchurch, during the start of our first innings, that I decided to pull out one of my favourite party tricks – the jumper challenge. This entailed putting on as many jumpers as we could muster between us, leaving me looking like I was wearing a fatsuit and unable to stand up again if I was pushed over. On this inaugural occasion of the jumper challenge, we managed 19, largely thanks to Vyv Pike having half-a-dozen old Gloucestershire tops which had been stretched in his 'fuller' years, and including players the size and shape of Darren Cowley in our number. It was all carried out with great hilarity, such that the players and spectators outside were increasingly intrigued to know what was happening in the away dressing room. When I eventually appeared, the game had to stop whilst our opening batsmen's attention was diverted, and then I proceeded to offer to the crowd a full warm-up repertoire with star-jumps, touching-the-toes, press-ups and more, all the time egged on by the rest of the team and even the announcer who made sure everyone was aware of who this clown was. Quite what ex-Warwickshire skipper and England one-day specialist Neil Smith made of this affair in his drop down into the amateur ranks one might only imagine, although he seemed a bloke with a sense of humour.

Someone who had a sense of humour failure during a Whitchurch trip was Vyv Pike, and the entire travelling committee, when they awoke to find our premier bowler's car had been completely 'camouflaged' during the night. I was among a small group of suspects who were on the receiving end of a 7am phone call from the club secretary, asking us to report in 15 minutes to the reception of the hotel for a 'hearing'. This did not last long as we were bang to rights, having spent a good hour under cover of darkness covering the car in grass clippings, branches, hanging baskets and flowerpots. The most amusing thing for me was that I got into less trouble than the rest of those identified, as 'being a student, it might have been expected of me'. On reflection, it shows you how low the expectations were of me, and students in general back then. Nowadays, we'd probably be on a criminal damage charge.

Superman v W.G.

One especially rainy day against Shropshire (it must have been August; it always rains in August), we were passing the time in our respective dressing rooms when one of the opposition players popped his head in to ask who our biggest joker was. For some reason – probably my proclivity for stupidity – I was named to take part in a race against Superman. That is, their all-rounder Jono Whitney, who was making it a habit of his to dress in Superman pants and using a Superman towel as a cape, to race against a nominee from the opposition when play was stopped for rain.

And so we set about finding me a costume, which ended up as a set of tight white compression leggings, and equally tight white top, a traditional woollen cricket cap in garish colours and, bizarrely, a Brillo pad I happened to keep in my bag which would act as a makeshift hook-on beard. The race between Superman and W.G. Grace was a longer-than-desired sprint across the field and back, with a Klinsmann dive to finish. It ended in a photo finish, but this one didn't go my way and still rankles.

The Honeymoon's Over

By sheer coincidence, it was an away trip to Shropshire again which forced me to book a truncated honeymoon in the summer of 2007. Six days on the island of Gozo (I had to Google this place to prove it wasn't made up) would surely be enough if I promised the trip of a lifetime at an unspecified future, winter, date.[7]

We married on a Friday – Friday 13th in fact, thumbing our noses at superstition – so that the majority of our guests could go off and play league cricket on the following day. It was a wonder that Farnham even fielded a team against Weybridge, let alone take them to the last ball, given that most of the top order had to be forklifted out of hotel bedrooms after dancing the night away, and our power hitter was said to have woken up in a rose bush in the churchyard. I was due back for the following week's fixture against Reigate Priory – the thought of missing two in a row never crossed my mind.

As it happened, this was the summer when flights were grounded owing to flooding, and although we did make it back for the match, it was after a flight into Bournemouth,

---

7   To date, this trip has failed to materialise, to no one's great surprise.

not Gatwick, and the prospects of play were about as likely as Kevin Pietersen winning an award for modesty. Nonetheless, custom dictated that both sides and the umpires would convene to spend a few hours wandering around a sodden field, shaking heads and sucking teeth in a knowing fashion, calculating new conditions of play which everyone in this great charade knew would never be used. There would, of course, be just enough time for a nice tea, several cups of coffee and for any player with a family, just enough time to miss any planned events or parenting responsibilities. You could tell the fathers – they were the ones nudging the umpires into a later decision, 'Give it another hour or so, Jim, it dries really quickly here,' so that they could avoid being called back to duty at an indoor play centre on an industrial estate near Camberley, or make it back in time for lunch with the in-laws. On the other hand, the younger, single players were just keen for a decision to be made which would allow the shutters of the bar to come up and the first round of several to be bought.

On this occasion, there were high jinks afoot, as the weather forecast suggested that not only would the Saturday match be off, but that the three-day county game would also start late, giving the green light to 'play the rain card' and gamble on a lie-in and day off. At least that was the theory in my head when I was encouraged to strip to my box briefs and join in the fun of slip-sliding all over the tarpaulin covers which covered the square, eventually opting for a night at home after several pints, and getting a lift at the crack of dawn to Shrewsbury.

Of course, my driver Tim Lamb and I had got the inside track from the players who had already gone to the hotel that the ground was waterlogged and if we arrived after the normal meeting time of 9am, we'd be OK. Indeed, the ground was so inundated that play was called off by the scheduled start time and the only decision to make was whether to stay for lunch or head back to the hotel to sleep off the rest of the hangover. So bad, in fact, were conditions, that it looked unlikely even that we would play on the following day, and so for the first and only time in my Dorset career, the players sat down for lunch and enjoyed the bottles of wine normally reserved for the official alickadoos. After a quick trip to Tesco for provisions (shed-loads of Coke, doughnuts and Doritos), most of the players snoozed and munched their way through a damp afternoon at a lovely country hotel, recovering just enough to be ready for a night out in Shrewsbury, safe in the knowledge that tomorrow was another rain-day. Never had so many golden tickets[8] come in one go.

This was the first night a young Max Waller was to enjoy on the town with Dorset. Waller would go on to become renowned as the finest fielder of his generation, and a decent T20 specialist leg-spinner, but at this stage he was as wet behind the ears as the pitch was that morning. He was a stereotypical young wannabe pro: all about the stash, the car, the cash, and was desperate to know how much our senior players were getting paid. Try as I might to explain that we were all just keen amateurs, he was not having it, and I am sure he still thinks there was more money in my expenses envelope than his. This obsession with material items meant that the rest of us found it hilarious when he dropped his brand-new iPhone into his pint. Max was not laughing then, but I suspect with a string of contracts under his belt in franchises including the new Hundred format, he is not too worried about the cost of a phone call these days. It was

---

8   A golden ticket (regional variation: pink ticket) is understood to have been taken by a batsman losing his wicket just before 'stumps' in the evening, allowing him the chance to go out until closing time and not have to bat in the morning. It is not unknown for fielding teams to take actual tickets out to the middle to offer to nightwatchmen or openers. In friendly 'jazz-hat' cricket, the equivalent is getting out just before lunch, during which copious amounts of wine, port and cheese will be on offer. It is frowned upon (but not unusual) for batsmen to take up the offer of a golden ticket.

a bit of an education into the way we played and prepared for cricket, not least when we finally decided to head home after celebrating our wicketkeeper Chris Park's birthday by popping him into a wheelie bin and shoving him down the high street, whilst our opening bowler stayed up for hours trying to hit the ducks on the hotel pond with stones from the driveway.

Beaten by a Girl

The next day – Monday – was another grim day of 'recovery', which was enlivened by a whole-squad squash tournament. It was rare for us to stay in a hotel with squash courts, and we thought this might just keep us out of the pubs with the prospect of a cricket match actually occurring the next day.

I said that my driver for the trip was Tim Lamb, although this was not strictly true. We were actually driven by his new girlfriend Lianne, whom he had met in Malaysia, and who happened to be the sister of the best women's squash player the world has ever seen, Nicol David. If you look up Nicol David's record, you will find that she was the top-ranked player in her sport for over a decade, and at one point had a greater points lead over her nearest rival than Tiger Woods had at his most dominant in golf. Not only that, having met Nicol on several occasions, she is a great character, full of fun and modesty who loves an English ale, despite being a billboard superstar back in her home country. Her sister Lianne is also a very good squash player – junior nationals and so on, but there is nothing to her: she can't be more than 5ft when she's uphill and light as a feather. Lianne is also lovely, but so quietly spoken that when it was suggested that she might want to join us on the court, it was hard to tell if she said yes or no.

You can imagine the scene: several burly sportsmen, all gym-fit and able to smash a little squash ball to a pulp, politely offering to have a hit against this girl who was half their size, thinking they would give her a good hiding. As it was, I've never seen a group of men so humiliated. I think between the 12 of us we took a total of four points off Lianne, and three of those went to one player and the other was a mishit into the tin. This tiny slip of a thing stroked and sliced and dropped the ball to all corners of the court, barely breaking sweat or moving from the 'T' whilst the blokes raced around, grunting and panting, sweating and hitting the ball harder and harder in their frustration. What made it worse was her embarrassed apologies as time and again she made us all look stupid. We played 'winner stays on' until she had dealt with us all, and then she meekly said thanks and headed for a shower, leaving us finally to do battle with each other, safe in the knowledge that we were all pretty bang average at squash.

Where's the Ring?

Tuesday finally came around and as we went back to Shrewsbury CC, I reflected on how much time seemed to have elapsed since our wedding day which had only been a mere ten days ago. There was also the realisation that not one ball of cricket had been bowled in that time, and we really could still have been on honeymoon. All I had done was basically come back for a three-day rainy holiday. This realisation was compounded by a phone call from my new wife in which she said: 'I don't care if you play or not, or whether you win or lose, but if the game is called off, you bloody well lie as we did not come home for nothing.'

'No "Good luck, Darling?"' But the line was already dead.

Under normal circumstances, we would never have played in those conditions. I stood at slip and as the overs passed, my feet sank further and further into the soggy ground, leaving prints at least an inch deep. I caught one catch, but dropped a sitter, and didn't bowl. We batted so poorly that we ended up blocking for a draw even in a shortened format, and my contribution was a golden duck, bowled through the gate by the off-spinner. Well worth coming home for, I don't think.

Oh well, at least it was back home that night to the warm embrace of the married home. But on the journey back, there was just a nagging feeling I'd forgotten something. An hour down the M5, I shot bolt upright from my back-seat slumber: 'My ring! I've left it with the scorer!' Less than a fortnight into a lifetime of marriage, I'd managed to leave my ring with another woman. This could be one of the shortest marriages in history. So, we called the scorer to arrange a meet at the next services, only for her to explain that she hadn't headed south, but north-west to Anglesey for a holiday and wouldn't be back until the next match in a fortnight's time back in Dorset. Explain that one away.

Bowled by Pete Trego Twice in Two Balls

Another game which ended up being horribly curtailed by unseasonable monsoon rain was against Shropshire's neighbours, Herefordshire, at the lovely ground of Colwall, down in the Malvern Hills. Batting first, we scored an absolute hatful of runs, with Glyn Treagus in particular going big, and Darren Cowley making mincemeat of the old ball, especially benefiting from the fact that not one, but two of their left-arm spinners got the yips and offered up a succession of long-hops and waist-high no-balls. Going in to bat in my customary lower-middle-order slot, I ought to have been able to boost the old average against a flagging attack on a flat pitch, but by the time I went in, the spinners had been put out to pasture and the opening bowler was back on. This happened to be Peter Trego, who went on to have a fine career as one of Somerset's longest-serving players, becoming great mates with Waller in the process. At the time, though, he was between contracts, trying to get himself back in the professional game, sporting pretty average-looking peroxide blond long hair. And although he later became a canny purveyor of slow-medium cutters and slower balls, at the time, he was also bowling at a pretty decent pace. Certainly decent enough for me, with my dislike of anything north of 75mph. I also knew Trego from youth days, when he had been a contemporary of my brother's, and so I was probably not in full battle mode.

In a bizarre innings, I managed to last just two balls and was bowled off both of them. The first saw me stuck on the crease, feet in the proverbial bucket, flailing hopelessly as the ball went through to the keeper with the sound of a big edge accompanying it. 'Not out', said the umpire – quite rightly – to the disbelief of the keeper, and with Trego in my face, laughing and asking if it had hit my stumps. On inspection, which we carried out together, there was a ripe red 'cherry mark' on the outside of the off stick. 'You'll have to bowl a bit straighter, Pete,' I chortled. What a wag. The next ball was a carbon copy, as was my effort to play it, with the only difference being that this time the stump was properly pegged back. 'That's much better,' I offered, nodding to him as I tucked my bat under my arm like the lord of the manor dismissed on his one outing of the year. It then rained for two days solid, with Tewkesbury (where we were staying) henceforth forever dubbed 'Dukes-bury'.[9]

Being Twelfth Man

During my early days playing for Dorset, I was in and out of the side, but loved being around the dressing room during and after play and picking up a few quid's worth of expenses. I also loved fielding, so I would be very happy to volunteer to be

---

9   This is cricket rhyming slang: *'Duke'* = *'The Duke of Spain'* = rain. Everyone knows there is no Duke of Spain, and that the King of Spain is Ashley Giles. 'Duke' can also be used as a verb, as in: 'There's no way we'll play today; it's properly duking down.' Heavy rain is known as 'Biblical Duke', whilst rain which will see an end to a day's play is referred to as 'Terminal Duke'.

twelfth man and feel well qualified to explain what constitutes a good or bad substitute.

Your primary function is obvious: you are there to deputise for any fielder who gets injured during play, so being a half-decent fielder is a prerequisite. It is amazing, though, just how easily some players appear to get 'injured' and how long they are prepared to stay off the field. There are many seam bowlers who deem it their privilege to simply wander off after their spell for a shower and a bit of a rub-down (if you were lucky enough to have a physio), despite not being injured at all. Also, one had to expect a call at any stage for players to nip off for a 'comfort break', on the premise of having slightly bruised a finger. Some players were notorious for absenting themselves from the field of play, and in the amateur echelons, I can certainly point to a half dozen who would happily tell an umpire they needed something sprayed or strapped and then would be seen on the players' balcony with a cup of coffee in one hand and a Silk Cut in the other moments later. Of course, should you, as twelfth man, be seen at any stage with your own coffee or in any way looking relaxed, it would be immediately picked up as laziness on the part of the eleven on the field and a spurious task would be found for you.

This second function can best be described as 'general dogsbody'. As twelfth man, you are essentially at the beck and call of the players from the moment you arrive in the dressing room until you head back to the hotel or hop in the car to go home. Anything from basic first aid, to endless supplies of drinks, sweets and other miscellany, it is up to you to have it ready from the word 'go'. Woe betide you if the drinks bottles are not kept filled, or if your response time is longer than a nanosecond in finding the captain's fifth pair of gloves, or the short leg's lucky box. I think I was a bit bullied by my team-mates, as I remember one session having to run jumpers on and off solidly for two hours straight, and then being fined when I told the keeper where to go, having run a helmet on and off for the eighth time. These days, you are expected to carry drinks on for everyone if a wicket falls, and you can bet your bottom dollar that as soon as you sneak off for a quick No.2 during a lengthy stand, that will be when the wicket comes, even if your team-mates have looked unlikely to make a breakthrough all innings.

If your team is batting, you must ensure you have a drink ready for the dismissed batsman. This can be fraught with danger: if you offer a drink to a bloke who has been cleaned up first ball, you can expect an earful for taking the proverbial, but it's probably worth the risk for fear of the potential repercussions of not offering a drink. Whichever way, you are certainly likely to be the first in the firing line for any thrown bats, helmets and other paraphernalia of your disappointed team-mate.

One might be forgiven for thinking that you would be able to get a decent amount of practice done as a reserve player, but think again. Your warm-up will consist of endless throw-downs – no sooner would you have finished throwing a set of half-volleys for one batsman than another would appear asking if you 'wouldn't mind doing a few more'. It starts to take the mick a bit when the tail-enders are at it, too. You can expect to spend a fair bit of time catching a ball with a baseball mitt as well, and a good twelfthers will develop their proficiency in this area, as it looks utterly shambolic to have a bloke missing balls from the bowlers in their run-throughs, and having to fetch them constantly from under parked cars on the boundary edge. A poor mitt-manager can expect to spend the first half hour of the day's play with his face in a bush searching for balls he has missed.

At the end of the day's play, I quickly learnt that it was the reserve player's job to collect orders for the post-play drinks from the bar. If you did not manage this in good time, you were likely to end up with some guessing to do, and you don't want to offer up a pint of warm shandy to a bloke who always has Lucozade, or fail to have a cold cider waiting for the alcoholic left-arm spinner. Not getting your order in on time for all the drinks to be poured was likely to cost you the first round that evening, which would be all your 'exes'[10] gone in one fell swoop.

Acting as 'Twelfthers', one has to be cognisant with the whole range of non-verbal signals which on-field players will use to request something from the dressing room. Some are more obvious than others, whilst some are like an arcane form of semaphore, or Morse code. All signals are preceded by the batsman waving furiously at the dressing room, trying to gain the twelfth man's attention. Quality mime show this is not. At professional level, this call is answered instantaneously by the designated twelfth (and probably thirteenth) man – who are easily distinguished by their lurid fluorescent training bibs. It can be a bit bizarre seeing some of the finest cricketers in the world performing this subservient function. I mean, it's not as if Cristiano Ronaldo or David Beckham ever ran a drink or the 'magic sponge' on to the football field if they happened to be on the bench. But with squads being rotated as a matter of course these days in cricket, it is not unusual to see a Jonny Bairstow or a Sam Curran trotting out with a towel and some squash from time to time. But at amateur level, if a poor twelfthers is in play, the batsman can be waiting minutes before someone eventually clocks his needs, which then will need careful deciphering from an expert.

Next, I will attempt to offer a layman's guide to the language of cricketing signals, in case you ever have the misfortune to

---

10 Expenses. Always in a brown envelope. Much safer if it comes in cheque form as cash will be gone by the end of the evening.

find yourself doing twelfth-man duties. It may save you a lot of pain.

Twelfth Man Signals: Beginner Level

New Gloves: the batsman will present both hands and proceed to offer what looks like a sock puppet show. The twelfth man is expected to dig around in the batsman's kit for as many as ten extra pairs of gloves. The one pair he actually wants has been placed carefully by the boundary, but he will have failed to inform you of this.

Helmet: Indicated by the tapping of one's head and the miming of a grille across the face. Most batsmen these days start their innings with a helmet on, so the signal is rarer. Calling for a helmet is regarded as a particularly cowardly act and any batsman performing this signal can expect sledging to highlight this deficiency of character for several overs thereafter.

Cap: Indicated by the miming of pulling the peak of a cap. This is the opposite to calling for a helmet in terms of bravado and can be regarded as a derogatory comment towards the bowler's lack of pace. A batsman calling for a cap must expect to receive nothing but bouncers for the foreseeable future. One must never, ever, revert back to a helmet having called for the cap.

Sunhat: The player requiring a sunhat should make a wide circular gesture around their head to indicate the brim of a 'floppy'. If a batsman calls for a 'floppy' it can be regarded as even more insulting to a bowler. Nonetheless, if the batsman does not proceed to bat in highly flamboyant Caribbean fashion, he should expect a volley of abuse from the fielding side (and probably his team-mates as well). Unless you are Richie Richardson, do not call for a floppy whilst batting. Sunhats should only be tolerated on fielders if the game is being played in the subcontinent, Queensland or the Caribbean. Anyone donning a floppy in England should be regarded with suspicion. (NB: I used to wear a floppy in the field, but then I would bowl in sunglasses as well, and if this book tells us anything, I could be a bit of a dick on the cricket field …)

Twelfth Man Signals: Intermediate Level

Jumper (short-sleeved): Indicated by the player stroking the length of their torso with the back of their two hands, from shoulder to waist. The twelfth man should be looking out for a bowler wanting a jumper at the end of their spell.

Jumper (long-sleeved): as above, with the addition of brushing the hands down both sleeves. Very few players actually own a long-sleeved jumper, so be careful that this does not represent a red herring for the twelfth man.

Towel: For drying the face of a batsman. Rather like asking for new gloves, this should only be performed by a player with well over fifty, or a highly-regarded 'gun' player. Tail-enders who attempt this should be fined for getting above their station and can be disregarded by the twelfth man in almost all cases. To indicate the need for a towel, the batsman will make a circular motion with his hand in front of his face. Be careful, or you'll end up with sun cream.

Paracetamol/Ibuprofen: Interchangeable as cricketers don't know the difference between what these drugs do. Indicated by the player pointing to his tongue with his forefinger. It is not the twelfth man's job to keep tabs on how many pills any player has taken, although it is accepted in every dressing room that the medical guidelines are only there for display purposes and a cricketer will know best how many to take.

Tape: A swift circular motion is described as if unwinding a spool of tape. To avoid confusion, the mime should encircle the object for which tape is required (i.e. bat tape would require a circular motion around a bat; medical strapping would see the same motion around a finger). The twelfth man must remember that a pair of scissors is implied in this signal and any failure to bring scissors with the tape will result in his looking foolish and frustrating the player who requested it.

Twelfth Man Signals: Advanced Level

Scissors: Not especially tricky to decipher – the standard scissor-finger gesture – albeit tricky with gloves on. However, one of the more bizarre moments of my early career came during the Under-15 Bunbury Festival right up in mining territory in Tynemouth in Northumberland, when I called the twelfth man to bring scissors to where I was fielding between overs at long-on. To this day, it is the only time I have seen anyone have a haircut during a spell of bowling. I was sporting the ubiquitous 'curtains' style beloved of teenagers in the mid-1990s, and just had the left-hand curtain lopped so I could see where I was landing it.

I actually bowled well on this day, and incidentally bowled my best ball ever, to remove Stephen Peters – later of Essex and Northamptonshire. Peters was one of the talked-about batsmen of my generation, and mentioned in hushed tones reserved only for the likes of Owais Shah, Zac Morris and Graeme Swann around the festival. Peters clearly did not think much of my flight and guile and had put away a couple of rank balls early on in my spell, before I dragged one wide of his off stump. Shouldering arms in the most derisory way, Peters looked at me with sheer disdain. Feeling about two-foot-tall now, the ball sticky in my twitching fingers, I tried my damnedest to get the next one right. But it was worse. High, wide and embarrassing – the sort of ball which is usually followed with the words of the bowler's death knell, 'Take a blow there, fella.' (Officially the second worst sound in cricket, after hearing your own stumps demolished. Well, perhaps third behind a Gatting fart.)

However, it had been a wet morning up north and there was a small damp patch half on, half off the pitch, seemingly out of harm's way. But anyone who has watched old footage of 'Deadly' Derek Underwood bowling on a 'sticky dog' will know that a drying pitch is the spinner's best friend. As Peters once more looked at me with the sort of pity only usually reserved for the homeless or bereaved, bat raised high above his shoulders, the ball broke back at an unfathomable angle and hit the top of middle stump. His jaw seemed literally to drop, I think I laughed out loud and all around me, my team-mates were cock-a-hoop with seeing the back of the best player on show. It has never left me. I wonder if he remembers it.

Glasses: My old Dorset team-mate Jack Leach has in recent years made batting in glasses the thing of cult legend, after he scored the most famous single in Ashes history in his support of Ben Stokes's heroic Headingley hundred in 2019. Several seasons before that, and before I took the plunge and had laser-eye-surgery, I used to bat in glasses, copping the sledging you would expect. Not least on the occasion when the screw came out of my specs, and I had to signal for a new pair. Only I didn't have a new pair. The closest thing that would help me see the ball was the pair belonging to my mum who happened to be scoring. And so it was that I completed a solid fifty wearing some pink and purple eyewear, with butterflies on the stem for good measure, looking like a poor man's Dame Edna Everage.

Although it's a dog's life being twelfth man, I actually got a lot out of it; I was on the bench for three Minor Counties finals, which was obviously not what I wanted but nonetheless I was part of the action and there when the trophies were handed out. Literally, in the case of the 2010 final for which my work had decreed I was unavailable (bitter, me?). But I was able to be on the field as sub when the final wicket went down and so, as club captain and leading wicket-taker that year, I was (rightfully, in my eyes) able to step up and collect the trophy. In my first final – 1998 – I took a blinder at short fine leg off Nigel Cowley, who took seven wickets in a losing effort. And in 2000, when Dorset eventually won their first title, I travelled with Tim Lamb to a birthday party in Wales (a long way from Bournemouth) and drank so much gin and tonic that the management didn't allow me to take the field the following day until after tea-time. A low moment, but I still have the medal …

You'd be hard pressed to find a young cricketer these days putting his hand up to travel for three days – they have so many more options for entertainment, but for me, the prospect of a few quid, time away with mates and the banter of the dressing room in the pre-smartphone era was like all my Christmases had come at once.

Chapter Ten

The Art of Captaincy – Amateur Style

MIKE BREARLEY is acknowledged as the oracle on cricket captaincy. Since winning the Ashes in 1981 from 1-0 down and helping to resurrect the career of Ian Botham seemingly in a matter of days, Brearley has been known as the man who made the cricket world realise that a good captain is worth more than his own runs or wickets. He would never have made the national side on talent alone, and cricket is probably the only sport in which the captain's job could be genuinely recognised as a discipline in itself.

Captaincy is so multi-faceted that you could write a book on it. No wait, he did. And it still holds true, even as the cricket world now seems to spin in a different orbit. However, captaincy of county and Test sides seems to me a whole different kettle of fish than taking charge of an amateur team. An old colleague of mine once suggested that there are two jobs in sport that everyone should try once, but never repeat. One was managing a non-league football team; the other was captaining an amateur cricket club. This is my experience of what it can be like.

The Off-Season

No sooner had I finished my degree course in 2002, than I was being asked to take over as captain back at my club – Farnham in Surrey. In many ways this was as much an honour as being asked to captain the university team. What I hadn't quite bargained for was just how much of a slog it was in comparison, nor just how young and inexperienced I still was at the age of 23.

Firstly, when you get the job in September, the next game of cricket is a long way off. The enthusiasm and folly of youth led me to believe that this would be a time for strategy, tactical planning, a pre-season programme which combined skills work, fitness and perhaps even elements of psychology. What it actually meant was turning up on a monthly basis to the freezing old pavilion to sit on plastic chairs for the club committee meetings. These summits tended to focus on such glamorous topics as:

- Whether we ought to invest our meagre funds in replacing a few roof tiles or focus on the scoreboard, which, although a modern electric version, has lost so many of its pieces that you could never tell if a team was one wicket down, or five, or eight.
- Who had the Most Improved Fielder cup, which was last awarded in 1993 and last seen in the kit bag of a disgraced overseas player?
- Could we manage another year with covers which leaked?
- Could our septuagenarian Sunday captain be persuaded to stand for 'one more year' for the fourth year running?
- Would there be hot water in the showers by April, and could the temperature be regulated?
- Whose job was it to ensure no dogs fouled the outfield: ours or the council's?

And so on. I quickly realised that there is more to running a social cricket club than just pitching up, tossing a coin and having a few beers after play.

I also lost several evenings of my life attending the League committee meetings, which would be held in a similarly bleak and cold pavilion at another club. As we were on the edge of the county, this meant a dreary trek up the A3 and back to listen to similar minutiae. I would return with boxes full of handbooks, fixture cards and match balls, which would then clutter up my house for the next few months. The romantic relationship of many a club captain will have been strained by the spare room being taken up with utterly unnecessary cricket paraphernalia, even months before the season itself drives the final nails into the coffin.

Primarily, it was my job to focus on cricketing matters, which meant setting up the winter net programme. Confirming the use of a local private school's facilities was the easy part. Getting players there, not so easy. The average attendance of a first-team player to the ten-week set of nets was about four weeks, but as captain you had to be at virtually all of them. So your practice consisted of trying to spread the various talents of the nine attendees (ages ranging between 11 and 60) across enough nets to ensure everyone got a reasonable bat and bowl, and that the younger lads did not get killed by the one first-team seamer who seemed intent on using the hard indoor surface to test out bouncers he would never bowl outdoors (like every seamer ever born, this would be off no more than 19 yards). You also had to accept that with such a mixture of talent, your ten-minute batting slot would mean switching between negotiating the aforementioned short balls one minute and picking the ball out of the side of the net the next, as your second-team keeper valiantly tried to get it down the other end in a straight line. And of course, there were never enough practice balls, as all the spares from last season had been smashed into the trees during the end-of-season six-a-side tournament. The seamer would have his own, brand-new cherry, whilst the rest of us would share three old balls – one of which would inevitably be a junior-sized ball while a second would have the initials of another club in marker pen on it. If we were lucky, the heating would be on, but I can remember at least one net session in the depths of January when the electric meter ran out leaving us fumbling around in the dark for our kit in Arctic temperatures. The carefully drafted strategy document I had planned to hand out remained apologetically in the bottom of my bag, getting more curled and soggy as the weeks went by, before being consigned to the bin somewhere in mid-March.

Another reason for the ditching of the battleplan was that the players I had expected to have at my disposal were no longer all available. 'Recruitment' feels a rather grandiose term for the begging and pleading which I was forced to do as the season loomed closer. Grand promises were made to waverers:

'Of course, you'll get the new ball. Downhill, with the wind, naturally.'

*'What number would you **like** to bat?'*

'If you do 12 games, I'll buy all your beers…'

Numbers that had lay dormant in my mobile phone were suddenly in action again as old team-mates and schoolmates, even passing acquaintances, were tapped up for their availability. There was charming of other halves to be done as well, trying to persuade wives and girlfriends that holidays in March and September were cheaper and far more relaxing than going away at the height of summer; weddings (and even worse, stag and hen dos) should be taken away from the cricket season, and any plans for home improvement, well, they would just have to wait.

Other unforeseen responsibilities which seemed to come my way were finding a sponsor for the shirts (achieved) and coming up with some fundraising events. And so was born 'Beryl's Bonus Ball' (a lottery spin-off named after the late chairman's wife) and the Farnham Fun Day which saw the players all take charge of a fun event like 'Splat the Rat' or hoopla. The 'Guess the Weight of the First XI' explained why we were not as successful as we ought to have been. I'd love to have seen old Brears persuading Bob Willis to run the welly-throwing contest.

Pre-Season

By the time we got to pre-season, I would be itching to get on with some cricket. Never mind that it would highlight how ineffective the winter nets had been. For one, the side which was selected barely resembled the bunch of keen beans who had given up their winter Sundays, and, secondly, any English player can tell you that there is a world of difference between flat, true indoor nets and the types of stodgy pasture which pass for a cricket pitch in April. Forget three slips and a gully, just post a ring of fielders and watch batsmen pop it up in the air off a slow, 'stoppy' pitch off the most mediocre medium-pacer. A staple of the early pre-season game is watching your carefully-honed cover drive lollipop to cover whilst you wipe a pitch mark off your face. Also, you are guaranteed to suffer horribly bruised hands since without actually catching a ball since the previous September, your palms are now as soft as marshmallows.

Pre-season matches are the very definition of a 'phoney war', as you are unlikely to have your ideal first team, and there is usually the added nuisance of having to find an umpire, scorer and someone to make teas, as these volunteers will have pencilled in the league dates and taken a final weekend away in Devon. Another certainty is that you will not have considered the need for a scorebook, and so will have to go to the local sports shop when it opens, meaning you will be late to pick up the 15-year-old whom you drafted in late the night before the game, and his dad who volunteered to umpire (and who will now be in your ear all season about how talented his lad is, until he gets the hump with him being in the third team and takes him to your arch-rivals in July). You will be doubly late as you will return to the sports shop to buy new cricket balls, which you will also have forgotten are required for a match and which of course are your responsibility as well. You may as well factor in a detour to the pet shop as it is inevitable that you will require sawdust when it starts to drizzle just as you are getting into your stride.

All of which just adds to the captain's burden and makes you wonder why you bothered at all. Your own game is so far down the list of priorities as to become insignificant. You won't bowl your normal quota of overs as you want to give everyone a 'run out', desperately hoping that the load of dross being offered up is just ring-rust which will have been dusted off by the following week. As for batting, again, you'll be in an unfamiliar position as you try to give all the players their preferred slot, if only just so there is no excuse for leaving them out when they, sadly, fail. Next week, of course, all the best players will be available and you'll have the unenviable job of explaining to the committed but average players why you have selected those who have only made a couple of cursory practices while they are forced into the twos having given up all their free time. Of course, the answer is obvious, but no one likes to state the obvious, especially when it means telling someone they can't bowl a hoop down a hill.

The sad truth of the matter is that, by the time the season proper rolls around, the preparation will have been exposed as underwhelming and all your recruitment dreams will have come to nothing, leaving you with the same team which scraped a mid-table finish last year, just a year older and more jaded, and without the overseas pro whose visa has been held up until after your first three inevitable defeats. As you do a final sweep of the pavilion, picking up a few fag butts from the patio, and try to mend the holes in the nets with a job-lot of plastic cable-ties, you can be forgiven for thinking that captaincy is not quite the glamour role which had been sold to you.

Match Day

This is what it has all been about. Actual competitive cricket. However, it's not as easy as it might be for the likes of Brearley, or even as it had been for me at Oxford. When winning is the only aim, captaincy is a comparative doddle. Every decision made is with that end in mind. But when you are in charge of a diverse bunch of amateurs who have made cricket their priority for every weekend in the summer, and are paying subscriptions and match fees for the privilege, there is a lot more you must keep in mind. Tactics are balanced carefully against the full gamut of egos. Asking someone to bat too low, or too high, may result in a sulk of epic proportions; woe betide you if you take off the seasoned seamer who feels he is just getting into his rhythm, and even asking someone to field at fine leg might result in their taking serious umbrage. And so your tactics are compromised from the start, and keeping an eye on your own game is nigh on impossible.

Pen-Pushers and Tin Men

What you must also remember is that it is not just the players you need to manage on match day. There is the scorer, if you are lucky enough to have one. Most clubs' first team will have a regular, and I was lucky that between my wife, my mum and my dad, we were usually well set. But, make no mistake, the average scorer is by no means the meek, mild number-cruncher that you might expect. No, they are very much one of the team of officials, along with the umpires, and they will be sure to remind you of this week in week out. Often they will 'pull rank' and get into the tea line well before any players, and you can be sure that they will give you their opinion of your tactics and the team's shortcomings before you've even managed to give your post-match team talk. But whilst they know their value, they are in fact invaluable, since a poorly-kept scorebook leads to poor records, and everyone knows that cricketers are all about the stats, even if they claim otherwise.

Your best scorer is also a repository of endless sweets, tissues, pens and pharmaceuticals. They will carry the significant responsibility of holding on to the 'vallies' (valuables) – a stinking holdall of assorted wallets, watches, mobile phones, keys and cigarettes. At a moment's notice the optimum scorer will be able to lay their hand on the right car key to silence some twat's Audi A3 convertible whilst simultaneously answering the phone to someone's mistress. They will keep countless supporters who could not be bothered to come to the ground up-to-date with an almost ball-by-ball account of the latest batting collapse. And they will maintain cordial relations with whichever poor sod had volunteered for the opposition, often in the most insalubrious of settings, since the scorers' box is usually a mere shed miles away from any other human contact and sheltered from any sun whatsoever. Without wishing to do the scoring fraternity (or indeed sorority) down, many is the time it has been reported to me by our scorer that they have had to endure an entire day stuck in a scorebox with a colleague for whom personal hygiene has been questionable at best. If not hygienically deficient, they will have verbal diarrhoea and spend the entire day rattling off endless facts and stats while our scorer has dreamt of a set of knitting needles to stick in their own eyes. Then there are the over-familiar; the space-invaders who try to turn on the charm. Or even worse, a combination of all of the above. Perhaps even worse is when a young child in a Chelsea shirt has been appointed to the role; and whilst I'm all for a development pathway for the scoring-minded, their chat is inevitably totally guff and the seasoned scorer will have to spend all day correcting their mistakes. At least with a youngster there is the chance of a brief escape at official intervals, whereas in normal circumstances the umpires and scorers are afforded their own separate table away from the *hoi polloi* in a universally accepted form of social distancing.

Perhaps the funniest scorer-related anecdote for me came in a county game taking place at a ground where the scoreboard was some distance across the ground from the pavilion. Having taken tea, the players and umpires were just returning to the field for the final session when the opposition scorer (a gentleman of ample build, shall we say) realised he had tarried over the rock cakes a little longer than he ought, and would have to get a shift on if he was to be ready for the resumption of play. Making a dash for it ('dash' is probably a little generous), our man made it most of the way across the outfield, before tripping a good pitch-length away from the scorebox itself. Being of rotund build, it quickly became apparent that it was going to be impossible for him to get himself back to the vertical without some aid. But before anyone could get close to him to lend a hand, the poor chap started to roll himself towards the nearest bench, in full view of everyone in the ground. It was like watching the Fat Controller on a spit. Whether the round of applause he received as he waved his funny luminous ping-pong bat thingy alleviated his embarrassment, I have no idea, but he can be safe that this story has kept us amused during many a long session in the slips.

It would be easy to be unkind about scorers (and many cricketers are), but when you think about it, they are seriously underrated. Anyone who has had to endure doing the book after getting out for a duck will know what I mean.

On the odd rare occasion, there might even be a team with the scorers. By team, I really mean someone whose sole responsibility is to keep the scoreboard up-to-date. Now, at some Test grounds, this role is legendary: some of the scoreboards in the subcontinent are behemoths, renowned for the speed, agility and daredevil bravery of their operators, and the famous old manual scoreboard at the Adelaide Oval is one of the wonders of the cricket world. More likely, in England, a scoreboard operator refers to someone who has nothing better to do with their weekend than change the 'tins' which hang from rusty nails on a painted black-and-white board. This particular set of cricketing memories would not be complete without a mention of two stalwart scoreboard operators.

Firstly, anyone who played at Oxford University around the turn of the century would remember 'Del Boy', whose toothy mug was ever-present poking out from the oblong-shaped hole in the Parks' scoreboard. No one knew what Del's full name was, where he lived, what he did for a living, or if he had any family. It was, I think, recognised that Del was rather simple in nature and that adding up in tens was probably the limit of his academic prowess. It was great theatre to sit in the press and scorers' box and listen to the running saga between Del and the scorer, Neil Harris. Neil was a typically proud scorer whose presentation was impeccable. He was the first I came across who would produce wagon wheels for both bowling and batting (even if you might not want to see it after being mauled for over a hundred, or out for less than ten). He was a staunch supporter of Oxford United and his claim to fame was being cast as a corpse in an episode of *Morse*. On weekends, he and his wife would volunteer to perform traffic surveys for Oxford Council. Not glamorous, but the sort of bloke that makes the world go around. Nothing was too much trouble for Neil. But his relationship with Del Boy was fascinating: the usually unflappable Neil would become quickly impatient, then riled, then apoplectic when his underling missed another single, or apportioned the last boundary to the wrong player, resulting in a ripple of applause for another professional's fifty, when really they were still on 46. Neil would curse and then miss the next delivery, all the while blaming Del, who would be serene in his box until the phone line between the two of them rang again to register the error. The sound of that phone line is as ingrained in my memory of the Parks as the sound of my arm-ball hitting the middle of a sponsored Gunn & Moore. However, he was universally loved and it did not matter that the tens and units were often the wrong way around. Just to see Del heading off after a good day's toil, always proudly dressed in his OUCC tracksuit top and with an enthusiastic thumbs-up, was enough to make you smile.

The other scoreboard operator who made an impression was Graham (or possibly Graeme; I never saw it in print), who manned the tins at Dean Park for many a year. Graham was as large as the poor roly-poly scorer who'd lost his footing, and would spend his winters watching AFC Bournemouth (long before they were Premier League material) and then summers at the cricket in his bucket hat, beer belly peeking cheekily out from a stained polo shirt. Always jovial, Graham was a cult hero in much the same way as Del Boy, and was easily persuaded into a beer. So much so, that during one especially long, hot summer, the team clubbed together to buy him a case of 24 Stellas, on the proviso that he finished them all by close of play. All of which went well, up until the final session when it became apparent that not only had the score gone horribly awry, but that Graham was now holding on to the scoreboard for dear life like Leonardo DiCaprio in the final scenes of *Titanic*. With 18 empty bottles around him, we decided that any more and we were likely to witness another natural disaster, and so Graham was relieved of his post and given time to recover before finding his way to wherever it was that he went after close of play.

The sad thing is that the custodian of the tins is a post which is in its final years, as scoreboards become electronic or flimsy plastic and go the way of linseed oil and the bat-knocking-in mallet. Again, the powers-that-be ought to consider if this is just another example of technology ruining the game as we know and love it. Eons into the future, I can see archaeologists debating the purpose of numbered tin squares dug up across rural regions of the old British Empire.

The Men in White Coats

The captain also has to spend a decent amount of time on match days with the umpires. Not only are there the official duties: the toss, making sure they have the stumps and bails, filling out a team-sheet and so on. But of course they will want a cup of coffee on arrival and since the tea lady only turns up to drop off the sandwiches and cake just before the tea interval, it will land on the captain to open up the kitchen, stick the kettle on and dig around for some sugar so the men in white coats can have a brew. This act of hospitality done, the carefully-planned warm-up session will have gone to the dogs, with the opening batsman now launching high catches at the youngsters, the spinner having a fag and the all-rounder idly flicking through a porn mag in the dressing room. The overseas will be having a natter with the opposition overseas, both pointing out just how rubbish their respective teams are and showing little sign of breaking a sweat or marshalling so much as a gentle jog around the outfield. When the skipper tries to gather the troops, he will be met with sighs and tuts at best; at worst he will be ignored entirely. This is a lonely moment. If you are the skipper in this situation, the safest thing to do is to wander over to the pitch itself and perform the pantomime of inspection: get down on your haunches as if to examine any grass on the wicket, lightly dig around any cracks you may find and generally give the impression of having some idea that this intelligence will determine what happens at the toss. If your players have not emerged after five minutes, you can extend this face-saving charade by doing some air-batting, as if 'visualising' yourself in play. This is what professionals do, so don't give your ignorance away by suddenly unleashing a repertoire of outlandish shots you will never play in a game. Stick to slow-motion defensive shots or little glides to fine-leg and hopefully you'll blend into the background long enough to then saunter back into the changing rooms and confidently announce that you've decided that 'individual warm-ups' are the best preparation for today.

Keeping the umpires happy is a key role of the captain, although a high-risk/high-reward move can be to persuade your wife or girlfriend to hang around long enough to entertain the umpires during the warm-up slot. The older gentlemen who take on the mantle of umpireship are usually the type who will enjoy female company and some well-placed attention and flattery early on could turn things your way. Even if this feels like a recipe for marital disaster, you can take the job on yourself: asking about the umpires' former glory days as players will doubtless open up streams of nostalgia and, if you can bear ten minutes listening, you'll go down as a good bloke, which is no bad thing when you need a decision to go your way in the final few overs. The savviest captains build up these relationships over a period of years and you must always be mindful that the opposition captain is probably doing exactly the same. It's also worth exercising caution in going too far. I have been embarrassed on one or two occasions when an umpire has got so pally that he has been almost itching to get the finger up. It's not a great look when you get a dodgy call go your way if it is accompanied with, *'That's out, captain!'*, or worse, *'That's out. Well bowled, Hicksy!'*

And you must buy the umpire a drink after play. In three-day games this is another good chance to butter them up, and you'd be a fool not to keep league umpires happy as you're bound to see them again a few weeks later. One of the few perks of being captain was the privilege of being able to buy a discretionary 'Captain's Jug' of lager if things had gone well. I certainly remember perhaps more than one Captain's Jug going down on the odd late night. It's no wonder our profit margins were so tight.

The club skipper is nothing short of a general factotum (a phrase that sounds more grand than it is, being a posh Latin term for dogsbody). It's hard to know when you feel this most keenly. If it's not replacing the little cubes of urinal freshener, then it might be having to do odd jobs between innings. When the likes of Michael Vaughan or Joe Root are getting a rubdown or discussing the finer points of tactics over a cup of tea or a Lucozade, the clubman may well be helping out to brush the pitch and re-paint the lines (if this was not done in our league, the club would receive a fine, which the captain would inevitably end up paying). Our groundsman at Farnham was also the opening bowler, in a weird echo of my childhood days at Child Okeford. This chap was all about the toys in his shed and preferred to use a leaf blower than a broom, which meant that at tea times, the ground resembled a Saharan sandstorm more than a leafy Surrey greensward. By the time we'd finished there was just a grassless dustbowl left behind: perfect for our spinners.

Of course, this was if the day was dry, which was infrequent, to say the least. More often than not, rain would affect play and then it was all hands on deck again, with the captain having to drag the troops out to pull on the covers (quickly if we were batting, at a snail's pace if we were in the field). Unless you are a club with lots of money, your covers will be impossible to move and a hazard to life and limb. Dorset keeper Chris Park almost took off trying to help put covers on at St Helens, Swansea, almost going as far as one of Garry Sobers's six sixes as he was flung into the air on a squally morning, holding on to the tarpaulin for dear life. The battle against the elements can feel like life or death when relegation or promotion is on the line, however, and I have seen on many occasions dozens of grown men wasting their Saturdays dressed in white clothing, attempting to dry a cricket pitch in the rain, sacrificing their towels, jumpers and any other cloth they can lay their hands on in the vain hope of getting a match started. Pet City in Farnham ran out of sawdust on one particular weekend, leaving hamster owners furious after we'd bought the lot to try to salvage a couple of points against Walton-on-Thames. But as a consolation, if rain does eventually stop play, there is fun to be had by using the sheet-style covers as an enormous adult-sized 'slip-and-slide', as has happened on more than one occasion.

And then there is actually a cricket team to manage. But to be quite frank, by the time all the peripheral tasks have been taken care of, the skipper has no more capacity for decision-making and so will stand at mid-off or slip watching helpless as the game passes them by, a million thoughts whizzing through his head, such as:

'I wonder what other blokes do on a weekend?'
'Chinese or Indian tonight?'
'How many weeks until September?'

It's all he can do to set a field and change the bowling once in a while. If, by some miracle, the game is won, it all seems worthwhile for a few drunken hours and by the time Tuesday comes around, he will have rekindled his enthusiasm for the game and get ready for the next weekly round of purgatory.

Post-Match

That alcoholic solace or celebration has to wait, though, until some more turgid jobs are accomplished. There is the collection of the boundary markers – not all club grounds have a rope – although this job can often be palmed off on a keen youngster, as it was delegated to me until I wised up that this was just a ruse to allow the old man a cheeky extra half pint. Those covers had to be rolled on again, and persuading the boys to do that after they'd showered was like trying to dislodge Steve Smith on a flat one. Umpires need to be watered, and you'll inevitably have to buy beers for the bloke who didn't end up in the top eight after all, the leggie who didn't get a bowl and that same dad of the keen 15-year-old, who has been there all day watching his son go from fine leg to third man and wanted to remind you that his lad had scored fifty for his age group in the week and that Guildford were offering to give him a run in the first team. Usually you'd be happy to let him go as it means not dealing with this ball-ache of a father, but you know he's better than most of your top order, and yet you can't risk a mutiny by demoting them. There are these types of politics facing every club skipper the world over.

Collecting the match fees is the worst, and a job often delegated to the scorer. You instantly become Public Enemy No.1 as you sidle from person to person like a Victorian debt collector, sending the impecunious or tight-fisted slipping out back doors and windows in an attempt to evade the inevitable. The weekly pantomime of turning wallets out to reveal no cash, or players 'just heading into town to get some cash' never to be seen again was as tiresome as it was predictable. As was the following *schtick*:

'Can I owe you?'
'No, because you still owe for last week.'
'What? I never! I distinctly remember ...'
'No you didn't, Gary, no you didn't.'

At our club, you also had to put the wooden shutters up on the front of the pavilion – another two-man job for which you had to collar someone early before you were left attempting the impossible on your own and with two jugs of Castle Lager in your belly. I say on your own, but there would often be one straggler – usually the overseas – who had passed out in the corner hours ago and would be left there until the following morning if there was a Sunday fixture.

Sundays, Midweek and Friendlies

These extra games have died a bit of a death in recent years. Back in the last century it was expected that decent players would play on Sundays as well as Saturdays, and cup matches might see us travelling all across the Home Counties. These days the expectations on people with families are different, and younger players have so many more options available to them socially that I don't blame them for not wanting to don a dirty pair of whites and spend another day playing cricket. But from the club captain's point of view, these games just meant even more begging, pleading and bribing just to scratch a side together. For me, they were just like another pre-season game, with all the attendant annoyances. And then there were the Tuesday night limited-over competitions, which were the same again, only with the added trauma of rush-hour traffic meaning we often started with eight or nine men as others rushed out of the city trying frantically to find a village green down a long-lost lane, where eleven locals had been practising for an hour since they all worked in the village or from home. Many was the evening that I contemplated my existence as I was bowled by a grubber delivered by some pub landlord to great adulation, watching our Premier League outfit humbled in the light of the setting sun, which was always behind the bowler's arm. In these games, rather like in friendlies, it was expected that you might 'drink back the fixture' (i.e. you'd be crap on the field, but you were a decent bunch and put a few quid behind the bar so you'd get invited back). Sadly (or rather, sensibly), people are much less inclined to drink and drive than they were in the Eighties, and so this sort of socialising is rarer, and usually it's a can of Coke and a meek apology.

Dropping Players

Whilst most of my tribulations as captain of Farnham came in the form of having to find players, occasionally we would be in the enviable position of having too many players available. Of course, for your professional captain this is described as a 'nice problem to have'. But when you know that you will be grovelling for players only weeks later, it's not quite so easy to give people the bad news that they are surplus to requirements for that weekend. I am well aware that there are many people who would have cursed me to anyone who would listen after they'd been dropped. After all, no one ever feels it's they who should get the axe. And I learnt some valuable life lessons from this unpleasant aspect of cricket. I made the mistake more than once of not being up-front with people and just telling them straight, and in person if possible, or at least on the phone. And there were also times that I left this job to the coach or manager, which is a big regret of mine. Now, if I have bad news to deliver, I'll always try to do it face-to-face and just get to the point. It's just a matter of respect. But that's the great thing about sport: it teaches you many things in so many ways.

Club cricket is just perfect for stories, scandal and intrigue. It's a wonder more books aren't written about it. About the best book I've read on this subject is *The Grade Cricketer*, coincidentally co-written by Ian Higgins, who has really made a name for himself in the Australian sporting media, and who also spent some happy seasons at Farnham. His take on Aussie grade cricket has different nuances to the English game, but the characters are the same the world over.

The Cricket Week – a Rite of Passage

I have been lucky enough in my cricket-playing days to captain sides at almost every level: from school to Premier League, junior county, Minor County and at first-class level. But perhaps the biggest challenge in captaincy is not in going higher up the levels, but actually having to take charge of friendly games, in which you have to try and get everyone at least a bowl or a bat, whilst manufacturing a declaration to coincide with tea, and a finish ideally in the final over of the 20 allotted in the last hour, by less than ten runs, with one wicket to spare. And if you didn't understand all that, imagine trying to remember it all as well as the names of the blokes you've only just been introduced to, on three hours' sleep and an almighty hangover, especially if you are on tour. You can read as many manuals and attend as many three-day conferences as you like, that is leadership training, right there. Friendly it may be, easy it is not. But I love it, and in my experience, it doesn't get much more friendly than the school old boys' cricket week.

For 60 years, a rag-tag assortment of reprobates has been making its way back to deepest darkest Dorset to represent the Clayesmore Cormorants in their annual cricket week, normally coinciding with the hottest week of the year in early July – that glorious early part of the holidays when summer seems to stretch out endlessly in front of you like a tropical sandy beach, when the Wimbledon champions have just been crowned, The Open is on television and cricket pitches are at their flattest. Tucked away amongst the greenest and most pleasant land of the Dorset countryside, you are so far away from the rush of civilisation that you could be forgiven for feeling as if you've stepped back hundreds of years, or stumbled into the Shire of Tolkien's Hobbits. And when you re-enter the picturesque village of Iwerne Minster, a festival of hanging baskets and thatched cottages welcomes you. The earth is happy and it feels good to be back on familiar ground. And as dozens of millennial newcomers to the cricket week have found to their horror, there is zero chance of getting a Wi-Fi signal or telephone reception. For five days, it is utter, disconnected bliss.

For the cricket week, we have been lucky to enjoy cordial terms with one of the boarding housemasters, who lets us make use of the boys' rooms for a peppercorn rent every year. We have the great fortune to play on some of the finest grounds in the county as we take part in a four-way festival alongside more illustrious public schools in Sherborne, Bryanston and Canford, fitting in another fixture against a wandering side for good measure.

For me, having already passed the 25th anniversary of my debut, the week means many things. As a fresh-faced 13-year-old, I picked up four wickets against a Canford side who got very red-faced and grumpy at getting out to a loopy off-spinner whose voice hadn't broken, so I became a tourist early. But prior even to this, it represented a chance to play on the boundary whilst my father played either with or against the Purley Strollers, whose south London accents seemed somewhat out of place amid the local drawl. But quickly I got my chance to play. What a thrill! Men's cricket, with a ball bigger than I was used to, and players who hit it so hard I had to be hidden in the field. But I found that I could still get wickets, and my insatiable love of the game meant that, once the actual match was over, I would immediately start up a new game with my younger brother, who would be green with envy that I'd been allowed to play with the grown-ups. It was a great time for boyhood heroes, too, and just being in the presence of the likes of Graeme Owton, who'd broken all the school records, was like tripping around Mount Olympus.

You soon get acclimatised, though, and before long, the cricket week became a chance to enjoy the pleasures of the post-match, and the extra games with my brother gave way to my first pints of shandy, which soon became lager-tops and pretty swiftly a refined taste for Badger Best. For these weeks are as much about the social as the cricket. Growing up, this was a safe place to learn about the ritual of post-match fines (first paid by your old man, but as soon as you could have a beer, you were paying your own way); to learn drinking songs and to learn that teachers were actually human beings. These weeks were a rite of passage, and as good an education into the grown-up world as I could have wished for. And given that as a youngster I would not be putting away beer in the same industrial quantities as more seasoned tourists, and had the healthy young organs to ensure hangovers were a thing of the future, I also found that I could have lots of fun scoring runs and taking wickets during the day. Even more bliss.

As my cricket became more serious, the Cormorants Week was still the first thing pencilled into my calendar every year; it was the first place I went after three-day Minor Counties games, and after my lone professional game for Worcestershire, I didn't bother going home, but headed straight down to the Talbot Inn to see how we'd done against old rivals Bryanston. It was more of a chance to remind myself why I loved the game, and to play for fun (and hopefully to keep in nick) rather than worrying about selection or tactics for the club or county. And of course, for the banter. It's a truism of good mates that you don't need to speak to them or see them regularly, but when you do, you just fall back into the same old comfortable patterns. And cricket week is no different.

To my mind, the week will always be official manager and financial advisor Andrew Beaton, heading off for his *Daily Telegraph* in his red polo shirt, Dennis Taylor glasses and socks-with-sandals fashion faux pas; Terry Morgan – the debonair developer from Oxfordshire who was not really an old boy of the school but had been invited once and never stopped coming; his son – Alex – who became a partner in all sorts of crimes, and could always be relied upon to suggest we 'get a cab to Bournemouth to see if there are any birds about'. In 25 years, we never made that trip! There will always be Terry's sidekick – Blanty – an antique dealer who looked a bit like the chap from the old TV series *Lovejoy* (if he was in a hall of mirrors). Blanty was, as they say, a 'character'. Among his party tricks was taking out his false teeth and dropping them in your pint, and he it was who cajoled an 18-year-old me up the clock tower at the school in the dead of night to ring the bells, giving the residents quite a shock. And it was Blanty with whom I stayed up until the sun rose and whom I had to fish out of the stream in the village, still in his whites at 5am. Of course, I've mentioned my hero Graeme Owton, and my brother would always be there too, and the amount of 'wisdom' we've shared after a box of Cabernet on tour could fill volumes, if only I could remember any of it. Other key players were the Dike brothers – famous in the county for their wonderful cakes, and Andy's utterly unorthodox yet ruthlessly effective chinamen. And the Lack brothers also go down as long-term servants, and decent cricketers to boot. There are so many more names and characters who deserve mentioning, but we'd be here forever if I listed them all.

I will mention one of our umpires who joined the tour for several years, for which we were very grateful. However, there was probably a reason why he had been 'retired' from officiating competitive cricket several years earlier, and you had to take the rough decisions with the smooth as part of the amateur fun of the week. On one occasion, he made a decision so woefully awful, we couldn't let it slide. My brother Guy was attempting a spell of military medium-pacers, as part of his long-term recovery from the yips which meant when he bowled spin his body seemed temporarily abducted by aliens and you had to run for cover if you were anywhere near him. And he was surprisingly getting it pretty straight on this day, eventually finding a thick inside edge which cannoned into the batsman's inner thigh pad. Being cricket week, some occasional cricketer offered a rather hopeful appeal from deep square leg, even as Guy was returning to his mark for the next ball, so obvious was the edge. But to everyone's horror, our umpire shot his finger up, giving the batsman out. This left us in a pickle, as etiquette would say that you ought to call the chap back, but this also meant casting aspersions on the ability and eyesight of the umpire. Of course, we all knew he was pretty terrible but the dread thought of us having to umpire our own games was enough for us to be desperate to keep him onside and happy to umpire the next day. So politely, Guy suggested that we hadn't really appealed and maybe he should reconsider his decision. To which the umpire, now realising his egregious error but not wanting to show weakness, replied, keeping his finger raised: 'I wasn't giving him out, I was pointing at that aeroplane up there,' which was a complete lie, but it meant he saved face, the batsman came back, and we had an umpire for tomorrow.

Undoubtedly, though, the thing which people look forward to the most on tour is Waffleball. Established around the turn of the millennium, Waffleball is essentially a game of ping-pong played using a tennis ball and two circular waffle-irons designed for toasting waffles on an Aga. No sooner has the pub kicked out, than the Cormorants will head back to the boarding house, charge their glasses and take up a station around the kitchen table, where a 'net' will be erected from various ephemera such as cereal packets, pot plants, a wastepaper basket and always, but always, 'The Bust of Piers Sabine' (a clay model of a man's head which bears a passing resemblance to one of the elder statesmen of the club). It is winner-stays-on and a match is first to three points, with everyone circulating clockwise after each bout. After a few beers, it is the most compelling, and competitive spectacle, with its own arcane rules now well embedded and even a winner's hat which must be worn for the following day's cricket. Such has been the success of Waffleball that, at the 50th anniversary of the club, a Waffleball table was erected in the marquee and an exhibition event was held so that all the older members could see it in action. I fully expect it to be an Olympic sport by 2050.

Nowadays, I tend to get to the tour less regularly, and certainly feel older every time I go, as some players have retired from playing and prefer a brief hill walk, a spot of fishing and then to come and watch a few overs before a nice dinner and glass of wine in place of the old days of chips and a barrelful of Badger (so central is the local ale to our fun that we even redesigned our crest to incorporate a barrel in place of the stumps behind a cricketing seabird). Other players seem much younger and will happily tell me that they were not even born when I was at school, or even when I started teaching. Such is the passing of time, I guess. Although there are still times when the sarcasm slips and a respectful nod is given to the fact some of the records I and my era left behind at the old place still stand. Much as I love cricket (and can't stand losing to the other schools), this week has never really been about the game itself, but more what it represents and can do for people. Here there is no hierarchy, just a great group of guys coming together for fun, camaraderie and no little nostalgia. And Waffleball. Always Waffleball.

Chapter Eleven

In the Club – Becoming an MCC Member

BY THE time I'd finished at Oxford, I'd been persuaded that joining the MCC would be a good idea. Qualifying as a playing member would open up the chance to jump a 25-year queue to join the club, meaning access to Lord's and the chance to play great cricket at superb grounds and even perhaps to do some touring. For me, it's been worth every penny, and I even managed to do some time behind the scenes as Area Representative for the London Suburban (South) region, which meant time spent in the corridors of cricket power at one of the great venues. Every time I go to Lord's feels special in its own way, and it has given rise to some great memories as well.

Lunch at Lord's with Mike Gatting

There are many rumours that abound about Mike Gatting which pertain to his predilection for eating (most of which I think have been propagated by Sir Ian Botham). There is the classic comment when Gatting was bowled by Shane Warne's 'Ball of the Century' that 'had it been a cheese roll, he wouldn't have missed it'. And there is the possibly apocryphal story that when offered the steak or the salmon for lunch at Lord's during a Test match, Gatting answered 'Both', without breaking stride. Then there is the exchange between Chris Cowdrey and David Gower: when Gower asked if Cowdrey would 'like Gatting a bit wider at slip?', Cowdrey responded that 'if Gatt was any wider, he'd explode'. All of which are pretty unfair, given that Mike Gatting scored the thick end of a hundred first-class hundreds, brought the Ashes back from Australia and later became one of the most influential administrators in world cricket. But I guess that bullies love a fatty as a target, and he was never the lithest, even when diving forward memorably to scoop up the ninth wicket off Bob Willis at Headingley in 1981.

In 2005, I had the incredible good fortune to be able to put to the test just exactly what the Middlesex and England legend does order during lunch at Lord's, when I was selected for the Marylebone Cricket Club to play against the other MCC – the Melbourne Cricket Club – the day after the Lord's Test.

The story begins with a phone call I received whilst on one of those old boys' tours, when the Cormorants were up against the Free Foresters at Seaton in Devon. Coming as it did on day four of the tour, and being a good two hours' bus ride from our base in north Dorset, I was feeling a little jaded from a long stint in the sunshine on the English Riviera, when the phone rang. A London number. Odd. I picked up, intrigued, and was connected to one of the sundry cricket administrators in St John's Wood, NW8, who informed me that my application to play for the club secretary at Lord's had been successful, and was I still available?

I learnt very quickly during the phone call that my newly gained membership to 'The Club' might open more doors than I had envisaged. Of course, I would be free to play (I didn't have my diary – well, I didn't even have a diary, but I knew I'd be free for this one). But there was more.

190

'And will you be attending the black-tie dinner on the evening of the match, Mr Hicks?'

'Erm, possibly *(mentally checks bank balance)* ... how much are tickets?'

'Oh no, it's all part of the game – no charge at all.'

'*(Relieved)* Oh, in which case, yes, I'd love to attend.'

'And will you be bringing a guest?'

'Again ... is there a charge?'

'No, Mr Hicks, you can bring one guest.'

'*(Again relieved, but now a little embarrassed.)* Great! Yes, I'll probably bring my girlfriend, but will have to confirm. *(Embarrassed, maybe, but thinking this might just impress her enough to win some brownie points)*

'And, Mr Hicks, will you be requiring a room in the hotel after the event?'

'*(Once more, embarrassed and feeling pretty much a total tight-wad, but thinking of cashing in the brownie points pretty quickly after coffee in the Long Room.)* Erm, is there a ...'

'No charge, sir.'

'In which case, yes. *(By which I mean, 'Yes, I would like to play at Lord's, take advantage of an all-expenses-paid black-tie dinner and stay the night at your expense, and bring along a guest. Could I also please have champagne sent to my room, a rub-down from a Swedish masseuse and VIP entry to a nightclub of my choice after dinner? Oh, and if I can open the batting and bowl with the slope, that would be lovely, thanks, Darling).*'

This was going to be one hell of a day.

* * *

And indeed it was an incredible day, which just kept giving.

Although I had played at Lord's before – for Oxford University – I had never changed in the home dressing room. And on this occasion, we were literally stepping into the dressing room just vacated by the England team who went on to win the incredible 2005 Ashes – Pietersen, Flintoff, Strauss et al. In fact, only six days previously, I had been in the Long Room experiencing first-hand the electric atmosphere which marked this series out from day one as something which would be exceptional. I had been in the pavilion to see Ponting take one on the grille from Harmison, and later in the day had been in the newly-opened champagne bar in the pavilion turret as Glenn McGrath produced a masterful spell to reduce the England top-order to rubble. So good had the day been to that point, and so popular was the new bar, that I actually had to phone home to get an update on what was happening on the pitch – a phone call which did not go down well, to say the least.

Days later, and now the Aussies had restored what appeared to be normal service by winning comfortably within four days, Lord's was almost back to normal when I rolled up in my Citroën Xsara (only a marginal upgrade from the Citroën AX I'd ragged around at the turn of the century) ready for the MCC match. However, we still had a live TV feed rigged up in the dressing room, and the stumps had gone back into the Test match pitch, still foot-marked by the great Australian pair of Warne and McGrath. We would be playing – quite literally – in the footsteps of cricketing gods.

Melbourne looked a strong outfit, with Andrew McDonald – who would return in 2009 as part of the Ashes squad – and Shane Harwood – a rapid bowler who also later represented his country – in their number. However, for once the Australians seemed overawed by the big occasion at the home of cricket, and capitulated for just 77 in response to our 250-odd. The day, therefore, offered little for me really in a cricketing sense. I did manage to get out to the middle in my pads, and spent three happy balls in a partnership with Gatting (I have a photo of the scoreboard with both our names adorning it – an equivalent of which I imagine sits proudly on his mantelpiece, too). I did not face a ball, and not running him out was about the extent of my contribution.

I did get a bowl as well, towards the end of the game, with our guests seven down. I got my wish of the Pavilion End and chucked down three passable overs of anodine off-spin, whilst Neil Kendrick – ex of Surrey – showed me how it was done by winkling out the last three poles for spit. At least I had a better time of it than our veteran keeper, playing his first game at Lord's – presumably as reward for long service to MCC – who was clocked on the head through his gloves in only the third over, and had to be taken to A&E for the remainder of the innings. Happily, he returned for the dinner and didn't let a head injury get in the way of a free bar.

Having gone through the slightly surreal experience of sitting around the Holy of Holies of the dressing room in our towels – a place which Gatting, more than anyone probably in history, could rightly call his own – munching sandwiches and enjoying a can of lager, we moved to the Lord's Tavern for some pre-dinner beers (remember the match had finished early) and to meet our guests. Following these snifters, we made our way back to the Long Room bar for the 'official' pre-drinks, by which point I was already pretty wobbly, and then we took our seats for dinner. The table plan read like a *Who's Who* of English cricket. I was sat next to Mrs Gatting, Penny next to Mike, and along from Graeme Fowler. The keynote speaker would be Tom Graveney, and there were Dexters, Frys, Cowdreys and Huttons all over the place. I have never felt like a smaller fish. My cricketing insignificance was compounded by the fact that Gatting called me 'Tim' all night, and I didn't have the balls to correct him, or even his wife, who was calling me Tim, too. Thinking back, may have even started calling myself Tim, for fear of upsetting such a big character on his home turf.

I didn't care a jot. I was properly sozzled, looking around at the amazing Long Room and at the Media Centre illuminated in various shades of purple and turquoise. How many legends had walked this hall? The special night improved even more when both teams who had been the 'day's entertainment' were invited to come up and receive from Sir Tom a solid silver, MCC-embossed champagne stopper. And as we were asked to leave, well after 11pm, Gatting pulled one last rabbit out of the hat. Not many people are bigger than the fusty Lord's management, but finding the bar closed for business, 'Gatt' called someone over and insisted that all the men be poured a pint of lager, and all the ladies a gin and tonic. It was a remarkable end to a remarkable day, and to have a hotel room to stagger back into just topped it off.

Such was our exuberance about the whole event, Penny and I went house-hunting the next day and put an offer in on a house which was just about the worst investment you could conceive. Some things are better done with a clear head, and in the cold light of day.

I suspect you want an answer about the lunch? Well, a gentleman never kisses and tells.

But ... there was salmon, steak and chicken on the menu that day.

And yes, he did.

Playing With Your Hero – John Emburey at Lord's

John Emburey would not be everyone's idea of a heroic cricket idol, but from the moment I made the fatal decision to become an off-spinner, the stolid, frowning Middlesex man was the guy for me. I sometimes wish I had switched to leg-spin when the Shane Warne effect took hold and every young leggie was suddenly regarded as a potential world-beater, but I was probably a good enough offie to make it to regional or national level, and so why gamble on a change? On the other hand, off-spinners are two-a-penny and so the chances of reaching the top are diluted. In the end, I chose the road more travelled, and so it was Embers who was the natural No.1.

To be fair to the man, he did win the Ashes in 1986/87, featured in the amazing Bunbury books as 'Ember-bunny' and wore a pretty stand-out crash helmet. He also had a bit of a weird slingy-type action and tended to do well in my games of pencil cricket. I have also seen him credited with the probably apocryphal diagnosis of a finger injury – 'the f***ing f***er's f***ing f***ed'. Hell, with that CV, how was he not more popular?

I had some weird heroes – Tim Curtis of Worcestershire was another, as was – inexplicably – David Leatherdale – whom I also met during my short stint with Worcestershire. I'm not sure my temporary team-mates understood why I had suddenly become tongue-tied when DL pitched up at Kidderminster for a net. I was also keen on Neal Radford (more so than Phil Newport, oddly) and I was also rendered slightly weak at the knees when I came up against Steve O'Shaughnessy in that Minor Counties final against Cumberland – quite why I didn't pick Botham, Hick or Dilley from that famous Worcestershire side of the late 1980s I'm not too sure. Probably my love of the underdog. Aside from the Pears, I had a bizarre ritual of saying goodnight to my poster of Wayne Larkins after saying my prayers – not that I thought he was the Lord himself, despite sharing similar epic facial hair. As far as off-spinners were concerned, Lancashire's Gary Yates got a brief look-in, and I did rate Tim May, but you can't really go for an Aussie, can you? So J.E. Emburey it was.

I didn't get to meet my idol properly until late in his career. I'm not even sure I saw him play live until he signed for Berkshire after retiring from Middlesex and joined them for a

three-dayer down at Dean Park, which I am sure he remembers
not one jot. I only remember two things about his part in the
game. One was his being deposited for one of the biggest sixes
even Cowley had hit at the ground (and he hit a fair few) and
secondly was a comment he made to my dad on the boundary,
about my bowling too slowly. This was a bit of a hammer blow
to me. I had secretly harboured the outlandish dream that
somehow Embers would take one look at my offering, realise
he'd unearthed a gem and drop everything to tell Middlesex
I needed to be signed on the spot and to send a taxi to take
me directly to Lord's, not passing Go. This did not happen –
clearly – and yet I was a bit gutted that he did not pull me aside
himself to have that chat. I mean, I was never going to listen
to the old man, was I?

Putting that disappointment to one side, a second
opportunity presented itself when I was selected to play at HQ
for MCC against a Minor Counties side in 2009. My spinning
partner for the day would be none other than my hero, who
announced that it was his birthday and would be his final
appearance on the hallowed turf – a moment of planetary
significance if ever there was one. And so it was that I found
myself bowling end-to-end with the great man on the Nursery
Ground in warm-up, and sharing the home dressing room.
Dreamland.

If ever I had wanted a confirmation of my own lowly place
in the cricketing pantheon, today was the day. Bowling on an
absurdly short boundary at the Grand Stand side of the ground,
I had been given the end which would offer me most assistance,
and I was keen to impress – imagine the firm handshake and
even perhaps the arm round the shoulder in the Tavern later,
the 'I'm surprised you never had more of a go at the pro game,
Hicksy' (for by now we would be three pints in and probably
planning where to go and continue discussing the difference

between an undercutter and slider). Imagine the regaling each other of chucking it just that bit wider to induce a creeping back foot and a stumping to remove Dean Jones in his pomp, imagine … I digress.

Sometimes the figures don't lie. My analysis for the innings was 4-0-39-0, including a six straight into the Tavern Stand – a country mile, and then some, from where we were. The old master relieved me at the Pavilion End and proceeded to land it on a sixpence, returning 4-40 from ten to the appropriate adulation.

I don't think we swapped notes after the game, which was kind of him. And in my embarrassment, I clean forgot to check out whether the rumour about his being longest in the shower was true or not. I suspect in every way, John Emburey is a bigger man than me.

The moral of this story is to leave gods where they belong and don't go getting ideas above your station. Leaving the Grace Gates that day, I felt like Frankenstein or Faust (or Scott Boswell). A humbling performance, but a huge privilege, nonetheless.

MCC Touring

Cricketing Croatia

Some 3000 years BC (my online guidebook tells me), the small island of Vis in the Adriatic Sea was first colonised. A tiny outpost some miles off the coast of Split, Vis changed hands over the centuries: once part of the Roman Empire, later from the Austrians to the Italians and nowadays to the former Yugoslavian state of Croatia. It is simply stunning, and in 2009, it was once again invaded. But this time it was probably by the least expected of marauders, as a small band of MCC cricketers switched their bacon-and-egg ties for sunhats and flip-flops, ready to take on the might of the national Croatian cricket team on what was my first experience of touring with the historic old club.

We spent a short week in Croatia, the trip being specifically organised to allow both school teachers and league cricketers the chance to represent the club during school holiday time. Falling into both categories and being at the time known as an 'A-list' player, I fancied my chances of being selected and duly got the call, looking forward to experiencing what was always spoken of as 'the reason you become a playing member'. With all expenses paid, this would make up for the last five years of eye-watering membership fees, and with a load of kit thrown in for good measure all was in place for a superb week. A harbourside hotel at the height of the Mediterranean summer – could it get any better?

Of course, there was the small matter of the actual matches, but I don't think the tourists were going to let that get in the way of what my wife tends to call 'stag weeks with pretend cricket thrown in'. The marker had already been laid down by the manager on the boat from Split, as the first of several cold beers accompanied the most cursory of team talks, reminding us of our 'ambassadorial status', which basically meant, 'Don't get lost, don't get arrested, and if you do, don't tell anyone.' I reckoned I could just about follow these instructions. On arrival, it was of course important to get the lie of the local land and with bars lining the harbour, it did not take long to establish that the hotel was well within staggering distance home, as long as you didn't veer too close to the luxury yachts moored on the water. The writing was very much on the wall as far as sobriety was concerned.

As a first-time tourist, my room-mate and I were told early on that we would not be required for the tour opener the following day, which was, as far as I was concerned, a green light for seeing last orders before my bed on the first night. We took advantage of a lie-in and then an idyllic trip to the Blue Lagoon on a speedboat to clear the head (and to clear out the insides of my room-mate, who was more green than blue for most of the choppy ride). After a leisurely lunch getting to know each other – remember that the majority of the tourists had only met for the first time in the departure lounge at Heathrow – we thought it would be the done thing to take a taxi to the ground to see how the lads were faring.

The ground was quite something. Roughly hewn out of a parched vineyard, it was no more than 40 yards to all boundaries, with a concrete pitch in the middle and a mat on top. The outfield – if it can be called that – was rutted in all directions, with dry thistles and weeds as a covering and not a blade of grass in sight. Just as at our home ground of Lord's, the MCC flag (mistaken the world over for the Spanish flag) was flying, except that rather than the stately turrets and red brick of NW8, our flag rather limply drooped from the solitary tree which offered the only shade from the 40-degree heat. Beneath the tree sat the Croatian opposition awaiting their turn to bat, as well as our twelfth man and scorer, who looked like they were about to pass out from heat exhaustion, or raging dehydration, not helped by the fact that they were sweating almost pure lager. I've been in cooler saunas.

The good news (depending on how you look at it) was the fact that this opposition did not seem to be up to much, and it looked as if we would come away with a pretty easy victory. The selection committee had chosen to send a couple of 'gun' players in the squad in the form of Darren Bicknell and Rob Turner, both of whom were recognised as former pros of the highest quality and unlucky not to have played for England. I guess this was an insurance policy in case Croatia had found some ringers and so as to avoid any embarrassment on our part. I suspect also that Turner, who also happened to be on the tours committee, fancied a week away in the sun. Either way, he played his part with a ridiculous 160, including more than 20 sixes, in a T20 match later in the week, and as a seasoned tourist who was great company. As it was, the fact that the match was pretty one-sided suggested that we could probably get away with a 'few beers' in celebration this evening as well. It is probably not giving away too many tour secrets here to say that 'a few beers' are had, and even perhaps expected, on every night, of every MCC tour.

'Great,' chimed in my room-mate, who had adopted a semi-prone position on a plastic patio chair, with a towel over his head.

Things had not gone so well for Bicknell. Despite a career aggregate of over 19,000 first-class runs for Surrey and Nottinghamshire and a reputation as one of the most elegant openers of his generation, he had somehow fallen victim to a combination of the only bowler with a modicum of pace in the Croatian attack and the fact that the concrete under the matting wicket had not been rolled absolutely flat. In fact, there was a genuine ridge on a length which made for a pretty hairy experience if the bowlers could get it above 65mph. Wary of this, 'Denz' (as he is affectionately known) contrived to be bowled for a duck, much to the delight of the bowler, who had an uncanny resemblance to a young Anil Kumble, with oversized spectacles held on with a sports band. It was not Bicknell's finest hour.

This ridge in the pitch became a recurring feature of the tour, not least when the English bowlers, with a few more 'wheels', got on to it. There is footage somewhere on YouTube of Simon Stanway – a superb Minor Counties bowler, but of what is known in the trade as 'rat's pace' – hitting a batman on the helmet off a good length for the ball to be caught at mid-off.

Another feature was trying to field on the aforementioned outfield, which looked more like a hard-baked vegetable patch than anything remotely like a playing field, let alone a cricket ground. So bumpy and cracked was it that you were as likely to get a broken nose as you were to perform an MCC textbook long-barrier. This is where I learnt a new game which I would take back for the Dorset lads, which was known as 'Snakes'. The rules are pretty simple. If you fumble, or misfield a ball, you are said to be 'on snakes' (the insinuation that a snake had come up and bitten you, I think). The player at the end of a 20-over stint – a drinks interval or innings break, say – would be deemed to be 'holding snakes' and would need to scull a bottle of lager at play's end. It proved a good way to keep people's attention toward the end of a long session, especially one which was going nowhere. And I'd like to take this opportunity to deny any suggestion that I ever asked anyone to pop into short leg in the last over of a day, just to drag one down so they'd get not only a bruise, but the 'snake', to add insult to the injury. I mean, who would do such a thing? Woe betide you, though, if you were holding snakes, or even two snakes, and had dropped a catch or got a duck – you could be staring down the barrel of three drinks before you'd even got in the shower. Not that showering was an option at Vis CC, Croatia, obviously.

Actually, what we tended to do was head back to cool off in the sea outside the hotel, which was a wonderful way to relax after the heat of battle and to put off the inevitable carnage which was to come after dark. And the tour continued in this vein, with cricket acting as necessary punctuation to the hearty socialising, which was enhanced no end by a trip to a renovated Second World War hangar which was now an extensive wine cellar run by Tony – the only genuine Croat in the team, which was largely made up of expat Aussies. Safe to say, Tony's *pinot gris* was better than his cover drive.

Fines meetings – a staple of all cricket tours – were held nightly and the punishments were merciless. My room-mate and I succumbed to the first sanction for not attending the match on day one. Of course, the fact that we had been given the morning off was neither here nor there as far as the fines committee (which Turner also appeared to run) was concerned. By the time everyone had been asked to 'see away' their share of the local brew, guilty of such crimes as dropping catches, having terrible chat and wearing the wrong kit (among other spurious charges), the team was ready only for staggering into the local bars again, presumably to try and drink ourselves sober. The potential monotony of the 'lads on tour' evenings was also broken by the arrival of an enormous cruise ship full of young and nubile Americans on the Tuesday, and a similar vessel full of Scandinavians on the Thursday. The local disco opened up for these nights and the single lads amongst us attempted to do their bit for international relations, strongly encouraged by the rest of the squad. Team spirit was soaring by now.

Bicknell's tour, however, was to get worse. Taking a day off for the second match and then watching as Turner dismantled the hapless opposition on the third day, Bicknell was left heading into the final game on the Thursday without a run to his name. It so happened that I had also managed not to trouble the scorers in my only innings to date on the island, and so it was decreed that Denz and I would open up together on the final day, in a shoot-out to see who would walk away with the 'worst batsman on tour' title, and no doubt a drinking fine to go with it. Bicknell was keen to take the first ball, which was fine by me, with the Kumble doppelganger coming downhill with a new ball towards the now infamous ridge.

The first ball was on a good length and my partner pushed gently to cover point. No run.

Or at least, I thought no run. As I looked up from the non-striker's end, all I could see was the large figure of an ex-pro bearing down on me, getting larger all the time, and on my side of the track, like a slow-motion scene from *Saving Private Ryan* or the last episode of *Blackadder Goes Forth,* screaming 'ONE RUN!!!!' Startled into action, and with the fear of adding to my duck with the ignominy of being run out without facing, I got off my blocks and tried to make my ground. Thankfully, the spiteful outfield did its job, and cover point now had 'snakes' whilst I had the strike. Bicknell could not contain himself at the non-striker's end, laughing hard and, more importantly, one not out. 'Your turn', he giggled.

Happily, I managed to tuck one off my hip for a genuine single which Bickers could not turn down, and so we had both avoided bagging 'em on tour. Now it would be a case of trying to cash in on a decent score to make the tour something of a success. I also wanted to witness one of the best batsmen of his generation from the best seat in the house.

How things can turn sour. Having had a little fist-pump and got over the adrenaline of the 'duck-off', the very next ball reared up off the ridge and clattered into Denz's glove. You know instinctively when something serious has occurred and the yelp he made when it happened left me in no doubt that he had broken his thumb. As was proven to be the case once he had been taken to the local hospital (hardly Harley Street) and been x-rayed.

The poor bloke had come on tour as the superstar and ended it with one run and a bust digit to his name. I have to say, though, that when he returned to the tour dinner – an unforgettable seafood platter from mine host Tony once again – Denz was top quality; all gallows humour and self-deprecating fun. How refreshing it is when top sportsmen turn out to be top blokes as well.

'A Star Is Barm': Lady Gaga and the Cumberland Wrestle

MCC Tour to Denmark 2015

In my last season as a Minor Counties cricketer, I decided it was time to try and make the transition to social cricket by applying for a tour in the summer to Denmark. It was – like the Croatia affair – less than a week long, but what it lacked in length, it made up for in fun, and again, alcohol consumption.

In contrast to Croatia, Denmark seemed to have a much better cricketing infrastructure and more active players. In fact, we were told there were 800 registered players, and a Premier League of eight teams. In addition, the first three of our games would be held at Svanholm Cricket Club in the outskirts of Copenhagen: a thoroughly up-to-date club with two-storey clubhouse, well-prepared grass wicket, a suite of artificial nets and even a 'Merlin' bowling machine in a small indoor school. Most English clubs would kill for these sort of facilities.

The make-up of our squad was much like that in Croatia: a few Minor Counties players and county second teamers, some top league cricketers and an old pro in Darren Cousins, late of Essex and Northamptonshire. It looked a rounded unit as we all swapped notes about mutual friends and made links over a civilised champagne in the oyster bar at Heathrow terminal five. The tone was also set when we were instructed each to buy a bottle of spirits for the trip, as booze was notoriously expensive in Scandinavia. It was easy to see how this would go.

What I didn't expect, though, was for the team to polish off an entire litre of Tanqueray gin between the airport and the hotel. Especially given it was only a 20-minute drive. It was becoming clear that our senior pro – Cousins – would be leading the charge off the pitch as well as on, and that this would be a long week.

One of the beauties of sport in general, and touring specifically, is how it can bring people from different backgrounds together. Alcohol seems to help, too. On that first night in Denmark, one team-mate told me he felt we would not get on as he was an Essex lad and I had been to Oxford. By the end of the night, I had been nominated to run the fines committee, instantly appointed him my right-hand man, and we got on like a house on fire for the remainder of the trip. Fair play to him, he set up his own coaching business and is now the brains behind the [Joe] Root Academy which gets millions of hits on social media. It shows that not all intelligence is book smarts.

After a first night of significant proportions, we got a proper wake-up call on day one of cricket, in which we were run ragged around the field and then knocked over by a well-drilled team of largely Asian expats. In that night's debrief the manager (dentist to Ian Botham and underwear model David Gandy, as it happens) made it abundantly clear that we were not to lose any further games on tour, or it would be viewed dimly back at Lord's. For the sake of clarity, I asked him in front of the team whether this meant we ought to take it easy that evening, or whether there would be a curfew.

'Of course the f*ck not. Just play better tomorrow. OK?'

With those instructions clear, we went about step one of the plan with gusto and got the glad rags on.

We'd got into general knowledge quizzes on that tour, thanks to Gus Kennedy – one of a rare breed who had managed to represent both Oxford and Cambridge – but there was an additional challenge offered up to two of our number, who happened to both be thick-set lads with ginger hair. They were given five minutes to answer a conundrum or the pair would pay the forfeit of having to wrestle each other – Cumberland-style – in only their jockstraps during the warm-up the next morning. For those of you quizzically-minded, the question was:

'Which two London Underground stations include all the five vowels?' Answer below.[11]

To our great delight, neither man got either answer (despite one of them actually living within a mile of the station) and so we were treated to the human version of two Jupiters colliding before play the next day. And we got our act together on the field to effectively level up the series.

As it is a central part of MCC touring to help develop the game of cricket in countries where it is less well-known, I spent a good hour or two after play working in the nets with a young German lad of 18 who was an aspiring leg-spinner. Amazingly, I was told this chap had travelled fully ten hours to be ready for play against us, which was enormously humbling. And he ripped out a pretty good leggie as well.

We had a third match at Svanholm CC – a T20 affair, which would be a tricky match, as our opposition had shown themselves aggressive players with no little ability. I remember this match for having a good day with the ball. Actually, having loved the long form of the game earlier in my career, I came to really enjoy T20. Every ball is an event and whilst as a spinner you can find yourself getting neckache watching the ball clear the ropes, it is also a great battle of wits and wickets are there for the taking. I'm so glad that spinners have proven their worth at the highest levels of T20 cricket and the game as a whole is richer for inventive and unorthodox spinners to counter the crash-bang-wallop of big bats and small boundaries. I can't remember if I got four or five wickets in my four overs, but I was certainly convinced that among a flurry of dismissals over two overs, I had registered a hat-trick.

---

11 Answer: Mansion House and South Ealing.

At least, that was what I was claiming as I walked off the pitch, with half the team congratulating me and handing me the match ball, and others certain that there had been a dot ball between wickets. The embarrassment of being shown the scorebook which clearly burst my bubble was exacerbated by the fact that I had just spent an hour being the judge, jury and executioner of the fines committee, and it would now be my turn. Penalties were in the standard 'finger' measurement of beer, but my penalties would be doubled as a matter of course, and this egregious showmanship would be met with the severest of punishments. Indeed, I am pretty certain there was not much air left in the top of my two-pint *stein* of Carlsberg when the 'weights-and-measures' official meted out the dose.

And so I was pretty well warmed up for another night in Copenhagen, which was becoming very familiar to us by night. What my body didn't need was anything too hectic. Like a rollercoaster, for instance.

The centre of Copenhagen is home to the world's oldest theme park – the Tivoli Gardens – which is the most bizarre mix of beautiful gardens, lovely restaurants and rollercoasters winding through it. We were there for dinner but most of the squad had a bash on the bone-rattlers beforehand, with at least one notable casualty. Dinner was long and beer-soaked (what a surprise), but when we emerged into the twinkling night air, a remarkable transformation had come over the park. Where there had been wide open green spaces, now there was not a blade to be seen as it seemed half the city had come to congregate in front of a stage. Every balcony in the hotels and restaurants had people dining *al fresco*, eyes trained on the stage, which we assumed would be for some local pop star, or Abba tribute act. They were awaiting the world's hottest A-lister of the time, Lady Gaga. We had paid the equivalent of a tenner to get into the park, and now would have the treat of a live concert by a global superstar, who had formed a ground-breaking duo with old crooner Tony Bennett. Or we might have done, had it not been for the fact that it was standing room only, and there were no beers within buying distance, and so the thirsty lads voted against the once-in-a-lifetime free entertainment in against out another venue for late-night refreshment. One-in, all-in, and so after one incredible number, we bade a 'Thanks-but-no-thanks' to the Gaga and headed off. The rest of the evening was not altogether lost in terms of cultural learning, as we all learnt that some northerners call a bread bun a 'barm', and that it is possible to order the culinary delicacy of a 'Pie Barm', around Lancashire, which constitutes a pie ... in a barm. Yes – a pie sandwich, ladies and gentlemen. This truly was an awakening for many of us, and 'Keep Calm, Pie Barm' became our unofficial tour motto.

Our final match saw us move away from Svanholm to play an afternoon T20 in the pouring rain on an artificial pitch. Probably the least pleasant conditions I've had to play in. But the host team were so keen to show their hospitality, which consisted of an enormous traditional Danish barbecue and yet more Carlsberg, that they would not take no for an answer. We won as well, to take the official tour results to Won 3, Lost 1. A passable result which meant the manager wouldn't be facing an inquest when he returned to London, and barring any misbehaviour on the final night, we would all be eligible for touring if we ever applied again. And aside from a minor mishap involving a fountain, one guy getting a lift home on a milk float and two ladies seen leaving the hotel in the early hours fully kitted out in MCC garb, we were as good as gold.

Staying Up Late in Sweden
I don't know if I had proved myself an expert in Scandinavian conditions, but my third and final tour for MCC saw me

selected to join another fine body of men in Sweden in the most unseasonably hot May Stockholm has ever seen. Getting a briefing phone call from the manager ahead of the trip, I was told that this was very much a 'thank you' tour for my years as a match manager and regional rep, and that I could take it easy and enjoy myself. Three years since I'd bowled a competitive ball and with a body starting to creak, as age and a family of five crept up on me, this was music to my ears.

And if Denmark had been a step up from Croatia, Sweden really had it going on as far as cricket was concerned: over 3,000 playing members registered and four divisions of league cricket across the whole country. Throughout the week we were there, the Swedish cricket authorities pulled out all the stops to ensure we were looked after and challenged on the field, in the hope that we would be able to help their development and profile. What was most noticeable in Sweden was the amount of Afghan expats who made up the teams we played against. Cricket was clearly a positive engine for social change, cohesion and integration, which is exactly what MCC was keen to see developing. And with this enthusiasm, our natural touring high spirits and a town full of beautiful people intoxicated by the sunshine and evenings which stayed light until 5am, all the ingredients were there for an unbelievable time.

Once again, MCC had ensured a strong unit, including a surgeon who probably overstepped the mark in telling us about how he had once had to remove a deodorant can from a patient, which had been 'self-inserted', shall we say, before having to put them back under anaesthetic to retrieve the lid. There was also an old opponent of mine who sat next to me on the flight and looked pretty forlorn when I told him the 500 Euros he'd ordered from the Post Office wouldn't do him much good in a country which uses its own currency. And in Nick Compton we could boast not only a captain whose ability should ensure we won our games, but a genuinely big name. I'm sure the oppositions were a little starstruck by the former Test player and member of one of the great cricketing dynasties, as indeed were a few of us.

The undoubted star of the show was an enigma of a bloke by the name of Jason Stocks – a left-arm spinner from Wales with hair like Albert Einstein after a walk in the rain. Whenever there was a lull in proceedings, a quiet moment on the bus for instance, or a gentle lap around the boundary, Stocksy would come up with some comedic pearl of wisdom or one of his extensive repertoire of impersonations. WhatsApp has been transformative for touring, and before every match we would find a video on our phones of Stocksy doing the full Geoffrey Boycott and Richie Benaud bit, having made his way to the ground while we were having breakfast. He chaired the fines meeting at the end of tour in a 'Bjorn from Abba' outfit which I am sure he brought along for the purpose. Not only did he keep us fully entertained all tour, but for weeks afterwards with his impressions from whichever ground he was playing or watching at. During the epic English cricketing summer of 2019, we would get match reports from seemingly every game during the World Cup. And it turned out that he had fallen on his feet by signing a contract to work for one of the title sponsors, which did, in fact, allow him 'Access all Areas' passes for every single match. This included the final, and it so happened that I ended up with the Welsh Wizard watching Ben Stokes's heroics and biting our fingernails to the bone in that unforgettable Super Over. But whilst I left for home on the train, Stocksy was still posting videos from the hallowed turf, accompanied by the soundtrack of Jos Buttler, Jonny Bairstow and the rest singing in the dressing room long into the night. His summer didn't quite finish there, though, as for some reason during the festivities after the final he had decided it would be a good idea to steal the top tier off an official cake which had been made depicting Eoin Morgan and Kane Williamson in icing on the top. Waking up to find this incredible beer trophy on his nightstand the next morning, Stocks was at a loss as to what to do. And the cake stayed there asking that very question right through the Ashes summer until the final Test at the Oval, another game for which he had been given tickets. Being unafraid of pushing the boundaries, he strode with the cake through the official corridors of the Surrey headquarters to the *Test Match Special* studio, where he presented the cake to Jonathan Agnew – live on air to the whole nation (and of course those who dip in before the shipping forecast).

Back in Sweden, Stocks and Compton were two of a five-man party who took to cycling around the city on a rest day, whilst the junior tourists had to spend an entire day running coaching for the eager Afghans. This was utterly idyllic and we thoroughly enjoyed our seafood lunch and ice cream. Thanks, lads. The jury had been out a little on Compo, who had given off the air of being pleasant enough, but a little aloof from the team, and doing interviews live for talkSPORT in the team bus on the way to matches seemed a bit unnecessary. His true colours came through during the 'Tour de Stockholm', however, and he emerged as quite the complex and fascinating individual, as he opened up about his Test career, injury troubles, mental health and hopes for future work in charity and photography. I guess he hadn't pictured his last year of professional cricket (he was still contracted to Middlesex) as including swimming in the Baltic Sea with a bunch of rogues and playing cricket on an Astro Turf pitch in the middle of a Swedish park. Given the circumstances, he did all right.

Indeed, we played all our matches at Gärdet Cricket Club, which was literally just a park, and you could count on there being at least two cyclists obliviously fizzing straight through the game and several groups of primary school pupils in high-vis jackets who didn't know what danger they were in when I was tossing up my filth. The cricket and the results were uncannily similar to my experience in Denmark, as we gave up a game on the last day, losing in the last over to a wonderful hundred from a chap who would not have been out of place on the Minor Counties circuit. Most of the time we were comfortably in charge and could cruise in third gear. Poor old Compton struggled, though, and failed to score more than about 30 runs all tour. Never mind: his off-spin was miles better than mine and my only knock was another golden duck which brought back memories of Vis.

The off-field antics were standard MCC fare, albeit with even less sleep as the 'white nights' near the Arctic Circle meant only two hours of darkness, which was dangerous, to say the least. I can confirm the stereotype that the Swedes are incredibly beautiful people. Not only are there some absolute stunners there, the average just seems to be several leagues higher than what you see on the streets back home. Certainly by the end of the week, the lads were almost in tears at the reality of having to go back to their home towns. Not that anyone had much of a chance of any romantic action, given that we were forced to wear replica football-style shirts for our last night, and the best chat-up line anyone could offer was our youngest player trying to impress girls with our teddy-bear mascot, nicknamed 'Freddie' (anytime the bear left his side would incur him a significant fine).

I'd love to manage an MCC tour one day. There is a lot of fun to be had, and yes, the alcohol consumption is probably higher than is sensible, but the cricket can be quite amazing and played in some of the most unexpected places in the world, bringing the Spirit of Cricket and the joy of the game to many people.

Look Up Not Down

It is an old adage at Lord's that if you win the toss, you should, 'look up, not down'. That is, look at the weather conditions before assessing the state of the pitch, especially when it comes to limited-overs matches, where the ball can swing prodigiously in overcast conditions in the morning session. Many a NatWest Trophy final was decided in the first hour with sides being skittled under leaden skies in September after a 10.30 start.

When I had the fortune to be invited to captain MCC at Lord's against the Minor Counties in 2012, I found myself reunited with Darren Bicknell, and this time as a room-mate in the 'dubious', the Danubius Hotel which overlooks the Home of Cricket. Bicknell was in my ear all night and in the morning about not batting first, even though the sun was shining, the odd marshmallow cloud was high in the sky, and it looked every inch the batting day (and I had no intention of wasting the chance of a good morning sitting on the home balcony enjoying the coffee and the cricket).

Everything went my way – the coin fell down nicely (I forget whether it was heads or tails; I always mixed it up rather than having a 'Tails never fails' approach), and we elected to bat. I knew I was right: the MCC scored a big total; Graham Grace of Wimbledon CC scored his second hundred in two games at HQ. Only Denz missed out, nicking one early ('the only ball to swing all day') and missing out on runs. He cursed me all innings. Luckily, the other batsmen backed me on this one, and we ran away comfortable victors. By beer time, he had forgiven me and admitted it was a 'look up' day after all.

Committee Man

I won't bore you with the ins-and-outs of trying to run a region of MCC cricket. Safe to say that it included making sure that nearly 50 games went forward in a competitive and good-spirited manner (with MCC winning the majority – results were definitely seen as important). It also meant you had the responsibility to assess people who applied to become playing members and then – most importantly – to recommend those players who after two years of 'probation' had done enough to warrant full membership, and who would then join the legions of old gents in salmon-pink chinos and egg-and-bacon ties on the benches at Lord's. The twice-yearly sub-committee meetings were fun for a while though, and I certainly enjoyed taking a day off work to sit in the committee room adjacent to the Long Room and play at being important. I say 'take a day off', but thanks to the wonders of modern technology and real-time document sharing, I did actually manage to deliver an entire A-level lesson during one of these meetings, whilst the rep for Scotland was arguing the case for someone in the Outer Hebrides to be given his membership. It was quite a responsibility running the London region, however, as many half-decent players would try their luck to jump the decades-long waiting list, only to play the bare minimum of matches and then settle into long days at the Test matches and finals, hardly promoting the actual cricketing side of the club at all. So our job was to be as rigorous as possible on selection.

The best part of the meetings had to be the meals, though, and we were treated to a slap-up dinner in the committee dining room, which is above the away dressing room. This was often better than a top restaurant in quality, with the wine selected to match. Business was deemed to be too difficult to do in a day, and so it was another night in the hotel on the corner and lunch the following day after proceedings had drawn to a close. A tab was set up for drinks after day one, and it would be fair to say that several of the area reps took the opportunity of a night away from home to get into 'tour mode' and often ended up heading into central London after dinner. As long as you could read your notes the following morning, you were OK. Only on one occasion did one of the reps fail to show up the next morning. Some investigation revealed that he had spent the night at Her Majesty's Pleasure and had opted out of arriving for the lunch. A good job he was stepping down, methinks.

Chapter Twelve

A Watching Brief

2007 World Cup, Barbados

The year 2007 in many ways was an *annus mirabilis*: it was the year Penny and I got married, the year I ran my first London Marathon and also the year Penny achieved a professional dream – working on a Cricket World Cup. Cricket history may dictate that the 2007 World Cup was not a triumph in organisational or administrative terms, which is unsurprising given that holding it in the West Indies meant having to share the tournament between many different island nations, each with their own idiosyncratic whims and wishes. But for Penny it represented the chance to live and work in Barbados for three months on a sport she loved, and for me, it meant the chance to have a holiday largely at the expense of her demanding boss.

It was a bizarre start to the trip for me anyway, as I'd literally just done back-to-back transatlantic flights, having spent my mother's 50th birthday in New York, along with my brother, seeing if it really was 'The city which never sleeps' (thanks to a terrifying goth bar in the Lower East Side of Manhattan which kicked us out at dawn, we concluded that it just about lived up to billing). This three-day jaunt to the Big Apple came on the heels of a 24-hour readathon at my school which meant I'd spent the last night of term awake all night reading *Hamlet* with a bunch of sixth-form students. I was also in 'tapering' mode ahead of the marathon, and so was assuming a quiet few days soaking up the sun and doing some gentle jogging and swimming was on the cards. I'd reckoned without Penny's workload and the lifestyle of business bigwigs at a major tournament.

I think the glamour of living in the Caribbean had worn off for Penny after a few weeks of 24/7 graft trying to herd cats and massage egos, and by the time I arrived for a week at the end of the group stages, she was at her wits' end. However, there was to be no rest for her, and on arrival, I was welcomed not by my beloved, but an unexpected substitute. Here was a bloke I'd never met, but who resembled James May from *Top Gear* – a big and imposing, yet genial, floppy-haired and loose-shirted character called Toby Brocklehurst, whose opening gambit was that his father had invented the Cricket World Cup. My first reaction was that this claim was rather like that of Dr Evil's father from the film *Austin Powers*, who claims to have invented the question mark – a ludicrous suggestion. But sometimes the most implausible things are true, and there you have it – Ben Brocklehurst – a former Somerset captain and owner of *The Cricketer* did indeed come up with the concept of a World Cup, which should have made him a household name in the sport.[12] A brief read of Brocklehurst senior's obituary tells me not only did he pass away just months after my meeting with his son, but that he was a seriously talented and interesting man.[13]

As in fact was his son. In one of those surreal experiences you look back on and think, 'Did that just happen?', Toby piled me into his car and told me I wouldn't even have time to unpack

12 https://www.thecricketer.com/Topics/world_cup_2019/world_cup_moments_-_no.48_1975,_prudential_cup_and_how_the_cricketer_played_a_part.html

13 https://www.telegraph.co.uk/news/obituaries/1555386/Ben-Brocklehurst.html

or see Penny until she finished work at six o'clock, which left us with a whole afternoon to kill. What would we do?

Well, like any self-respecting blokes who've never met each other before, we headed for the nearest place we could buy a drink, which meant driving up the idyllic west coast to find a rum shack. I believe I did have a look at a map and, in a pang of cultural conscience, suggested we aim for an interesting church in the far north of the island, to which my new friend agreed, as long as we could stop off for a brief sharpener *en route*. A brief sharpener turned out to be a full hip-flask-sized bottle of rum, topped off with a shared can of coke before we were on the road again, tongues a bit looser and seatbelts a bit tighter. We didn't manage to get as far as the church as Toby was clearly thirsty on that day and we popped into another rum shack for a repeat dose, at which point he felt he ought to keep reasonably close to the villa where Penny and her boss were staying, as driving was just starting to get 'a bit more risky'. No shit. I was already pretty toasted when Toby suggested we take it a bit easier by popping into the luxury resort of Sandy Lane. During our drive, I had found out more about this larger-than-life figure: he was a property developer and investor who was currently based in Panama, but had some interest in Cuba. I couldn't help but notice that there were a couple of fat Cuban cigars rolling around in the glove compartment in front of me, and, noticing my interest, he asked me whether I smoked Cuban cigars. I have to admit, smoking Cuban cigars was not a regular habit of mine, but in for a penny in for a pound, I'd be up for one, as that seemed to be the way the day was going. Penny would hate me rolling in stinking of smoke, but Captain Morgan was in charge of my decision-making now, so there I was, fresh off the plane into paradise, *cuba libre* in hand, cigar in mouth gazing at the azure ocean with a bloke I'd never met in my life. It wasn't long before a chilled-looking Rastafarian openly asked if we were looking for cocaine, which we weren't, but in that moment, it felt as if almost anything could have happened. If Angus Fraser had stepped on stage and done a pole dance, it wouldn't have fazed me.

By the time we did head back to see Penny eventually, I'd learnt all about international property, why Cuban cigars are smoother than regular cigars (it's all to do with the smoke being alkaline, not acid, apparently) and the fact that Toby had been to North Korea where he said he'd been in a museum which claimed Kim Jong-Il had hit nine holes in one on one round of golf and had been the first man on the moon. And you know what? After the revelation about his father and the World Cup, there was nothing I wouldn't have believed from this man.

The remainder of the trip was a little more like I'd anticipated, albeit I had to entertain myself for long swathes of time whilst my wife-to-be worked. Still, watching one-day internationals on my own in corporate boxes, spending hours by the pool or heading off to the beach to swim with turtles was no real hardship. Evenings were spent as the guest of the boss, or his colleagues, at some of the finest restaurants on the island, and the fully-stocked bar and fridge at the villa were at my disposal whenever I liked, as was the live-in cook. Ideal preparation for the marathon it was not, but I did develop a taste for Grey Goose vodka and helped buoy up the Bajan rum industry.

It was nice to be able to catch up with my old university team-mate Jamie Dalrymple, who had been a surprise inclusion in the squad, and who gave me a bit of an insider's view of life in the England camp. It certainly did not seem especially rosy, with the well-publicised rifts which would tear the squad apart starting to emerge and a culture of hierarchy and suspicion had taken root after the elation of the 2005 Ashes.

Penny had her own tribulations: being interviewed as part of the investigation into the tragic death of Pakistan coach

Bob Woolmer; tripping over while running on the day of the final, so that she had to perform all her official duties with bloody bandages over her knees; sharing the villa pool with a convicted murderer who insisted on swimming naked, and generally having to be anyone and everyone's dogsbody. Still, a spare winner's trophy adorns our mantelpiece and not many people can say that.

Jimmy Adams and the Post-Match Party – Goa, 2006

I remember having a VHS of Geoffrey Boycott's *Bats, Balls and Bouncers* in which there was a sequence about cricket in the West Indies and India – two parts of the world where cricket was seen as a religion and crowds were notoriously loud, colourful and a bit barmy. In the video, we moved from the antics of Gravy and Mayfield – the two long-time jesters and rivals of the St John's Ground in Antigua – to the dusty *maidans* of India, accompanied by the mystical music of the sitar and shots of English batsmen being tied in knots by the twirly spinners of the subcontinent. I had been to the Caribbean a couple of times in my youth and loved it, and yet India always held that charm, so when I got the chance to go and watch England play two one-dayers one winter with Penny and a couple of good mates, I jumped at it.

This was in the days when my wife-to-be was working in cricket and had some errands to run on the day we arrived on which England were due to play in Goa – namely dropping off some lime marmalade, marmite and cigarettes to the England team hotel in return for complimentary tickets from one of her contacts. Not a bad deal, in my book. Now, Goa is not a renowned centre for cricket in the country, but you could have fooled me. The stadium was flanked by an enormous field full of people who were evidently queuing, but for what, and in what order, was totally incomprehensible. What is more, despite the early hour (the match was due to start at 9am, I think) the sun was already hot and the dust oppressive after a long flight and no sleep. We had one small bottle of coke and no suncream between us – well planned, team.

Gambling on the fact we had our tickets already, we joined a snaking line of people, all intrigued by our whiteness, and eventually reached the gate. The organisation of seating in the ground followed the rules of queueing outside (i.e. none) and we just had to try pot luck. It later turned out that 35,000 people were there, which was going some for a stadium which had a 'capacity' of 28,000. So space was at a premium and the police were not a great help, being more keen to catch a glimpse of MS Dhoni at the toss than regulate the crowd. Huffing and puffing, we climbed to the top tier, where, at last, some space appeared. I dropped my backpack, straightened my sweaty t-shirt, turned to face the pitch and take in my first experience of an Indian cricket match, and realised that we had set up camp right behind the big screen. Super.

Eventually we did manage to blag our way into a VIP section of sorts, which meant seating and shade. It did not mean alcohol, which was a bit of an inconvenience and it also did not absolve one from having to listen to the incessant beat of drums and plastic bottles being banged together every ball. In fact, the Indian crowd was so into the match that even byes brought a cheer akin to a Premier League goal. I can't imagine what IPL matches or a World Cup final on the subcontinent must be like. We were certainly a long way from Lord's. Predictably, the Indians gave England a proper lesson in white-ball cricket, with Yuvraj Singh hitting a fine hundred and dispatching James Anderson out of the ground on one occasion. The crowd, however, loved Dhoni and we were amazed when his name was chanted at the fall of every wicket with seemingly the whole country desperate for the sleek-haired skipper to make his entrance. When MS did arrive, he treated us to one of his famous 'helicopter' sixes – again, Jimmy was the victim as the ball sailed back into the pavilion with the merest of cursory flicks as follow-through.

Game done, and England on the receiving end, we decided to take the short walk along the beach from our digs back to the Taj Exotica to drop more goodies off. Penny told us to wait in the lobby and keep a low profile and said she would not be long. However, it was day one in a new country and we were footloose and fancy-free; what is more, we got wind of the fact that a post-match reception was being held for the players in the hotel gardens. They wouldn't mind if a few fans (well, friends of the squad, really, given the lime marmalade) joined in for a quick one or two, would they? Security seemed pretty slack at the do, and we tentatively wandered in, and having taken advantage of a free beer at the first tent, the confidence rose and we eased into the evening. There were no signs of the England party whatsoever, so anyone there must have assumed we were some sort of net bowlers, or minor officials with the tour party. And this is the way we decided to play it when interest in our presence grew. We cooked up a story quickly in case we were rumbled, in which I would be me – a semi-professional out here net-bowling – one mate would be a kit-man and the last would pose as James Adams, of Hampshire fame, as he had similarly long-ish hair and we all knew Jimmy from school and junior cricket and could probably pull off his slightly foppish, public-school demeanour if challenged.

And challenged we were, or rather, not challenged but essentially fêted. As none of the England players ever did arrive, which seemed a bit off, but they had had a tough day in the dirt, the local fans started to flock around us and ask for photos and autographs, which we were only too happy to offer, as the free food and drink kept coming. 'Jimmy' was especially popular as some of the more discerning cricket nuts there knew who he was and that his name had been mentioned as a potential future Test player. So it was that Penny arrived at the end of the gardens looking for us, only to have that sinking feeling that we were about to permanently damage her professional reputation as she approached the growing gaggle of excited Indians around a small group of white men looking very pleased with themselves.

I got the message straight away from the less-than-loving look in her eyes and tried to haul the others away as the locals were phoning friends to invite them along to meet these minor celebrities. On the way out, despite Penny's protestations, we helped ourselves to a gift each from the pile of offerings for the tour party from their Goan hosts. Well, we figured we had earned it more during the evening session. Sadly, the local produce was edible and never made it through customs – a nice tacky plaque would have been the ideal keepsake from our brush with fame.

We did have a good laugh about this over the next couple of days and then forgot about the episode until we were awaiting a plane in Bangalore airport. Tired and restless, my friend Tom dropped his guard when from across the departure lounge came the excited cry of 'Jimmy, Jimmy! Jimmy, I knew it was you!' Against all the odds, in this country of a billion-plus people, one of the most ardent of the post-match supporters had recognised who he thought was James Adams and wanted to run him through some frame-by-frame analysis of Flintoff's bowling from the match. At this point, 'Jimmy' had to admit the game was up, and with some profuse apologies, we made our way on to the plane, leaving the poor chap wondering who on earth we were.

The flight we took was on Kingfisher Airlines. Kingfisher as in the fizzy, gassy stuff you order when your local Tandoori restaurant has run out of Cobra. A beer company, and an airline, eh? So free beer it was, and would you believe, immediately after the safety video, footage of a vintage India v West Indies series was broadcast to every screen. Truly, if Carlsberg did airlines for cricket nuts, this would be it.

The real James Adams is a true gent and a proper professional, as Hampshire members will attest. I'd also say he was unlucky never to be capped for his country, given the amount of opening batsmen England tried as partners for Alastair Cook after the retirement of Andrew Strauss. At his best, Jimmy was a graceful and elegant left-hander who became a lot tougher after a spell in Australia working with Justin Langer's coach, who apparently had him facing bouncer after bouncer from about 16 yards with a bowling machine in a brutal winter. This was a key moment in Adams' career, as he had gone through a rough trot of form, to the point where I think he was ready to pack it all in.

I know it was a rough trot for him, because he actually ended up playing under my captaincy for Dorset in the summer of 2008, against Wiltshire in the Minor Counties Championship at Corsham. This was quite a step down for Jimmy, and it is credit to his humility that you would never have known it; he just breezed into the changing room, asked where he could sit and could he help with the warm-up. He certainly wasn't paid by us for the privilege of three days of our average chat and questionable hotel etiquette.

Form, however, is a funny thing, and having spent some time in the field, in the first innings he was lbw for a duck. You can imagine what a pitiful sight it was to see a player of his quality trudging back to a dressing room of strangers, contemplating his career. And form being the fickle spirit that it is, this game represented my highest aggregate score in a two-day game. What he would have given for the two 70-odds I managed in the purplest patch of my life? (I averaged over

An early holiday in France. Looking at my pads, the locals thought my parents had dressed me in some instruments of torture

Even at the village fete I insisted on dressing up as a cricketer

Winning some early silverware with Dorset Under 11s in Cornwall, 1990

In my ESCA West of England cap – a prized possession, 1994

Jonny Wilkinson – schoolmate and role model.

Fidel Edwards put me on my backside with the fastest ball I faced. And in front of a big crowd too.

Dad – far left – and Mum – by my side amongst others. School coach Mark Russell next to Kevin Curran and Cardigan Connor, with Alec Stewart and Robin Smith in front

*The Parks, Oxford.
Many happy memories
and my name on the
same wall as Colin
Cowdrey and Imran
Khan*

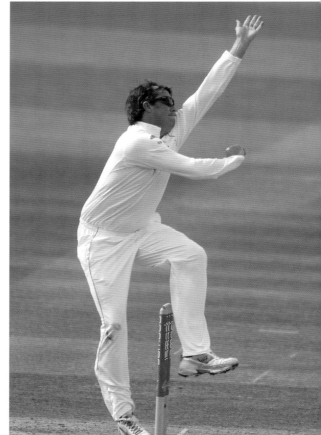

*Graeme Swann was an
age-group rival for me.
He always did get his
front arm higher than
I did.*

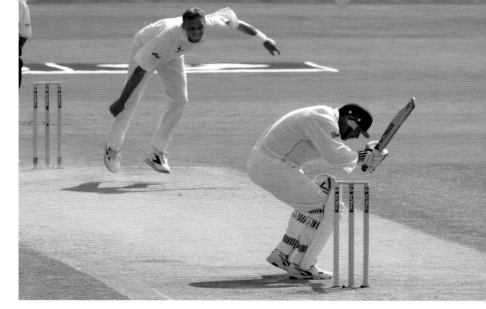

My off-spin was our plan A against Robin Smith for Oxford University. Luckily, I managed to avoid facing Allan Donald when Warwickshire came to town.

Always a really nice guy when I met him, Marcus Trescothick missed a rare one that turned from me on my first-class captaincy debut

Posing for the press with Robin Smith ahead of my second match as a first-class captain, The Parks, 2000

CRICKET'S BACK! It was an all-too-familiar scene in the Parks yesterday as Oxford Universities sat out the whole day in the opening home match of the season.
Watching the rain under the safety of an umbrella are Hampshire captain Robin Smith (left) and his Oxford counterpart Tom Hicks.
The match was officially abandoned this morning without a ball being bowled.

TELL-TALE SIGN: The bad news in the Parks yesterday

'Skipper Serious' Jamie Dalrymple showed us students what it takes to play for your country

Picking up an enormous trophy after our only win on tour in Pakistan, Karachi, 2000. We had to leave the ground under armed guard.

KARACHI: Administrator KMC, Brig Abdul Haq gives away the winning trophy to Tom Hickk, skipper, Oxford University, England

More silverware for Oxford University after beating the old enemy at Lord's, 2001

Douglas Jardine in his Harlequin hat. He would not have liked Oxford University merging with Oxford Brookes

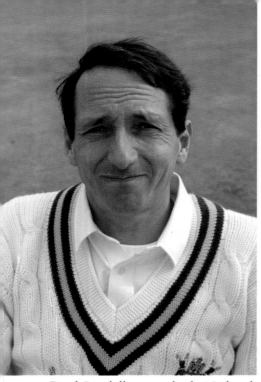

Derek Randall was coach when I played against New Zealand. He made me feel ten feet tall.

Dion Nash offered one of the more memorable sledges I faced, in the same New Zealand game

Dean Park, Bournemouth. Home of Dorset CCC and where I proposed to Penny. One of the finest old grounds in England, before it was sold in 2015. So many memories

60 with the bat in that season, against a career average of 20.)

In the second innings, we were all rooting for him as he'd come across as such a good lad. In fact, this came as no surprise – he had been a top schoolboy at Sherborne School, where he had been coached by the Dorset coach at the time, Alan Willows – which was the reason for him joining us in the first place. I had also known Jimmy as a youngster as he played with my brother.

Boarding Houses and Balloons

Corsham itself is a beautiful club ground set in the picturesque village near Bath, famous for its cherry trees which blossom in May, and for the golden Cotswold stone buildings which glow honey-like in the evening sunshine late in a day's play. I have some good memories of cricket there. For example, the Adams game was actually my own most successful one with the bat for Dorset, as we knocked off well over 300 to win after a Wes Durston (late of Somerset and Derbyshire) hundred had looked like putting Wiltshire in an unassailable position.

But Corsham is also what is known in the trade as a 'postage stamp': i.e. a very small ground, which I had also found out in an earlier game, back in our successful championship-winning year of 2000, when Roger Sillence (an old South Wilts team mate of mine who later went on to play for Worcestershire) kept launching me and Vyv Pike out of the ground as Wiltshire windows were imperilled for an afternoon. Because of the small size of the ground, there is inevitably a risk for spectators. In the 2000 game, Dorset again managed an implausible run chase, this time with Darren Cowley spraying projectiles to all parts. One six knocked a rather portly elderly member off his plastic patio chair, to have it land on his back; he ended up looking like some sheepish giant tortoise. And the danger to visitors almost ended in personal tragedy when my ineptitude with the ball almost caused the death of my own mother, who, quietly playing with my baby daughter under one of the cherry trees, had the ball thump into her chest after Ed Young (who was moonlighting for Wiltshire during his stint at Gloucestershire) plonked a rank full toss over cow corner. Time really did seem to stand still as we both shouted in unison, 'No, No, No … Heads, Heads, HEADS!' Luckily, she lived to fight another day; she ought to have known better than to take her eyes off the game when I was bowling.

Young's six came in my last game there – a rather depressing defeat in 2014 when I was really starting to feel as if my days at this level were numbered. By this time, I was a well-established housemaster at Wellington College and, no longer captain, and with three children in tow, focus had drifted away from cricket, and it was becoming increasingly hard to justify three days away from work and the family. This didn't stop me trying to roll back the years off the field, though, and I had my rubber arm twisted by some of the more outgoing younger lads to join them in a night out in Bath. It was not a venue I had notched up in my career thus far, so why not?

Several Jägerbombs later – with half the Wiltshire contingent, I may add – I found myself in another nameless sweaty nightclub on a Monday night, listening to the DJ giving a 'shout out' to Emily (or someone or other) on her 18th birthday. At which point I sobered up pretty quickly at the thought that I really ought to have been teaching someone of her age the next day in school, and that this probably wasn't an appropriate place to be for a schoolmaster of one of England's most traditional boarding schools. Not to mention the fact that all the other lads were insistent on taking selfies and getting pictures of 'old man Hicks' posted on social media. This was probably the moment when I realised that the world had moved on and that retreating quietly into the background would be the more dignified thing to do, although the old devil on the shoulder would reappear from time to time.

The following day brought my future and my past together in an odd way. Although we were losing heavily, there was the usual post-night-out buzz about the dressing room. Batting in the rarefied position of No.3 (which tells you about the strength of the side at the time), I had committed to making the most of the flat pitch and small boundary which I had enjoyed so much in 2008. I also wanted to sweat out as much of the alcohol as I could, rather than fester away in the pavilion. It was not long into the morning before I heard my old mate and rival Michael Coles muttering at me from first slip as I took my guard, 'Oi, Hicksy, careful with the pitch mate, you're dripping Jägermeister everywhere.' This, of course, from a bloke who'd been tucked up in bed early, like any grown adult should have been.

I did manage to see off the new ball, but succumbed to the spinner and had to watch the rest of the game from the balcony, which is where I learnt something which would be an eye-opener in my other life as a housemaster. The lads drew my attention to the slightly bizarre behaviour of one of our number, who seemed to be propositioning people around the boundary. He then disappeared through a gap in the wall into the village for a few minutes, returning on the other side of the ground, approaching more people (mostly those whom my mother-in-law would term 'youths', in a rather judgemental tone), before he eventually turned back to the balcony with a big grin on his face and a punched fist of triumph in the air.

'What's he up to?' said I innocently.

'Balloons, Hicker.'

'Balloons. Right,' said I, none the wiser.

'You've got to see this. You'll love it.'

'Will I?' said my internal housemaster monologue, sensing something nefarious afoot.

By this time, our jubilant team-mate had reappeared, and I was about to witness for the first time someone taking nitrous oxide (laughing gas, nox, or hippy crack, as it is also known, I believe). For the uninitiated, essentially what you do is fill a normal party balloon with the gas and then inhale in and out, which apparently induces a light-headed buzz.

Although most of the boys were in fits watching this young fella experience the temporary high of inhaling the gas, which is easily bought from food stores as a way to create whipped cream, and was not illegal at that time, I have to say I felt a little queasy at the experience. It was as if he was some sideshow, a peculiarity, a way for the others to experience vicariously a sense of the thrill and danger of substance abuse. I can't say I liked it, and I certainly did not want to try it, despite being strongly encouraged to do so. Give me a few pints of Badger Bitter any day of the week. Again, just like the night before, I knew that my time was up and I belonged in a dressing room from a different era.

The episode did, however, give me some justification to the school for continuing to play. In the same way that I justified to my wife that playing MCC cricket was really beneficial for networking and could almost be considered 'work' (something, unbelievably, she still disputes today), now I could justify to my superiors that hanging around teenagers and lads in their early twenties would give me a privileged insight into the dangerous habits of the day. And whilst I myself would raise a sceptical eyebrow at this logic, it didn't take long to have some concrete evidence to back this up.

On returning to the boarding house the evening of the match, I made sure I spent a good amount of time in and around the boys' quarters, catching up and ensuring that I had my finger back on the pulse of what was going on (like football and politics, a day is a long time in a boarding school, and much can have gone on between 60 boys). On visiting the boys' rooms, I knocked on one particular door and got no answer. Popping my head in to see if the lad was there, I happened to notice on his desk an open packet of balloons. Twenty-four hours ago, I would have walked away, oblivious. Now, though, my interest was piqued and I had a closer look, to find alongside the balloons some instructions for whipping cream, and I knew immediately that the scourge of nitrous oxide had made it under my roof. The next day, I was able to inform all the other houseparents about this new craze, and suddenly we were ahead of the game. In fact, this new habit was only reported in the national press a week or two later, before it took off massively on the festival circuit later that summer. But as with all these things, pride comes before a fall. You may feel ahead of the game, but teenagers are slippery creatures and my self-satisfaction at thinking I knew what was going on was swiftly pulled from under me when, investigating a loose tile in the boys' bathroom, I heard the tell-tale chinking of vodka bottles before a deluge of metal gas canisters clattered on to my head from the cavity in the ceiling. They'd been at it for weeks and I hadn't had a clue.

The Best Match I Ever Saw – Oxford v Cambridge Women's Varsity Match, 2000

Even though I've had the great fortune to play and watch cricket on several continents, I have to come back closer to home to relate the best match I ever saw. You could debate for hours what constitutes a good match: is it the skill of the players, the atmosphere, buckets of runs and glorious stroke-making, individual battles, inventive bowling, age-old rivalries? Yes, all of the above. I was there on day one of the amazing 2005 Ashes series, and at Trent Bridge when Ashley Giles's nudge to leg saw England home after Shane Warne had threatened to break home hearts; I was at Lord's in 2019 to see what many people would cite as the most dramatic conclusion to a tournament, let alone a match, when Ben Stokes's heroics and unfathomable good fortune saw us win the World Cup (as Ian Smith's now timeless commentary attested 'by the barest of margins'). I'm also proud to have been the last person to be ejected from the ground after Stuart Broad made his one and only Test hundred. But the Women's Varsity Match of 2000 remains for me the most implausible of finishes, and the most tense of atmospheres.

When I arrived in the Parks to see the concluding overs of this match, it looked all over- bar the shouting. Playing in a longer format than normal, a full 50 overs, Oxford had been bowled out pretty cheaply and Cambridge were cruising. In fact, if memory serves me correctly, they needed just eleven runs to win from the final ten overs, with seven wickets in hand. Had the WASP win predictor been invented in those days, you can be sure it would have given Oxford barely a 1% chance of turning it around. But nerves are a funny business, and as dot-balls mounted up, and the Oxford fielders kept stopping the ball in the infield, it quickly became a question of who would hold theirs.

Runs on the board have never seemed so crucial. The old cry of, 'We've got 'em; they've got to get them' (which you only ever hear when you've horribly failed with the bat) seemed to be the mantra as the Dark Blues put the squeeze on. The two bowlers – nothing more than slow-medium – both bowled with metronomic accuracy, and it really was a 'You miss, I hit' scenario as the Cambridge batters opted for extreme caution waiting for the bad ball to put away. It never came. And then the wickets started to fall. Straight balls seemed to take on a more threatening quality and wickets four and five went down to a bowled and a leg-before. No.7 arrived with more intent –

surely a couple of lusty blows would see the game done – but swinging across the line, she was bowled as well.

The game plan changed and the lower order looked to see if they might do it in singles. But a horrible mix-up led to a run-out as the Oxford ring tightened like a constrictor, slowly squeezing the life out of the batting side. And still every ball stayed on target. Every fielder stood ready, poised, and they stopped everything. Two more wickets and now eight down, the game looked in the balance. Nevertheless, a boundary would get Cambridge close. And there was always the danger of wides and no-balls. Should the keeper continue to stand up to the stumps, or take the safe option and go back? No. Stick to your guns now. Back yourself.

A two. Was the momentum shifting? A dashed single to follow, and now it was within one hit. But overs were also ticking away. Whatever happened now, this would go down as a nail-biter. I looked down at the textbook in my hand which had now been screwed into a tight cylinder, and I realised I was utterly absorbed in the match, as was everyone in the ground now.

Another run-out. Panic had well and truly set in. And now only the No.11, who surely hadn't expected to bat, had to make the long walk to the middle, looking for all the world as if she'd never worn pads before. The fielders inched closer: 'Eleven versus one' you could hear someone cry. The smell of blood was in the nostrils of the ring fielders, who must have looked less like genteel young ladies in culottes and more like predators going in for the kill. The first ball was trapped at the last minute by a borrowed bat clamping down just in time to stop it thudding into a pair of nervous knees which hadn't moved an inch from the crease. Next ball. Again on target. This time it did hit the pads. 'Howzat!' The appeal for leg-before rang from every fielder, and the rapt spectators. And the finger had to be raised, sparking utter bedlam, as victory was snatched by a single run. It was all the things your prep school coach had told you coming true in spectacular fashion. Bowl wicket-to-wicket; use the long barrier; back up and take the game as long as you can. Pressure brings wickets. And boy did it. I wish you'd seen it.

Chapter Thirteen

Signing Professionals, Sponsorship and Skodas

A False Economy – The Club Pro

In 2007, I swapped the captaincy of my club side for that of my county, handing over to my brother at Farnham. My taking over as captain of Dorset coincided with a change in coaching staff as well. Having taken us to Lord's the year before in the knockout cup, Richard Scott had been asked to join Middlesex, where he spent a good decade and won the County Championship. In his place, the Dorset committee opted for Alan Willows – another ex-Dorset player, who had played first-class cricket for Sussex as a batsman and left-arm spinner. He was also master-in-charge of cricket at Sherborne School and would continue this role, as well as coach the county side.

Willows (or Wills, as he liked to be called – surely there must be a better nickname for someone with such a cricket-themed surname?) could not have been more different in approach than Scott (humorously nicknamed 'Dog', in typically inventive cricket fashion). Whilst Dog was of the old school and would join us for a few beers after play to chew over tactics and let off steam, Wills was much more into new innovations, keen on detailed training plans and marginal gains. Cynics of the modern propensity for Thera-bands, medicine balls and the multitude of plastic paraphernalia which tend to appear on outfields before play might claim that there is an inverse correlation between the number of cones on a field for a warm-up and the quality of the coach. If this is correct, then Scott certainly had the edge on Willows, although that is unfair on Alan, and I learned a great deal from the methods of both men. I think Wills learned a lot from working with the Minor Counties team, and certainly found them a very different breed from the schoolboys he was used to.

It became apparent early on that although I was happy as captain, the new coach was going to instil a new level of professionalism in the squad and we would differ on various aspects of managing a successful unit. I will spare you the intricate details, but one aspect I believe is worthy of comment as it is replicated in many club teams across the country: this is the employment of professional players in amateur clubs.

Go to almost any ground in England on a Saturday and you will see, amongst the ranks of the talented youngsters, gnarly experienced clubmen, hopefuls dragged up from the second team and the chap who has been cajoled by the skipper to make up the numbers on a promise of a couple of free pints and a waived match fee, an individual of a different ilk who stands out a mile. This is the club 'pro', most often an overseas player (known just as 'the overseas') who has no real links to the club but has been offered several hundred pounds a week to turn out in some parochial league for a side he hadn't heard of until he chanced his arm and sent a few hopeful emails to clubs in the off-season. Hence, you end up with random Kiwis in the nether reaches of the Birmingham leagues, Pakistanis with dreams of being the next Wasim Akram, plucked from obscurity straight into the Test team, doing their best to impress in division five of the West Kent league and countless Australians, cursing their way through a season for various outposts from coastal Cornwall to not-so-sunny Cumbria.

Some overseas professionals are a good investment; they get fully involved in promoting the club and coaching young players, acting as role models and ambassadors for the game. These are the sort of players who often spend several seasons at the same club and recognise that the money they are earning is only in part for their performances on a Saturday. It is as much for the wider picture of what they offer the club and the community it serves.

Others, however, show little interest in the club and are happy just to take the money and run. And in the worst cases, they can actually detract from a club as they bring an attitude which is counterproductive and can be destabilising and cause factionalism in the dressing room. Without careful management, these players can be extremely damaging as they can be hard to argue with, given that they are often the best player. It can come down to luck as to what type of character a club ends up with in any given season, and clubs are often under real pressure to pick anyone who is willing to take whatever they can offer (of course, some clubs have many more resources than others), as not to pick a professional cricketer can severely weaken your chances of success. The net result in cricketing terms, though, especially further down the leagues, is that you end up with a bizarre 'Overseas v Overseas' situation – a game within a game which leaves most of the other players as mere bit-part players. It can also breed resentment, if the overseas pro is an unpleasant mercenary who does not actually cut it on the pitch, yet benefits from the cash provided by the match fees and subscriptions of everyone else's hard-earned salaries.

It is not so much the players themselves with whom I have the biggest issue; most of them are decent cricketers and decent blokes, keen for a summer exploring a new culture and developing their skills in an alien environment. In the top divisions, I would argue that their influence raises the level of the leagues and allows good home-grown players to test themselves against a higher calibre of player. But in the lower leagues there can be such a gulf in quality as to make it laughable; this probably doing nothing for the development of the individual's game either.

No, my issue is with the clubs and leagues themselves. I cannot, in an era when clubs are increasingly strapped for cash, understand why a committee would decide to spend a good part of their annual income on a player when there is little chance that this investment will be paid back in any financial way. Few leagues have prize money, few charge entrance fees, and I doubt that sponsors are really bothered about who a professional is, unless in one of the very few cases where it is a really big name. Surely it would be far more sustainable and successful to invest the money – often well into the thousands – in youth cricket, coaches, infrastructure, improving the facilities, pitch, nets etc, or subsidising match fees for committed players. I have seen some creative thinking from some clubs, who cover the cost of travel for a handful of young players, who have left the area to go to university to come back to play at weekends. This has the doubly positive effect of keeping a successful team and social unit together, whilst ensuring that once they finish their studies, they feel a responsibility to come back and play in the future. Since they are usually in their late teens and early twenties, much of the cost probably comes back to the club over the bar as well.

Another very successful club in Surrey chose not to pay one person a big stipend, but spread the earmarked money as a win bonus between all members of the team on a Saturday, which engendered a spirit of teamwork and collective responsibility. It is no surprise to me that this club were serial championship winners in my time as a league cricketer.

The employment of professionals – be they indigenous or overseas – is a discussion which could fill a whole book, or a discussion paper at least, and I don't intend to labour the point too much here. I ought, also, in the spirit of addressing hypocrisy, admit that I spent three years of my league career as a paid player.

Sas Vegas

The first time I was paid to play club cricket was in my Jekyll-and-Hyde year at the turn of the millennium. The year 2000, in which I captained Oxford University at Lord's and led them to victory over Northamptonshire, but also was dropped from the Dorset side which won the Minor Counties Championship for the first time in their history. Having become a bit disillusioned with the Surrey Championship, and what I seem to remember perceiving as a lack of respect for, and interest in, the first-class university scene, I decided to take up an informal offer to join some of my West-Country team-mates at South Wilts CC in Salisbury.

I thoroughly enjoyed being around a different dressing room (and it is remarkable just how different in tone the banter is in different leagues) as well as adapting to a slightly different format. The Southern League at that time was just experimenting with a new format which saw the season split into half limited-overs, win/lose matches and half more traditional declaration matches with no limits on bowlers and the chance for a draw. Half the limited-overs games would take place at the start of the summer, and the second half would come after a declaration 'season', so to speak. I like this format for a Premier League – and there are all sorts of variations to be found still around the country – as it means that for half a season clubs must select a bowling attack of at least five bowlers, such that often the best overall team will win this section, whilst the longer format allows for spinners to have more of a say and for batsmen to build longer innings. The chance of a draw also means there is a premium on match-winning bowlers, so genuine quicks are more valuable than traditional club seamers.

In any case, at South Wilts I enjoyed the Minor County banter with colleagues such as Roger Sillence and James Tomlinson (later of Hampshire) and several other great characters like Jamie Glasson, Russell Rowe and Tim Lamb. The highlight for me, though, was playing with our overseas pro, who was a real cult hero for the season: a Pakistani ex-Test player called Manzoor Elahi, whom I recognised from my *On Top Down Under* video. Not only was I mildly starstruck, but Manzoor was the embodiment of the word 'mercurial'. He would look for all money as if he couldn't lay bat on a bowler, and then launch him into the houses for consecutive sixes. He was a bit like MS Dhoni in the way he approached a run chase – you never quite knew if he had a clue what was going on, but would then get you over the line with seemingly no issue at all and return with a 'what's-the-problem?' look on his face. And although not really a bowler, he had that Pakistani confidence to demand the ball from the captain and would as often turn the game with a key wicket as he would be carted for two overs then take himself off and hide at fine leg for an hour. Mansoor definitely added colour to that summer for me and I can still never listen to Dean Martin's *Mambo Italiano* without hearing Jamie Glasson's voice singing, 'Hey Manzoor, Manzoor Elahi-hi-oh'.

Sadly, my form was little more than woeful for South Wilts. So much so that when the end of the season came, the chairman somewhat apologetically handed me a cheque for half the fee we had agreed when I signed up. To be honest, I was equally apologetic to accept it, and it was mutually agreed that I might be better off returning to Farnham the following year.

Brook CC – A Skoda But No Sightscreen

My second foray into playing as a club professional came in the 2009 and 2010 seasons when Farnham had been relegated two years running to Division Two of the Surrey Championship. In that season and the previous one I had arguably been at my peak and took the thick end of 100 league wickets. In fact, I was the leading Premier League wicket-taker in 2007 after going past 50 with a five-wicket haul against Wimbledon on the last day of the season. I then took six five-bags in 2008, bowling more overs than anyone else in the league (something which would not have happened under the Southern League format). But despite this, we were doomed to relegation again.

It was during a rain break against Brook CC that I was approached by my old mate Matt Swarbrick, who suggested that his new club was willing to forgo an overseas pro for the following season and to instead direct the funds my way. They reasoned that they would be getting a tried-and-tested Surrey League performer rather than gambling on someone they did not know and for whom they would have to find accommodation and gainful employment. My instant reaction was to say no, especially as it felt like something of a betrayal, not least as the question had been popped in our own clubhouse and we were not at that point yet relegated. I was also wary of being considered a mercenary, and at worst a 'Judas', and wondering whether I'd be welcome back at Farnham if I were to switch allegiance.

Some frank conversations with my brother, who had replaced me as club captain, ensued, and as I considered the idea more deeply, I began to wonder if this might not be a good move both for me and the club. I would still be able to play at a higher level (albeit not the Premier League) and would welcome the chance to test myself in different surroundings, as well as the fact that the money on offer, whilst not life-changing, would certainly come in useful with our first child due in the winter of 2009. As far as letting Farnham down was concerned, although I am sure my wickets and runs would be missed, actually there was an argument to say that with me out of the way, it would allow more opportunities for other players to bowl a bigger quota and for the team to regroup as more of a unit. If this sounds like someone trying to justify themselves, it is worth noting that this is what eventually happened, with the first team getting promoted in the following two years, and a new atmosphere developing, built around a team ethos rather than individual performances.

I would highly recommend a visit to Brook Cricket Club. Sitting in the leafiest of south Surrey villages, it is a ground which exudes character. At one end, the straight boundary is little more than 40 metres, and so I reckoned that I would probably be better served bowling from the other end, where the straight boundary extended up a hill so steep that the club had actually gained special dispensation not to have a sightscreen, as it was a physical impossibility. Fielding at long-off, you would be fully ten metres above the batsman and it was possible to see the ball roll around the boundary rather than go over it at times. To add to this, at deep midwicket the boundary swerved dramatically to avoid the walled garden of a neighbouring house, such that deep long-on would be unable to see a fielder at cow corner. The pavilion, like so many others at English village grounds, was picture-postcard lovely, but was actually also the village hall so the space was shared with the plastic toys of the day nursery and discarded tickets from the most recent local tombola. The changing rooms were tiny, but, as I had found at South Wilts, nothing breeds team bonding more quickly than having to deal at close quarters with someone else's sweaty jockstrap as they rummage around for some Tiger Balm, or to find your towel has been 'shared' by four team-mates whilst you are still batting, or worse still, has been used to dry off the plastic garden chairs before play on a drizzly morning. Some of my worst recurring nightmares are punctuated by recollections of the tattoos of team-mates and the bodies of middle-aged men gone to seed, with the unmistakable 't-shirt tan' which marks one out as a fellow cricketer.

Across the road from the ground sits a charming, if overpriced, pub, the Dog and Partridge, which served well after the game, but which also represented one of many infrastructure issues which would be detrimental to a small club like this. Without a bar of its own, I am sure the club missed out on crucial income, but more significantly, there was no youth section, which had immediate and more long-term implications. For one, in the height of summer, when less committed members of the club decided, inexplicably, to head off on family holidays rather than stand in the field for the second XI against Stoke D'Abernon, or some other such opponent, there were no willing youngsters to step in and fill an eleven. This situation can only last a few weeks before administrators become twitchy and, before long, Brook found themselves without a second XI, and a few years after my stint, they actually dropped from the league altogether, to regroup as a village club in the bottom tier.

Secondly, without a youth section, the club risks losing its role as a community venture. In clubs where junior cricket thrives, you will see dozens of parents volunteering to coach, sell raffle tickets, man the bar and so on, with others happy to meet up and put money in the coffers whilst catching up on the local playground gossip. At Brook, you ended up with a weird hybrid club where the Sunday side retained some classic village cricket matches against colourfully-named clubs such as the Arabs, the Grasshoppers, and even MCC and I Zingari, whilst on a Saturday, the premium put on climbing the Surrey Championship saw a team drawn increasingly from a pool of public schoolboys, only a few of whom had any allegiance to the club, beyond wanting to play with their bunch of mates. By the end of my second year, I found myself captain of a side comprising me and ten Carthusians (ex-Charterhouse pupils). Clearly something had gone awry, and when these lads headed off for university, the club faced a gaping hole.

I was pleased with my performances for Brook – I managed 44 wickets in year one and 20-odd in half the games the following year, once I had started as housemaster at Wellington and could no longer take every Saturday off to play. Perhaps more importantly, I saw it as my role to encourage the younger players to recognise what it takes to run a small club, and would try to lead by example off the pitch by being there first, to put out the boundary markers, make tea for the umpires, hitch up the advertising hoardings and help the groundsman with a few final preparations before starting the warm-up. I also tried to insist on players staying for a beer after play and for those who had performed well to buy a jug of beer for our team and the opposition. Sadly, these traditions seem to be evaporating from the game, to its detriment, in my opinion.

I suppose it was easier for me to buy my jugs, given that the club was subsidising my appearances, even if the prices at the Dog and Partridge didn't leave me much change. It was also easier for me to get to the ground early as I was now not dependent on the shared family car, having somehow managed to avail myself for the only time in my career with a brand-new sponsored car. Yes, for the season, I would be zooming around the Surrey lanes and the South Circular in a Skoda Octavia, garishly branded with the garage's logo, the legend 'Brook CC' and a silhouetted cricketer, playing the sort of expansive drive which was categorically not my signature shot (a nurdled single to third man would have been more appropriate). All it needed to be completely tasteless would have been my name on the side. Which, of course, I would have lapped up. I remembered years before seeing Andrew Flintoff's name on a car during an England Under-17 trial on an adjacent pitch to the one I was playing on at Oundle School, and also that of the perhaps lesser-known (at least outside of Glamorgan) name of Steve Barwick pulling into one of my first games for Dorset as twelfth man, and thinking that to have a car with your name on it was to have made it as a cricketer. I guess the fact that this was a Skoda and I didn't warrant a name-check tells you all you need to know about where I stand in the grand pantheon of cricketers.

Sent Packing by David Sales

Thinking about that Flintoff moment takes me back to my trials for England Under-15s. I remember when this was, as it coincided with the incredible Oval Test match against South Africa in which Devon Malcolm was riled up by being hit on the head by a bouncer and proceeded to take nine wickets, bowling at the speed of light.

As I recall, two squads were selected who would take on the England Under-16 team and then battle it out against each other to see who would then make the final eleven and get the much-coveted navy blue ESCA (England Schools Cricket Association) hat to go with their regional coloured one of the same design (mine was black, for the West of England). There were several players who were considered as nailed-on certs for selection, such as Graeme Swann of Northants, Zac Morris of Yorkshire and Stephen Peters of Essex. However, I might have had a shot at the second spinner's slot, with Swanny nailed-on as an all-rounder.

In the match against the Under-16s, I came up against David Sales, also of Northamptonshire, and who had already developed a reputation as one of the hardest-hitting young batsmen around. That he never won a cap for his country will have surprised many who knew him as a 16-year-old, but I guess it just wasn't to be for old 'Jumble'. Nonetheless, he became the latest in what was to become a long line of players to put me squarely in my place, dispatching my beautifully flighted off-spin with little respect for the subtle variations in pace and guile to all parts of the Oundle School second-team ground. One over went for 29, for heaven's sake. I'm pretty sure at that point, I knew this was not going to be my year. Not even my dad – my biggest supporter – could sugarcoat this particular turd of a bowling spell, and I think he probably spent most of it watching through his hands from behind a tree, it was so painful.

Normally, I would say that cricket is easier for bowlers, as you always have a chance to come back and get a wicket, however badly you may have bowled to begin with, whilst batsmen only get one mistake and it's curtains. But when you know your captain is more likely to get the wicketkeeper to unpad and have a trundle before calling on you again, and yet you still have to battle through a few more balls which could end up anywhere in a 100-metre radius, it can be a pretty cruel place for a bowler. It only gets worse when the ball is having to be retrieved from bushes and car parks, with you standing at your mark wishing you were anywhere else. And the final ignominy is if you have been hit for so many sixes that you have to join the hordes of dispirited team-mates searching for a ball hit off your own bowling, whilst the umpire trots off to the scorers' hut to fetch another spare. You can try making a joke about how the new ball you have had to take might bring more luck, but no amount of wry humour will make this better. By this point, everyone basically hates you, not least the seamer from the other end, who has been working on the original ball for an hour and it was 'just starting to reverse'. I'm afraid this has become a pretty familiar scenario, and I wouldn't wish it on anyone.

Much like those extra few balls of a spell which you wish you could forfeit by putting on a fake groin strain, I had to deal with the fact that I had another trial game the next day. The feeling was like fielding under what is known as 'grade rules', where a side can chase down a score, win the match, but then keep batting for bonus points with the beaten side having to continue to bowl. I knew I had no hope of selection at the end of the day, but had to front up against the other eleven. So, brave face on, I hoped I could somehow conjure up a spell of such wizardry that the previous day's mauling by Sales would be glossed over by the selectors as a mere blip.

I was thinking this through at my station at long-on, desperately trying to visualise my best ball, while the captain was no doubt having to work out when to bring on this complete liability. Snapping out of my reverie, I noticed that the ball had been hit in my direction. And not only that, it was airborne and very catchable. The batsman was Zac Morris – the biggest fish of them all at under-15 level – and I had the chance to look calm under the high ball, re-establish myself as a big-match performer and put everything right again. I gauged the flight of the ball, ran in several yards, steadied myself under it, committing to the Australian fingers-up technique which would be an added nod to the selectors that I was a player for the future, and got ready to do what I had done hundreds of times in practice. Only in the rush of adrenaline, I hadn't judged it at all, and heard the ball plop on the turf a few metres behind me. Oh dear, oh dear. As anyone who has dropped a catch in the deep knows, the thing to do is to try to compensate by working really hard to get the ball in and save the two, and as I pitifully turned to retrieve the ball, I could see two of the selectors in my eyeline on the boundary. There were not even any head-shakes, quizzical looks or extravagant crossing-outs of a name on a clipboard. I'd been cut long before this, which only made it ten times worse.

* * *

Following my two years at Brook, I returned to Farnham who were back in Division One and looking for promotion under the new regulations which matched those of the Southern League. However, despite the odd good match and individual performance, I was now committed to schoolmastering on a Saturday, which meant at best half a season of league cricket. With the family growing, this was becoming more of a chore than the thing I used to live for. I was suddenly something of a veteran; the changing room chat had changed, or rather, it hadn't changed, but my interest in nights out, who was stalking who on Tinder and who was top of the averages just didn't hold the same allure and so I gently started making myself less available. Holidays took priority and I basically became that bloke I'd always complained about as captain, who could make a big difference, but was rarely there and generally didn't live up to past glories when he was. And so my club career petered out, rather than ending with a glorious finale.

Nonetheless, I was keen to prolong my career with Dorset for as long as possible, trying to cheat the cricketing gods by relying more on nous and experience – smoke and mirrors – than decent match practice.

Chapter Fourteen

Keeping Up With the Joneses

Getting the Selection Balance Right

Coming back to the difference of opinion I had with Alan Willows as to what Dorset's strategy for signing players from outside the county ought to be. A few issues were raised. For one, and without wishing to upset those associated with it, the Dorset League was of such a low quality that it appeared hard to produce a Minor Counties team which would be competitive, drawn just from teams within the county, compared to the relative strength of the Cornwall and Devon Leagues and the fact that counties such as Berkshire and Wiltshire benefited from having clubs in ECB Premier Leagues. So whilst it might have been a nice idea, and politically acceptable, to adopt a strategy of only picking 'home-grown' Dorset players would have severely hampered our ability to challenge meaningfully in competitive games. This meant we would need to recruit more widely.

My view was always that if we were to do so, then players ought to have some link to the county, be that through work, birth, family or being recommended by one of the existing players. I was keen to avoid a selfish, mercenary attitude and wanted my players to show pride and passion for the county they were representing. Equally, I wanted to avoid paying anyone, which might lead to a split in the dressing room, even if this meant that some match-winners would be out of our reach.

Generally, then, the imported players who represented Dorset during my tenure as captain were friends of friends, drawn mainly from the Surrey Championship, where I plied my trade on a Saturday; the Southern League, where most talented Dorset players would end up if they wanted to play Premier League cricket; or the Northamptonshire Premier league, where my vice-captain Chris Park was captain of the Northampton Saints, having moved from Dorset some years before.

We also benefited from a symbiotic relationship with our local major counties – Somerset and Hampshire – by which they would be able to take our best young players on to their academies whilst we would be able to offer a decent standard of cricket to players who were on the fringes of the professional game, or between contracts.

Some examples of where this worked well for us was in the cases of Jack Leach, who took 6-21 to help us win the 2010 Minor Counties Championship final as a budding left-arm spinner, before becoming a key part of Somerset's success and then on to England honours. Another was Lewis McManus, who attended my old school – Claysmore – before being picked up for Hampshire and becoming their first-choice wicketkeeper.

Chris Jones was another case-in point. Jonesy (another genius piece of nicknaming) was a Dorset youngster who went on to the staff at Somerset and seemed likely to make a career for himself as a classy batsman when he scored a hundred against the touring Australians in 2013. Willows was desperate to have Chris in our side and was adamant that we do everything to look after the youngster, particularly when on tour with some of the slightly less professional members of the squad (myself included). So some senior players knew we could use this to our advantage to get one over the neurotic coach when we took a 17-year-old Jones on tour to Herefordshire in 2008.

Following a day in the field, we planned on a team meal and a couple of quiet beers at a local pub. Willows was delayed for some reason and so we decided to wind him up. Knowing he was already concerned about us leading him astray (probably due to the fact we had mentioned it constantly in the dressing room at Brockhampton all day), we talked Jonesy into playing along with the trick which would involve one of us keeping lookout for Wills, whilst we would have a tray of shot glasses around a group of players with Jones in the midst. When the coach arrived, the plan was to have the young lad finish what looked like a pint of beer, but in reality was just the dregs of a shandy, and then as the coach walked in to have a crowd chanting 'Jonesy, Jonesy' as he necked a shot of water made to look like vodka. Hook, line and sinker doesn't do justice to the reaction of our gullible coach, who still wouldn't believe us when we explained the joke was on him. Jonesy was a true pro, and kept the joke running by slurring his words and staggering around, just to keep Willows in the dark.

That evening was also the scene for one of the more bizarre, and worrying, conversations I have ever had with an umpire. A lovely Welsh chap called John James was officiating the match and happened to be at the same pub for his dinner (there not being a wealth of options in deepest Herefordshire, something our management had presumably taken into account when choosing our hotel). James was in his last few years as an umpire and some of us knew him quite well, and so we bought him a beer, investing a few quid from my 'Captain's Allowance' in the cynical hope it might pay dividends in the event of a close decision on the pitch. And whilst I felt bad in thinking these upright custodians of the game could be in any way manipulated, James surprised me with his comments that evening.

We were discussing the 50-over final in 2006, which we lost to Northumberland, and in which he was the standing umpire when the final ball was bowled. As it happened, a chap called David Barrick had put in a man-of-the-match performance for them and was 97 not out with two to win, and a century at Lord's in the offing, when our big opening bowler Martin Ford slung one down the leg side which ran away for four to give the game to the opposition, but to leave Barrick a frustrating three runs short of a once-in-a-lifetime achievement. This had clearly been bothering John, who wanted to know from us whether Fordy had done this deliberately. We were quick to reassure the worried Welshman that Fordy was one of the most honest blokes around and that it was highly unlikely that he would have done this on purpose.

'I'm so relieved,' a visibly calmer James exhaled.

Something was nagging at me, though, as I replied:

'Out of interest, John, what would you have done if you thought it had been on purpose?'

'Oh, I'd have called him back, Hicksy.'

'But that's not really the law though, is it?'

'No, but some things are more important than the laws of the game.'

Wow.

This really got me interested. An umpire telling me that the laws of cricket – which as far as I was concerned had been handed down like the Ten Commandments to W.G. Grace as if he were some cricketing Moses – were open not only to interpretation, but could be discarded on a whim. I had to push him on this.

'What do you mean, John? You're saying you'd break the sacred laws which govern our beloved game?'

'Well, Tom, for instance, it's like …'

I couldn't imagine what was coming here. I knew of players who would happily push the boundaries of the acceptable, but an umpire?

'… it's like when Darren's batting …'

Hang on, he's talking about my team-mate Darren Cowley here…

'… I'd never give him out lbw …'

Thunderbolts and lightning. Had I heard this correctly?

'Sorry, John, did you say you'd <u>never</u> give Darren out lbw?'

'That's right. Well, he's just too good to watch, isn't he?'

This was quite remarkable news, and he was adamant about it. Of course, I pushed him as to whether the same personal rule applied when I was at the crease. He gave me a sort of sad-looking smile, a pat on the arm, no words, and turned to get himself another pint while I picked my jaw up off the floor.

A Missed Talent – Darren Cowley

I should say a few words about Darren Cowley here. DC, or Tucker, as he was known from schooldays, is the son of former Glamorgan, Hampshire and Dorset off-spinner Nigel Cowley, who later became well-known as a professional umpire. 'Dougal', as he was known (I believe after the *Magic Roundabout* character), was a self-confessed 'not-outer', which I learned on that bitterly cold day in Bristol playing for Oxford against Gloucestershire after several unsuccessful leg-before appeals against Kim Barnett. Even after reminding Dougal of the time I took a blinding catch as twelfth man in the Minor Counties final of 1998 off his bowling, he explained that as a young pup bowling to an old pro like Barnett, my chances of success were marginal, at best. Again, nice to know every umpire is entirely neutral …

That is to be a little unfair on Nigel, who was a top bloke and father to one of my best mates in cricket, whom I first met on an ill-fated school tour to South Africa in 1996/97. For some reason, our school coach had told the tour organisers that we were one of the strongest school sides in England. This was about as misguided as the time I told the Oxford University team that on our day we could beat Australia if we just got our skills right. And it meant that we would have to face some of the hardest cricket of our lives, including a memorable game at Amanzimtoti CC in Durban, where Darren was one of several players sporting age-group Durban or South Africa shirts. We were in for a rough ride, chasing over 300 from 40 overs. I was relieved, batting at No.4, when their rapid opening bowler seemed to break down, but couldn't understand why the slips were giggling so much. It turned out that they would replace him with a chap called Gary Gilder, who any South African of that generation would recognise as a very swift left-armer, who had actually been told he could not bowl as he would be too much for this hapless bunch, but who would now get the chance to make us hop around. Which he did. And made his debut for Natal that season.

It was men against boys. A theme which was followed up after the game when I was first introduced to the post-match entertainment that is the 'stump game'. A relay race in which two teams line up facing two stumps about a pitch-length away and each person in turn downs a beer, runs to the stump, puts their head on it and has to circle it ten times before attempting to run back to the team, usually ending up in hilarious collisions and fallings-over. Unfortunately, the Castle Lager and the stump game were probably too much for some of our number, and I remember the bathroom in the coach back to the hotel being required by at least one inebriated schoolboy.

This was the early days of tours going to South Africa after apartheid and it is fair to say the logistics didn't always quite go to plan. For instance, it had been organised to put us up in a hotel on the beachfront in Durban for New Year's Eve, which in itself is not a great plan, given that all of the white folk shipped out of the town for new year, leaving the beach a seething mass of black people, with hundreds of VW camper vans blaring out extraordinary bass notes and firecrackers being let off all around. Can you imagine the sight of 16 white English public schoolboys walking a mile on the promenade in order to reach the Indian nightclub 'Stringfella's' where we were due to see in the new year? And the 'hotel' we were staying in? Well, not only was it infested with cockroaches and bed bugs, but whilst the first floor was a hotel, the ground floor was actually an old-people's home and the second floor was – for want of a better expression – a knocking shop. So as we gingerly convened for our big night out, the traffic in the lobby in the early evening was a bizarre mix of zimmer-frames, blue-rinse hair and ladies of ill repute. As someone who works in safeguarding in schools now, this gives me nightmares and I'm sure my parents would have been having kittens as the designated staff on tour.

To add to an already difficult tour, on the way from Oudtshoorn to Cape Town, on the famous and beautiful 'Garden Route', our team bus not only broke down, but fully burned to the ground, leaving us with no luggage, cricket kit, water or shelter in the midday African heat, as the driver saw his pride and joy go up, literally, in smoke. We made the best of it, and when the list came around for us to say what we had lost for the insurance company, it's incredible how many pairs of new Oakley sunglasses and expensive watches just happened to have gone missing. We even became the charity of the week on Good Hope FM radio station, with black bags of t-shirts and odd and ends of cricket kit being donated for the last leg of our tour. If they could have donated us some batsmen it would have been nice.

Back to Cowley, and the next time I came across this barrel-shaped, shaven-haired bully-boy of a batsman was in the 2000 season, when he appeared in the Dorset squad after having sharpened his skills as a left-arm spinner and big hitter in the South African Under-19 side which included – among others – Mark Boucher. There was no coincidence that Darren's arrival on the scene was in the season that Dorset eventually broke its duck and became Minor County champions for the first time in their over hundred-year history. He top-scored in the final and had become probably the most feared batsman at this level in the country.

Darren was quite the phenomenon, with an ability to hit the ball I have rarely seen matched, at least until the IPL era of enormous bats and a better understanding of the biomechanics of big hitting. The only player who really challenged him in my experience was Julian Wood of Hampshire and later Berkshire, now a 'range-hitting' guru. Cowley was equally effective against the short ball, hooking and pulling fast bowlers for fun, as he was on the front foot, where his ability to clear not only the ropes, but also many fences, hedges and walls was the stuff of local legend. He had no truck with playing himself in; in his mind, 'if it was up, it was off'. He reasoned that if you could get to the pitch of the ball to defend it, you could just extend the arms from there and hit it for four or six. And it didn't matter who the bowler was. Even John Emburey, playing in his latter years for Berkshire, was dispatched out of the park in his first over by the 'Barton Barrel' (a nickname garnered from Cowley's Devon club side).

The 'Cowley Leave' – as it became known – consisted of a huge attempted airshot at a lofted drive, usually first ball of his innings; and batting in the slot below Darren in the order (usually five or six) became known as 'riding the Cowley rollercoaster' as whilst you enjoyed the thrills of his expansive batting, you felt you could be in at any moment. Usually, though, he came off, and we were delighted to have him in our side. Indeed, the biggest shame really was that despite the advent of T20 cricket during his time playing for Dorset, he was never picked up by a county. As his team-mates, we always backed him to do well and we also valued his loyalty to the Leopards, since we knew that he would have had regular overtures from rival teams. There is much more one could say about this talismanic cricketer – his bowling and slip-catching for two, and the way he took his no-holds-barred approach into post-match affairs was as much part of what he meant to the team as some of his big innings.

DC was an opportunity missed for the professional game, but don't take my word for it, just listen to John James.

Even Better than Caddick?

Dorset coach Alan Willows was desperate to sign some big-name players to help us establish a winning culture and bring some silverware back to the county for the first time since we had our legendary leg-spinner Vyv Pike bamboozling batsmen from Thame to Thirsk. And at the opening of the 2009 season, we were preparing for our first three-day game, against Oxfordshire at the beautiful ground of Great and Little Tew, when I received a phone call suggesting that Somerset needed a couple of seamers to get some overs under their belt, and would we be interested in Andy Caddick for a game, or Steffan Jones perhaps for a few more? Despite my normal, emotional reaction of protecting our own players and worrying about how an interloper might upset the dressing room, I have to say I was pretty excited at the prospect of having someone of Caddick's calibre, and Jones would be a good option, too, as he was known to bowl pretty good 'wheels'. Essentially it was a no-lose situation, so when I was later told that Caddick would be turning out for Wiltshire, but that Steffan would be joining us, I was only a little disappointed.

It does not surprise me that Steffan is now a big name in the fast-bowling, biomechanics world – this big, burly Welshman with the broadest of shoulders arrived with more bags even than our wicketkeeper, and proceeded to set up a corner of the modest dressing room with an array of supplements so vast it was as if he'd just ram-raided Holland and Barrett, as well as an assortment of different coloured, different weighted balls – some for throwing, some for stretching, some for, well, I never found out about some of them. It was certainly a different approach from some of my older colleagues whose kit bags tended to contain mostly Lucozade, Mayfair cigarettes and porn mags. Dorset had gone professional.

And the big man did not disappoint. He fairly roared in and ripped through the Oxfordshire batting, setting up a comfortable win for us and putting us on the path to a successful three-day season. And he was no sufferer of fools. Also in our attack that day was a young lad called Mitchell Wilson, who could also get it down there at a decent pace, but who had the tendency to drop off in the field. Wilson had misjudged a catch in the deep in the first session, and was collared by Jones at the lunch break to be frogmarched to the adjoining second team ground where the Somerset man proceeded to launch high catches at him for half an hour whilst we all quietly sniggered over our salad. It was a great statement about the standards he wanted from his team-mates, and I probably didn't do enough to encourage and support him as captain in his mission.

This is a bit of a regret of mine, as I did find Steffan a very different character from me: whilst I was keen that the boys had dinner together and shared a beer or two, chatting about the game, Steff tended to keep himself to himself off the field and ordered room service rather than join us. He was also very difficult to persuade tactically, having that self-belief that if only I'd give him the ball, he would inevitably take a wicket. I loved that attitude, but didn't always share such faith in his ability, especially in his second spell at the club when the pace was down and the X-factor seemed to have gone. Nonetheless, had I given him more of a chance to impart his professional experience on the squad, we may have had more success. We live and learn. And we certainly got more out of Steff than we would have from Caddick.

Hollywood and the Murray Mints

I should be clear that even though many people may have thought we were paying players, to my knowledge this never happened at Dorset (indeed, we lost out on several signings because we refused to do so, for financial, as well as moral reasons – the committee and I saw eye to eye on this). That didn't stop me winding up a young Max Waller, who would not believe that at least four of our team were not getting paid, and this became a periodical theme of the banter when he or I were bowling. If I took a wicket, Chris Park would pipe up with 'Twenty quid in the pocket, Hicker', or if Cowley was on 40 not out, one of us would comment, 'Ten more for his bonus', if Max was in earshot. I'm sure he still suspects we were paid, but I doubt that he cares a great deal, having made a great career for himself as a T20 specialist for Somerset and other franchises as a reliable leggie and one of the finest fielders of his generation. One of my proudest moments was taking a couple of pretty steady catches off my own bowling in a one-day game against Wales, with Max screeching 'That's a worldy, Hicker!' in my ear from extra cover as I surprised even myself. High praise from someone of his ability.

The rumours of payment were certainly in the air when Steve Selwood joined the Dorset squad in 2005. Known by many as 'Hollywood', I'd known Steve as a junior player at Middlesex and he had always come across as a huge show-pony: highlighted, 'surf-dude' hairstyle, top off for tanning at any given occasion, and a stylish left-handed batsman. Now I got to know him, Hollywood proved himself to be … a huge show-pony with highlighted surf-dude hair, keen to tan himself at any given occasion, and a stylish left-handed batsman. He was just what we needed, and home games at the beach resort of Bournemouth suited him down to the ground.

And I am probably doing Sellers a disservice; although he was certainly quick to ask the questions about the frills of Minor Counties cricket (How much are expenses? What stash do we get? Do any teams pay?), once he understood that he had a place with Dorset only as long as he was willing to fit into the dressing room, and that all we would offer was the chance to prove himself to the professional counties so he could get back into the game, having been released recently by Derbyshire, he was good as gold. Not only that, he was a real character in the dressing room. It was Sellers who introduced the boys to Bluetooth – the first time technology allowed you to share files over the airwaves at the advent of smartphones (the X-rated content of most of the files would have got me sacked from school, if not arrested, so I steered clear of that). He was also mad keen on the animated film *Team America* – a sort of spoof *Thunderbirds* full of inappropriate jokes about terrorists. It was from the film's title song that he developed our team motto for that season: 'Leopards: F**k yeah!' Subtle, isn't it?

Another thing which Sellers brought to the table was an uncanny ability to shine the ball so that it swung prodigiously. Our seamers in that era were very successful, not least a young all-rounder from Weymouth called Dan Belt, who had the Botham-esque knack of taking wickets with bad balls and who seemed to be able to swing the old ball both ways at some pace, with a slippery bouncer in the armoury as well. To compare to the successful Ashes-winning side of 2005, Belty was our Simon Jones, keeping up the pressure once the new-ball attack had come off. It was some time before we realised that although he was undoubtedly a skilful bowler, he was getting a great deal of assistance from our bleach-blond, unpaid 'pro'.

Sellers would become highly protective of the cricket ball, not allowing anyone else to shine it, and getting very angry when the rough side got damp through sweat. He insisted on it coming to him after every ball and he would vigorously rub it to get it hot, applying saliva all the time. Eventually, it dawned on us that this was no ordinary shining, but there was dark magic in his method. It was the Murray Mints, you see. Full of sticky sugar, Steve was applying liberal amounts of polish, essentially, to the ball, whilst keeping the other side dry, which had the effect of making what should have been a soft and easy-to-bat-against ball into a looping, hooping grenade. The odd umpire would have a quiet word, and so he would ease off for a while, but mostly we got away with it.

It is interesting to reflect on this in the aftermath of the Australian 'sandpaper affair' for which Steve Smith was stripped of the captaincy, and David Warner and Cameron Bancroft were banned for a considerable amount of time. Whilst sandpaper is most certainly beyond the pale, this application of a 'foreign substance' was definitely also cheating, and I guess we all (once we worked out what was happening) colluded in a sort of collective amnesia, blinded by the success we were having as a team, and perhaps a feeling that we were somehow being more 'professional' than our opponents. The post-Covid era has reopened the debate about what is acceptable practice and what is cheating, in just another stage in the ever-evolving story of this great game.

I think the moment at which I felt that we might have gone too far was when, standing next to Selwood at slip, he had his palm flat with the ball stuck to it, defying gravity, with him grinning from ear to ear.

Chapter Fifteen

Smells Like Team Spirit

Dressing room Japes

Pages and pages have been written over the years about the 'locker-room' spirit. Whether it be the legendary 'boot room' at Liverpool Football Club, the Crazy Gang spirit of the Vinnie Jones days at Wimbledon FC or the intensity of the players' locker room at the All England Tennis club during a Wimbledon championship, there is something quasi-mythical about what goes on in the inner sanctum of a sports arena. And a cricket changing room trumps any other sport.

The sheer nature of cricket dictates that players spend an inordinate amount of time off the field and in the dressing room (or 'sheds' as they are affectionately known in Australia). The length of the match, and the fact that for large parts you are waiting to bat, or rueing getting out, means that it is quite possible for a player to spend more time off the field than on it during a declaration match, if that player is a poor batsman but part of a strong bowling unit. Is there any other sport where this is even remotely possible? Far from being incidental, and just the place where you change and shower, and maybe receive a brief team-talk and a soggy orange at half-time, the cricket changing room can be the centre of your universe for days on end. I imagine this is even more the case for Test cricketers, who can hardly just wander off for a game of boundary bowls or nip to the Co-Op for a coffee and some Haribo. They are not even allowed their phones, for goodness sake, for fear of match-fixing.

So the cricket changing room takes on a shared significance for the team, and breeds its own atmosphere. I mean this as much literally as metaphorically, since with eleven players, substitutes and coaches all changing, showering, sweating, farting, and applying endless lotions and potions throughout the day in a confined space (they are almost always too small, of course), not to mention spilling tea, energy drinks, beer, and leaving ends of sandwich, melon, crisp packets all over the place, the pungent aroma of the changing room is something altogether unique, and probably best avoided.

It may help to paint the picture if I try to describe a typical scene in the Dean Park dressing room during a three-day county match.

In the corner, by the loos, is Cowley. Why he changes by the ablutions I have no idea, as after three days of cricket teas, post-match lagers and takeaway dinners, that part of the room is more, shall we say, 'fragrant' than elsewhere. Cowley will happily sit in his jockstrap rolling a cigarette. Once he has drained two coffees and stubbed out his second 'oily',[14] his hangover has eased off enough for him to go and hit a few throw downs, chewing an out-of-date Co-codamol on the way. He will almost certainly smash a run-a-ball hundred later, despite having had to shave his teeth and wash his eyeballs before facing the first ball.

Next to Cowley is one of the new lads, who has not worked out that this will not be a good place for three days, since whilst Cowley is the most popular bloke in the team, no one wants to

---

14 Rhyming slang: 'oily rag'= fag.

get near that corner. The new lad is the only one who has read the instructions from the manager which says he must wear a shirt and tie. He will continue to do this, despite seeing the state of Cowley and witnessing our first-change seamer fall out of the back seat of a Vauxhall Astra as the warm-up starts. He will also probably not bowl and score very few. I suspect he will get a game in an away match against Shropshire at Telford in a couple of years and then disappear without trace despite having turned up for every winter net for the past three seasons. Nice chap, though. Shame.

Along the bench from the new lad is Masoor, who is from Gloucestershire and desperately keen to make his way in the game. He has even spent the winter out in India for the experience. After three seasons, Maz has been accepted into the fold and is becoming a solid opening batsman. His biggest mistake is sitting next to me, as after three post-match ciders, I am prone to getting into a deep conversation about the Quran. Maz is polite, and sober enough to humour my spiritual musings, whilst all the time hoping that I don't drip my drink all over his kit. He looks as if he should be a world-class left-arm spinner. He is not.

For an educated fellow, I am a messy changer. I kid myself that I know where everything is in my area of the dressing room, but in reality, I have just stored up so much Dorset stash over the years that I can usually lay my hands on something approaching the right kit. I might have to pull a couple of old lemon sherberts off the bottom of my t-shirt and use yesterday's socks, but by and large I'm in decent order. Nothing matches though. The good thing about being such a mediocre batsman is that I rarely got through more than one pair of gloves in a weekend (let alone an innings). But boy will you know about it if I've scored runs on the Saturday. On those weekends, I'll ensure I'm first to the ground and will leave my entire padding array 'out to dry', on display in front of the dressing room, so everyone is aware that I may just have carved my way to a fifty the day before. During throwdowns on these days, the coach has to deal with me analysing my game in minute detail, before inevitably having to watch me nick off for not many later in the day. For me, the changing room is extremely familiar.

Moving round the room, we come to the old stager, who I am sure still models himself on the old cigarette cards. His shirt flaps open like Dennis Lillee and he wears permanent five-o'clock shadow. He is the only player still using the old-fashioned coffin-style case, which is home to a multitude of sins. A seemingly endless supply of paper-based pornography sits alongside league and county handbooks going back decades. Boxes of playing cards muddle in with the cigarettes and, incongruously, the *Telegraph* crossword, which he will casually finish whilst commenting sardonically on almost anything. The old stager hates football and anything to do with it, has presented *Homes Under the Hammer* and has a mate in every town south of the Severn estuary. No one really knows what he does after the game, or for a living. It is amazing that he is still getting picked – he has that uncanny knack of producing an airy fifty just when the selection committee are starting to sharpen their pencils. With this sort of timing and something of a debonair spirit, he has been dodging the axe for years and holds the record for appearances, despite an average of about 20.

Beside the old stager we move into the more professional zone where two opening bowlers – thick as thieves – have staked their place. Both well over 6ft 4in, they are affectionately known as the 'Twin Towers'. They have all the gear – two sets of Oakley glasses (one for fielding, one for leisure), bowling boots, batting boots, trainers – all size 15; the best batting kit of the entire team, despite being ten and Jack. Happily, they are both generous enough to lend their bats out. Cowley has not bought a bat of his own in years, and they are happy to see him go through two a season, they are such nice chaps. However, all this kit means the coach and twelfth man have to share a holdall and change in shifts, but who's going to argue with the fast-and-nasties?

The two opening batsmen also dress next to each other (there's definitely some strange camaraderie between openers of both disciplines). Both are extremely well turned out (one was nicknamed 'Labels' as everything was a top brand name, even his golf clubs were top of the range and when we could get him to come out for a beer, it was only ever an expensive, bottled continental number – no warm Carling for him). Labels is dead calm all the time and after a couple of sighs after getting out, he will dutifully put all his kit away in the order it went in – he even uses one of those bat sleeves, of which dozens are strewn in cricketers' attics the world over. As an aside, bat sleeves are singularly the most useless piece of kit ever invented. I would not be surprised if all these campaigns to clear up the oceans find the issue is a floating mass of these useless oversized condoms clogging up the Bay of Bengal.

In contrast to Labels, his partner is a notorious bat-thrower and if he gets out, the word will quickly get around to vacate the premises, and a swift exodus will ensue as he starts launching projectiles from the moment he nears the boundary rope; gloves, bat, box, the lot is raining in worse than a barrage of bumpers from Brett Lee.

Spare a thought for the poor soul who is now next in and has to pad up. He cannot escape the onslaught, which continues with a tirade of expletives once the ammunition to throw has been exhausted. What must he do? Does he pretend to be invisible and go about his own preparation in silence, avoiding eye contact as if his team-mate is Medusa? Does he hazard conversation?

'Didn't nick it then?' *(No, best avoid that.)*

'Bit high?' *(Obviously, you ignoramus, even a blind man could see that.)*

'Can I borrow your box?'

No. In circumstances such as these, one must get changed as promptly as possible, say nothing and quietly, apologetically slide past, leaving the human tornado to whirl itself out of energy. I have seen mirrors smashed, toilet seats demolished, picnic chairs obliterated, and even one player who had a spare bat expressly in his bag for throwing and smashing when he was out. Of course, whilst this is going on, all the blokes on the balcony are pissing themselves laughing and have to put on the straight faces again when he eventually emerges.

Now you could tentatively hazard a question:

'Didn't nick it then?'

'Smashed it, mate,' he will finally admit.

Arriving in the final part of the dressing room you come across bowling coach Julian Shackleton (son of the legendary Hampshire seamer Derek) who is so thin if he turns sideways he literally disappears, apart from the permanent cigarette drooping from his lips. Ever the entrepreneur, he will only dispense his best advice if you agree to buy a pair of overpriced cricket socks from his car boot. And beyond him, by the showers, are the keeper and all-rounder. These two secretly think they run the show and keep the team together. The fact is, they probably do, and so they are pretty much untouchable. No one will challenge them as long as they keep digging the top-order out of trouble with doughty middle-order partnerships, and producing the goods in the field. Of course the keeper has some odd habits (they all do), and the all-rounder hasn't done a team warm-up since he topped the averages three years ago and was approached by Hampshire. We're just happy to have them both and so they can keep their kit how they like, where they like.

It goes without saying that there are three showers, but only one works properly and the temperature ranges from freezing to scalding and only the second team vice-captain knows which knob to turn to achieve a happy medium, and he is on holiday with his missus for a fortnight. Everyone's towel (those who remembered to bring one) is damp and cold as no natural light penetrates the changing room, and water seeps through to soak the underside of at least two people's bags. I once ruined a bat which was standing upright by the shower overnight, the end of which soaked up so much water it was twice as thick by the morning. That was when I moved to my current position. On reflection, I don't have it so bad, even if when the door is opened, I am in full view of everyone outside. Our poor scorer has seen more full frontals than is healthy for a woman of a certain age. I shudder to think how many times she's also copped the view from the back.

If the physical atmosphere in the sheds is a grim cocktail of farts, Tiger Balm, mouldy tuna sandwiches and the stale odour of 11 sweaty jockstraps, the pervading tone of what sometimes passes for 'team spirit' is something equally intangible and esoteric.

Behind Closed Doors

Much like the old adage of 'What goes on tour, stays on tour', there is much which goes on behind closed doors in the changing rooms which must stay sacrosanct. However, the sheer amount of dead time during a cricket match makes it fertile ground for banter, themes and practical jokes. Here are just a few of the old 'classics'.

The Sausages in the Gloves Trick

There are multiple variants on this simple, yet thoroughly irritating prank which consists of secreting mini cocktail sausages in various parts of a team-mate's kit. An obvious place is in the fingers of batting gloves where they typically are only discovered at that crucial, adrenaline-filled moment when a wicket has fallen and the victim of the prank not only has to try and get mentally prepared for battle, but finds the job all that harder by having to try and remove a bite-size pork treat. The job is, of course, almost impossible as – like a Chinese thumb-screw – the more you try to wiggle a sausage out of a glove, the more it becomes wedged. I have found the only way to get one out is by scratching it out bit by bit – not ideal when you only have three minutes to avoid getting timed out. You can extend the cocktail sausage prank by using a whole pack of sausages, leaving them in shoes, socks, blazer pockets, the glove box of a car, and so on. And if they go undiscovered, the more chance they have of starting to smell a bit rancid, so you get good long-term bang for your buck. Couple this by hiding 19 but telling your victim there were 20, so they continue to look for the last one long after the match has finished and everyone has gone home. And do feel free to be creative with this – substitute prawns for your sausages for extra pungency.

A poor 17-year-old Lewis McManus fell foul of a variant of this on his Dorset debut in a game against Wiltshire at Devizes when he made the rookie error of leaving his wicketkeeping gloves on the floor during a drinks break when he left the field to answer a call of nature. Being the supportive, responsible senior players that we were, Cowley and I deemed it part of this young player's wider cricketing education to have to deal with some gummy bears in his gauntlets, and for five minutes after the break, all the players had to wait while poor Lewis (or Justin Bieber as he was known to us) scrabbled around, mortified with embarrassment, trying to extricate the sticky sweets. To no avail – he finally settled for jamming them as far up the gloves as he could and hoping not to break a finger until the next break in play when some tweezers were located.

I'm not sure they do this stuff at Hampshire. I hope they do.

I suffered an extreme variation of the sausage prank at the hands of my mate Tom Caines, after one of many hot summer weeks at his parents' farm in Dorset. On the way home from one of these vigils, reluctantly pushing the trusty Citroën AX to its absolute limit on the A303, I noticed a strange aroma. Of course, after days on end at my mate's house during the cricket season, it was quite possible that this was just of my own personal making, with stacks of damp, musty kit in the boot, but it was not a smell I recognised. Only after stopping on the hard shoulder and exploring every inch of the car did I put my hand under the passenger seat where I had the nausea-inducing, stomach-turning experience of feeling the mangy fur of a dead, flea-ridden rabbit he had retrieved from the road somewhere and hidden the night before. Let me be clear: roadkill is not part of the deal when it comes to changing room pranks.

Cutting Off the Trouser Leg

This was a trick which was played on our lanky opening bowler – Paddy Murphy – at Farnham. Murph was one of those highly intelligent people who seem to exhibit very little common sense. A high-flying corporate lawyer in Dubai, Paddy (or 'Posh Bloke', as he was also known to some of our players without letters after their name) failed to realise that he was the butt of an ongoing prank which entailed cutting the bottom few centimetres from one of his trouser legs. This would typically happen just before he put them on for the game, so he would either realise just as the umpires' bell would ring – too late for a change (and no one ever really takes a spare pair of whites anyway), or he would bowl a couple of balls of his opening spell before feeling the breeze around his ankles and shooting a frustrated stare at the giggling slip cordon, who couldn't quite believe this had happened again.

Deep Heat in the Box
Not sophisticated, and with a lasting effect which could really piss someone off for a whole day. Expect a backlash.

Shampoo in the Shower
One I learnt in my very early years of village cricket at Child Okeford, where the joke was on a bloke called Martin Oliver, who would love to spend time in the shower after matches and ended up spending longer than he planned as no sooner had he managed to rinse the shampoo from his hair, but his team-mates would discreetly pour more on his head so to rinse it out became a Sisyphean task. I don't know. It made me laugh.

Superglueing Socks
Two of funniest cricketers I played against were the Cheshire double-act of Nathan Dumelow and Ben Spendlove, who had been team-mates at Derbyshire and seemed made for the slightly lower grade of repartee which Minor Counties cricket had to offer. Spendlove did have his own moment in the sun and was probably the most famous England twelfth man for his sharp catch off Hansie Cronje at Edgbaston in 1998 until Gary Pratt came along and almost bagged an MBE by running out Ricky Ponting at Trent Bridge during the 2005 Ashes. Incidentally, years after that run-out which sparked Ponting's furious tirade at Duncan Fletcher, Pratt single-handedly stood in the way of Dorset reaching a Lord's final under my leadership by steering Cumberland to victory with a gritty knock in a low-scoring semi-final at Dean Park in 2012 (looking at the scorecard for

that game, a young Liam Livingstone was bowled for a 12-ball duck by Jack Leach – how their careers have moved on).

I had also had some previous with Spendlove in our junior days. Both he and I had fallen at the final hurdle to make the England team at under-14 level, and we shared a gloomy bus ride back to our hotel from Jesmond. He won't forgive me for mentioning that he was in floods of tears that day (of course it was mentioned on the pitch when he walked out to bat …) Spenny was great value and a good player to boot, and I enjoyed our games against Cheshire, who seemed to share our 'play hard on and off the field' attitude. Ben and his mucker Dumelow certainly enjoyed a trip to Bournemouth, and could be relied upon to take full advantage of all the entertainment available in a big seaside resort in high summer.

Back in the dressing room, superglue was their go-to, and opening bat Danny Leach was often the fall guy. I remember furious yelling from Leach one lunchtime:

'Not a fookin' gen, lads!'

Laughter.

'Me fookin' socks, you c***s! You superglued me fookin' socks to the floor agen.'

Laughter now from both dressing rooms amid a hail of shoes and gloves as Dumelow and Spendlove fall, hysterical, through the door.

They would also glue a 20 pence piece to the floor and watch as passers-by stooped to pick it up. Again, simple but effective and it'll keep you and your mates amused all day.

Apparently, the former South African batsman Neil McKenzie was on the receiving end of something similar at Hampshire. McKenzie was well-known to suffer from OCD – a sort of obsessive attention to detail. Cricketers – like bullies – have the sharpest radar for any sign of weakness, and so McKenzie found his bat taped to the ceiling of the dressing room as he desperately tried to go through his rigorous pre-innings routine.

What Colour?

Of course, so much of this is puerile and annoying, which is kind of the point. When you reduce cricket to its bare bones, it is really just a bunch of grown men playing bat-and-ball with each other, so why would you expect anything more grown up off the field?

Talking puerile, part of the standard chat in the Dorset dressing room was to answer any request with the question: 'What colour?'

As in:

'Have you got any bat tape?'

'What colour?'

'Has anyone got any suncream?'

'What colour?'

'Anyone got any chewing gum?'

'What colour?'

Annoying, isn't it?

And any sense of an irritated response would be met with an enthusiastic 'Gottim!', as if a wicket had fallen.

As I said, there is a lot of dead time during cricket matches.

The Overworked Postman

One happy by-product of the many hours spent on the side of the cricket field for me has been honing my skills at cryptic crosswords: a skill nurtured by erstwhile Dorset skipper Stuart Rintoul. I used to get a real hard time from Rints as a junior player and regular twelfth man, and he took the chance to humiliate me on one rainy day on tour in Neston, on the Wirral. Most of the team were nursing huge hangovers after a night out in Chester on one of the 'Northern tours' which saw back-to-back two-day games against Shropshire and Cheshire, this time on our way to the Western Division title in 1999.

Sensing I'd be keen to show off my intellect, he gently lured me in with a couple of easy clues, before posing this one:

'*Overworked postman?*'

I asked for clarification, '*Overworked postman?*'

'*Overworked postman.*'

And then a long, pregnant pause, before I blundered two-footed into his trap.

'*How many letters?*'

'*F***ING HUNDREDS!*'

Changing room Cricket

Most teams and clubs will have their own traditions of how to while away the time during long batting innings, or on those interminable rain days. Changing room cricket is a classic – batting with a stump, using a tennis ball or windball (the olden days equivalent of an Incrediball) with all the other players acting as close fieldsmen. The batsman is only allowed to defend, but that doesn't stop the game always ending with someone failing to control themselves and winding up a massive shot which pinballs around the changing room, off the strip lighting and into someone's face.

Or there is the game where you have a player at each end of a long table (there tends to be one in the middle of most dressing rooms, with bags on top) and you throw a ball to each other and must not catch it above the level of the table. Both games are actually pretty good for your skills. I also enjoyed playing with a windball on wet days, skidding it as hard as you could over a short pitch with plenty of slips in place. The same effect can be produced by hitting a tennis ball with a racket. Staying in line with your eyes on the ball is the key, so again, it's actually not bad practice, but you can expect a few stingers on the way.

Ssssh!

On the pitch things can get pretty tedious as well and keeping a team interested and energised through long sessions in the field can develop into something of an art form. OK, yes, there were times when the focus of our attention would be on the batsman and the state of the game, but often, once the shine had gone from the new ball, and especially in multi-day cricket, you need to make your own entertainment if the game becomes attritional.

One game we played was to find a theme for the 'encouraging' comments in the field. For instance, if Martin Ford – opening bowler and one of the 'Twin Towers' – happened to be playing, we might try to get in as many references to Ford cars, or cars in general, as we could.

'Come on Fordy, escort him to the boundary!'

'Let's go up a gear, Fordy!'

'Take the handbrake off, big guy!'

All of which would become more and more obscure…

'Like you're bowling from the Vauxhall End, fella!'

'Metro-nomic line-and-length!'

You can see the sort of nonsense which could come out. Although at least it was sort of original, unlike some of the generic nonsense I have to endure every week listening to schoolchildren, whose wit just about extends to, 'He's fishing, boys!', or 'Big swing, no ding!'. Umpiring to this claptrap makes Saturday afternoons pretty painful, but I guess that's what some umpires felt about our inanities.

Other attempts to stave off the on-field boredom included the silent over. This was a genuine tactic to unnerve batsmen as well as keep all the fielders involved. The signal would be given, and on the point of the umpire calling the end of the over, all the players had to remain silent until the next call of over. This meant no talking, clapping or other noise. The only exception was that you were allowed to appeal. On one occasion I remember a moment of real controversy during a silent over. It was during the fateful game against Berkshire when Julian Wood fell out with the umpire, who subsequently refused to stand for the rest of the game. Before Wood had been given out, we had called a silent over with Stuart Naylor at the crease. Naylor – a hard cricketer who gave no quarter – clearly nicked the ball to the keeper standing up to the stumps. There was a huge, audible edge which clearly couldn't have been anything else given that it was as silent as a churchyard during that over, and yet the umpire missed it. We were apoplectic, but such was the guys' commitment to the silent over cause that whilst there was much holding of heads and gnashing of teeth, we limited our sledging and obvious dissatisfaction with the umpire to complete mime show, which in itself was pretty funny. Happily, we removed Naylor two overs later and he copped a fearful barrage on his way to the pavilion.

Anyone failing to adhere to a silent over would suffer some kind of fines punishment at the end of play.

Scatter!

Another thing which got us in a spot of bother but which was again original and (we thought) hilarious, was the 'scatter wicket'. Based loosely on a football celebration where the scorer pretended to evade his team-mates, we came up with the notion that when a wicket fell, rather than heading to the bowler to congratulate him, everyone would feign towards him before flying off – arms aloft, or circling, or punching the air in delight – to all corners of the field.

The World Cup of Cricket Teas

Many readers will be aware of Richard Osman's (The *Pointless* guy from TV) book *The World Cup of Everything*. For those who haven't seen it, he basically takes a whole range of ideas and plays them off in a hypothetical knockout format. For example, ice-cream flavours, chocolate bars, cities: it works for anything. I've had great fun with teaching colleagues arguing who would win in 'battles' between famous authors (Shakespeare tends to come out on top most times, but Charles Dickens and Jane Austen have undergone some epic contests over the years ...) And it's a great way to pass time on countless rainy cricket days and long fielding sessions. Cricketers love a list and there are so many imaginary teams you can come up with (best ever England team, best World XI, fattest Minor County team etc.) Some friends and I even picked a full 15-player rugby team composed entirely of fruit and vegetables. But one of my favourite conversation starters is, 'If you were only allowed three items in your cricket tea, what would they be?' Oh, it's a goody, and I've known voices raised, people storming out of rooms and even threats of violence over this conundrum. I got a couple of close cricket mates together to see if we could sort this one out once and for all, using the World Cup format. And here it is.

Sandwiches

We decided to split the tea into its key constituent parts, starting with the sandwiches. There was some early backing for the sausage sandwich, which led us to establish a general rule that although some items were good, if their natural habitat was not the cricket tea table, they would not qualify. And so sausage sandwiches, and bacon, were out: good for pre-match, not for tea. Some more exotic fillings were thrown around (not literally), with prawn cocktail and coronation chicken mooted. Seafood tends to divide and it was deemed there was too much risk with the chicken as often it can be overly full of fruit – apricots and raisins – and the fruit/meat combo is definitely a splitter, so they were out. Although it's a cliché, I've never seen a cucumber sandwich at a cricket tea so they were not discussed. Jam sandwiches were roundly shouted down as being fit only for children's parties and so we were left with three solid stalwarts in cheese and pickle, ham, and egg, with an honourable mention for roast beef. But we had to get it down to two for the quarter-finals. The finer points of all three were put under the microscope: should it be egg on its own, or egg and cress; should cheese and onion be considered; surely ham is only good if it's good and not the wafer-thin supermarket version? (Another clear rule was established here, that we would assume the best version of every item.) In the end, it was ham which had to fall by the wayside, as the jury could not decide which mustard goes best – grainy or English – if indeed one wanted mustard at all. And so cheese and pickle (Branston, of course) and egg (no cress, on white) would represent the sandwich fraternity in the final stages of what was already becoming a mouthwatering (sorry) tournament.

Savouries

Whilst sandwiches are a staple of any tea, the savoury assortment can be the difference between a great tea and mid-match disappointment. The sausage roll entered the draw as a red-hot favourite, although it was pointed out that they do have to be warm, and that there are often not enough. So, tea-makers out there, you have been told: if you are offering up sausage rolls, don't skimp on quantity. Other big players were expected to be the rival cousin to the sausage roll – the cocktail sausage (a side question about how many you could manage in one sitting is worth considering if you are playing at home); also the Scotch egg and pork pie, the pizza slice and quiche were in the running, with chicken drumsticks or wings, samosas (the overseas pro of the cricket tea), satay chicken, chicken nuggets and a big bowl of hot chips, offered up as a staple of Northern cricket grounds especially. This would sort the wheat from the chaff, and some heavyweights would fall at this hurdle. Whoever mentioned the cheeseboard was clearly mixing their lunch with their tea.

No one could look beyond the sausage rolls and these breezed through the play-offs, with the Scotch egg looking good as well (not the savoury eggs with chopped up egg, mind you). Pork pies fell down due to the jelly, pizza was felt also to be more of a party item, even if everyone agreed they were guilty of 'going large' on pizza if it was hot. Crisps were out. Quiche, samosas and other 'exotic' items were shelved early doors, leaving chips with Scotch eggs as possibles for qualification to the final stages.

Healthy Options

Then someone threw in the controversial healthier items in the form of a fruit platter and a range of vegetable sticks (celery, carrot, cucumber, peppers etc). Now, it could be easy to dismiss these options in the face of some more obvious high-calorie, high-meat content, high-pastry content items, but this being the 21st century and attitudes now much more open-minded, we lingered on the fruit platter, ditching the crudités when someone mentioned hummus (clearly we're not that modern just yet). The fruit platter (to include melons, bananas, strawberries and grapes as standard) would be put up against the hopefuls from the savoury list once we'd interrogated the sweet end of the table.

Cakes

If you were to draw your archetypal English cricket tea, you would have a vast array of cakes adorning a checked tablecloth, but the truth is that no one really needs more than one (OK, maybe two slices of cake between nicking off for nought and standing at slip for the afternoon), and so we knew we had to be ruthless and whittle this down to just a couple of champion cakes, to be accompanied by some of the other sweet items on offer. It didn't take us long to get down to three. Fruit cake, chocolate cake and Victoria sponge. I think you'll agree these are the front-row forwards of the cricket tea. Not to be messed with. And homemade, of course. Once again, we had to make a very clear rule that anything that came in a packet should be unceremoniously binned and anyone offering this up should be sacked on the spot and barred from the clubhouse until they've learnt their lesson. Mr Kipling can frankly eff off.

One of the judges argued persuasively for fruit cake, although the claim that it might represent one of your 'five-a-day' was perhaps a step too far, and may have cost the cake dear in the final reckoning. The Victoria sponge is an absolute classic and perhaps on a different day might have won through. Tough really, there was nothing more that old Vicky sponge could have done, she just came up against a more worthy opponent in the chocolate cake, which was presented as a glorious centrepiece that would draw the eyes of all and sundry as the tea was being laid out. The key advocate for the chocolate cake is actually an opening batter who suggested that she would arrange with the tea ladies (or, indeed, men) to have a slice of cake put aside if he was going to bat after the break. This raised all sorts of questions of etiquette and big-gun behaviour, with the upshot being an agreement that tea should be consumed without exception in the pavilion where it was served, and within the time constraints of the interval. So, no bananas taken to the dressing room for later, no plates put in the fridge, and no popping items in your pocket as you go out to field. Nonetheless, the chocolate cake came out a worthy winner. We also enjoyed the fact you can spot the guilty chocolate-cake-eaters by the tell-tale stains on their whites. What larks! And the fruit cake also sneaked through by the skin of its teeth.

Sweet Treats

This is where the fun really starts. But again, anything in a wrapper needs to be discarded out of hand. I don't mind a Penguin or a Kit Kat with a cup of tea at home after dinner, but putting them on the cricket tea table smacks of laziness (you've had a week to come up with an alternative, for goodness sake). Like the sausage butty, biscuits do have their place at the cricket, but only with your pre-match coffee. Don't try to pass them off as a genuine tea item. Three major front runners leapt forward in this category: the scone with jam and cream, the chocolate fridge-cake or 'Tiffin', and the flapjack. Rice-Krispie cakes were rejected as masquerading as Tiffin, and jam tarts (a particular favourite of mine) were not given a look-in. It's incredible, really, that the scones did not prevail, but I think it came down to the perennial argument over whether to put the jam on first (the Cornish method) or the clotted cream first (the Devon way). We didn't want tea causing a row and so we left the cream teas for your summer hols. There was nothing between the others, though, and we all wanted the Tiffin and the flapjack to fight it out in the quarters.

So, at this stage we had seven definites: egg sandwich, cheese and pickle sandwich, sausage rolls, chocolate cake, fruit cake, Tiffin, and flapjack.

Which meant we had to choose one of the following: Scotch egg, chips or fruit platter.

Although to my mind the balance of the overall tea had me leaning towards the savoury items, the panel felt that with sausage rolls already through, another sausage-based snack would be over the top so the Scotch egg faded away, and the clincher for the fruit platter was less that it represented a future-facing move and more that we felt that chips would be on offer during your extended cricket day ... alongside your kebab as you fell out of the pub at midnight. And so, against the odds, the fruit platter went through to the final eight.

This is how it played out:

Quarter Final	Semi-Final	Final	Winner
Egg Sandwich v Cheese and Pickle	Egg Sandwich		
	v	Egg Sandwich	
Fruit Platter v Sausage Roll	Sausage Roll		
		v	Flapjack
Chocolate Cake v Fruit Cake	Chocolate Cake		
	v	Flapjack	
Tiffin v Flapjack	Flapjack		

And just for good measure, we played a 'control' version with the items in a different draw, and again the egg sandwich and flapjack prevailed, giving us the incontrovertible conclusion that the flapjack is the champion tea item. I look forward to hearing your versions. Play nicely.

New York and the Banana Stab

Fun and games was not limited to on the field and cricket has long been synonymous with overindulgence (what more would you expect from a game which involves at least one meal and whose most famous protagonist was a portly bearded doctor from Bristol with a penchant for port and cheese?)

While not wishing to descend too far into tales of stag-do misbehaviour, I do feel that the 'Banana Stab' is worthy of a mention, as a tradition born out of necessity one happy post-match evening at Farnham CC.

'What is a Banana Stab?' I hear you cry. I will start from the presumption that all readers are familiar with the 'Suicide Tequila' or 'Tequila Stuntman', which involves snorting a line of salt, then drinking a shot of tequila before squirting a wedge of lemon into one's eye. Don't ask me why this is a thing, but I believe it is generally well-known. But on this particular evening, when it was generally decided that Suicide Tequilas would be a good idea, we found ourselves bereft of any lemon behind the bar. By some quirk of serendipity, there was a platter of fruit left over from tea, which included several halved bananas. One thing led to another, and not long after, I found myself with my top off at the bar next to our loose cannon of a fast bowler – Richie Norfolk (so-called because he came from Norfolk) – also topless, faced with the challenge of snorting the salt, drinking the tequila and then, rather than a lemon in the eye, it became *mano-a-mano* contest of who could stab the other in the eye with the banana.

What ensued was a chaotic half hour of head-to-head stab-offs with banana everywhere and drunk cricketers stumbling around with dripping noses and eyelids stuck together with exotic fruit. It became a hit and, I believe, is still played at least once a season at the club, showing greater longevity than the experimental combinations of the 'Gazoo' (Guinness and Yazoo chocolate milk) or the 'Pinness' (Pimm's and Guinness).

Quite by chance, my brother and I found ourselves with the opportunity to take the Banana Stab Stateside – our attempt to 'break America' like the Beatles – when we found ourselves in a margarita bar in the Meatpacking District on a holiday to New York. This bar prided itself on being pretty 'out there', with a female MC armed with a megaphone hauling people up to the bar to scull cans of beer to enthusiastic whooping and hollering and all-American high-fives. As lads brought up during the height of UK drinking culture in the late 1990s, Guy and I were pretty underwhelmed by the efforts we were witnessing, and fuelled with the cocksuredness which comes with being abroad and with a couple of cocktails inside us, called over the

MC and explained that we had a way of upping the ante, if she were up for it.

We described how the Banana Stab worked, and she looked at us aghast, saying that Health and Safety would never allow it, and anyway, they did not have any bananas. 'Fine,' I said, 'if I can source some bananas, would you let us demonstrate?'

'OK,' she agreed, reluctantly.

With this, I legged it out of the bar and found the nearest 7-11, which, improbably, but which I took as a sign, had a mountain of bananas on special offer in the very doorway. It was meant to be.

Returning to the bar clutching as many bananas as I could, I think my determination persuaded her to let me have the megaphone and I was given the floor to explain to the clientele how this ridiculous game worked. Of course, she had sold it as something which was a national tradition back in the UK, which was something of an exaggeration in that we had not managed to persuade anyone outside of Farnham to take part other than under duress at some stag do or other. So here I was, suddenly centre-stage, having to do my best – *Coyote Ugly*-style – to whip up a cynical crowd into taking on the challenge of the Banana Stab for the first time on American soil.

To begin with, it looked as if this would fall really flat as no hands were raised, but just as I was contemplating that this had all been a terrible idea, a cheer came up from one of the rowdier tables. A champion had been found!

Now, seeing the man who had been selected to be my adversary for this inaugural and groundbreaking event, I wished that I'd never even stepped into the bar that evening. Clad in a cut-off t-shirt which exposed a pair of enormous biceps, and wearing a stars-and-stripes bandana, sat the Goliath to my David – a fully-stacked Puerto Rican, weighing at least 200 pounds and easily my equal in height. Gulp.

To be fair, he did look a bit nonplussed and sheepish. He had clearly been pushed forward reluctantly, like the kid who has been told to confess to the teacher on behalf of his friends, but even so, I was already concerned for the potential state of my face if he had anything about him.

The long table was cleared and we sat face-to-face across from each other. This was my OK Corral, my *go-ahead-punk-make-my-day* moment. This was for transatlantic glory; the Ryder Cup; for good old Blighty; for Queen and Country. Hell, I could be a national hero if the press got wind of this.

The salt was lined evenly, and cut with credit cards as if we were both hardened cocaine addicts; we each rolled our dollar bills and placed our tequila shot and banana within easy grabbing distance, eyeballing each other with intent like two heavyweights, as the atmosphere gained in intensity. Vision tunnelling, pupils dilated and eyes narrowed to slits, we tremblingly awaited the countdown.

And then we were on. Heads to the table, snuffling like pigs after truffles, and I came up first and could tell he was struggling. Clasping the shot glass, I could sense he was in my sights and as the acrid spirit hit the back of my throat, the adrenaline of victory welled up inside of me. Experience would win out over brawn tonight. He had barely put the little glass to his lips before I was grabbing the back of his bullish neck with my left hand, banana poised for the *coup-de-grace*. I jammed the fruit into his eye, expecting it to disintegrate into mush like it always had in previous bouts. But now, at the moment of my finest triumph, disaster struck. The New York bananas were firmer than I had imagined, and rather than plunging into his eye socket, my weapon slid off the bridge of his nose, out of my grasp and went spinning down the end of the table, out of reach. I groped for it, but found my movement arrested as my head was clamped in front of his gleeful, grinning face. There was nothing to do but submit as the man-mountain smeared his banana, somewhat apologetically, all over my defenceless face.

'*Sorry, man,*' he offered, a total gentleman, who appeared more confused than triumphant.

'*No hard feelings,*' I replied (lying). We embraced, wiped our faces and joined their table for the rest of the night as dozens of the other drinkers bought us drinks and wanted to hear more of this crazy British tradition which was, surely, on the point of going global.

Hotel, Motel, Holiday Inn

It has been well documented that the treadmill of professional cricket can have an extremely detrimental effect on mental health. High-profile players such as Marcus Trescothick and Jonathan Trott have eloquently and heart-wrenchingly described the depression and crippling anxiety of professional life lived under intense scrutiny, often being away from home and family for weeks or months at a time. And for every Trott and Trescothick you can be sure there are dozens of lesser-known cricketers trying to make their way in the game, living life in the dead-eyed purgatory of England's arterial roads, surviving on service-station suppers and staring at the walls of countless faceless Hiltons, Holiday Inns or Best Westerns, with only the memory of their most recent failure for company.

And these days, this also comes hand-in-hand with attempting to find some shred of comfort and positivity to offer your Instagram followers. I shudder when I read the ubiquitous hashtag *#wegoagain*, which seems to say it all. Win, lose or draw, the professional's life seems to be one where it is always about the next day. No wonder the grind proves too much for some.

On the other hand, one of the joys of my cricket career (playing and watching) has been the opportunities it has afforded me to visit places I may otherwise never have seen.

But for cricket, I might never have been to the Caribbean, Sri Lanka, South Africa, Pakistan, Sweden, Croatia, and I have also developed a deeper affinity for the less-travelled corners of my own country, having played God's game anywhere from Penzance to Penrith. But the difference here is that an average summer for the likes of me would amount to around three weeks on the road, factoring in three three-day away matches, three or four away one-day matches, a tour of some kind and various MCC or representative games. And to be honest, a few days here and there away from work and the family can feel like a bit of a holiday. Take me away from my loved ones for weeks or months and it would be a different story.

This does come with a caveat. Resources are not extensive in the nether reaches of elite amateur cricket, and so the range of hotels I have stayed in in the name of cricket vary wildly. At the high end, if we were very lucky, we might find ourselves in a four-star hotel with pool, gym and even spa facilities. Some might be attached to a golf course, although the only chance you'd get to play would be if rain had stopped the cricket, which would mean less-than-ideal golfing weather, too. This sort of luxury stay was as rare as hen's teeth. More often, we would stay in a generic chain hotel: a Hilton, a Travelodge, which were comfortable enough, but offered little other than a Hungry Horse or Beefeater-style restaurant attached and likely the gentle murmur of the motorway to lull you to sleep. It's hard to get excited about this type of home from home, although you could be almost guaranteed that there would be a wedding taking place on the Saturday night, and we would regularly arrive after a long drive from whatever league match we had been playing in to pass groups of short-skirted girls, addled on Blue WKD and smoking in a group on our way to check in, whilst a staggering second cousin of the bride would collar you to inform you that either a: he hated cricket and it was the most f***ing boring game the world had ever created, or b: he was a pretty fast bowler and if we needed any help, he'd be happy to step in. Either way, running the Saturday wedding gauntlet was a pretty common occurrence.

There were times when after a long day's cricket and travel, you quite fancied a beer or two and there were times when a hardcore of the team would join in the nuptial festivities. I reckon we may have taken this one step too far during a game against Cornwall at Penzance, when Cowley produced, from under his pads on day one, the top tier of the previous night's wedding cake, complete with icing bride and groom, which we then wagered our young twelfth man – Dan 'Battler' Britton – to try and eat within ten minutes at the end of the day's play. If the happy couple are reading this, years on, I apologise on behalf of the team.

And then there is the other type of accommodation: the independently-run hotels and guest houses which still retain an element of local charm and character, and which tend to throw up the best stories, too. These establishments are often found in the more out-of-the-way backwaters – lands which time forgot, in places many people have never heard of. To give you a flavour of the Minor Counties landscape, here is a list of some of the places I have played, in no particular order. See how many you recognise (and bonus points for naming which county they are found in): Trowbridge, Truro, Abergavenny, March, Benwell Hill, Challow and Childrey, Neston, Whitchurch, Kendal, Shifnal, Weymouth, Budleigh Salterton, St Just, St Fagan's, Eastnor, Abergavenny, Devizes, Nantwich, Sevenoaks, Tring, Thame and Brockhampton, to name but a few.

Talking of Brockhampton, this is a great case in point, where the hotel we stayed in – in deepest, darkest Herefordshire – had the look and feel of *Fawlty Towers*. You would be welcomed at reception by a portrait of the Queen, circa-1970, by the landlord or lady, who would also be running the bar, serving the meals and who would also be cleaning your room the next day, replacing the antiquated shower cap and impossible-to-open bar of soap. On a moral note, I'm sure we could solve the world's ecological crisis if we stopped bed and breakfasts from providing single-use coffee creamer sachets. Every room in this particular hotel came with a set of stag's antlers as standard, and there was high emotion when our scorer – Christine – came into the hotel bar shrieking and waving a long piece of tubing with two attachments which would convert the bath taps into a shower of sorts. If any of us wanted a shower during the week, we had to pass the tubing on, as it was the only one the hotel owned.

This sort of shambles was not uncommon, but did seem to bring out the worst in the team, as we could essentially take over a hotel (and frequently did).

In full flow for Dorset in the Minor County Championship Final against Cumberland, Netherfield, 1999. We lost this one but got our revenge a year later, although I was dropped for the final.

Darren Cowley and I shared many years, beers and good times for Dorset CCC. One of the best players and blokes you will meet. I was very proud to be his best man

Jos Buttler hit the best shot I've witnessed off my bowling in a T20 for Somerset against Dorset. Another annoyingly nice guy.

Max Waller in Somerset action but he also played a decent amount for Dorset. An amazing fielder, he couldn't believe none of us were getting paid

Jack Leach won the Minor Counties championship with Dorset under my captaincy in 2010 before becoming an Ashes cult hero

Tossing up with Keith Parsons at Lord's in 2012 for MCC v Minor Counties. Not a bad home ground

MCC v Minor Counties: Lord's, 2012. Batting under the gaze of the famous Media Centre and wishing it was a Test match

The fastest I faced? Not quite, but Simon Jones was a handful off 19 yards in the nets.

Farnham Park. What I would consider my home club. Rural England at its finest

My final game as captain of Farnham CC. A special picture with my mum one side, my wife the other, and my brother on my right

THE COOPER DEAN PAVILIO

With the family after my last game for Dorset, at Dean Park nine years after popping the question. I was proud to be made a life member after an 18-year career for the Leopards

It was handy having the Curran brothers to net with at Wellington College.
Their dad would be proud of their success

I met Allan Lamb as a close friend of
the Currans. One dinner with him was
possibly the best night of my cricketing life

Lara and Walsh: two legends of the
West Indies whom I met in differing
circumstances

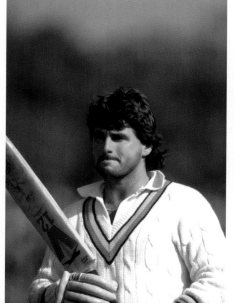

Henry Olonga: a man of immense moral courage, but not a fan of fig tart

With Graeme Swann in the Long Room, Lord's, 2018. What I would have given for his cricket career!

Chapter Sixteen

Who's the Fastest?

WHEN THE majority of your non-cricketing friends know you have come up against some household names, this is one of the first questions you get asked. For many years, my answer remained the same. I had the (mis)fortune to be in the same school year group as Simon Jones – the so-called 'racehorse' from Glamorgan, who became a national hero as part of the pace attack which wrested back the Ashes from Australia in that glorious summer of 2005. With Wales being classed as a West of England county for the purposes of regional trials, it meant I came across Jonesy annually in county matches, but more significantly in the indoor winter nets, where he was blisteringly quick, and nasty with it.

The indoor school at Taunton was notorious for being hard and fast, and Jones was notorious for being quite prepared to inflict physical damage. It was not that he was a bad bloke, far from it, but with a red cherry in his hand, the bloodlust was in him. The story goes that in one school match on a pudding wicket, he gave up trying to bounce out the determined opener for Sherborne School – my old pal Charlie Warren again – and took the pitch out of the equation with a deliberate beamer. He had also bent the grille of John Claughton – one-time England age-group captain and later my predecessor as Oxford University skipper. Also, like every single seamer I have ever netted against, he was quite prepared to ignore the front-foot no-ball rule, so making the pitch effectively 18, rather than 22 yards, and in the nets there was no prospect of nicking a single and getting down the other end. At least I didn't have to face him weekly at school, like my mates from Millfield. Not that being his team-mate mattered that much; it was rarely in your half.

Coward that I am, I did have one escape plan up my sleeve to keep out of the way of these illegal Exocets. You see, Jonesy, like me, was something of a lower-middle-order batsman, and the way indoor nets traditionally work is that the openers go in first and then it tends to follow in something like batting order with the tailenders having a swish against the non-bowlers towards the end. Anyone who has pitched up for club nets will attest to this universal law of cricket. So at Taunton, I just kept an eye on when the coaches tipped him a wink to pad up and made damned sure I was in their eyeline ready for a hit. In this way, I did, for the most part, manage to do a fair bit of batting alongside him, obviously encouraging him along from the next net (*'shot, Jonesy!' 'sounds like you're in great nick, fella'*) in the hope he'd be lenient if the next round of nets saw me in his sights. I would wager I am not the first or last bloke to do this, but it's not my proudest confession.

However, I could run, but eventually I ran out of hiding spaces as far as Jones was concerned and it was with Warren again that I found myself opening up the innings on a quicker-than-usual deck in an under-16 game in Jersey for Dorset against Wales. Bear in mind, now, that whilst Jonesy will be forever known for his injuries as well as his reverse swing, at this age he was already pretty much fully-grown and his body was working well. It certainly felt that way when we both copped a barrage of bruises, but in a funny way it was enjoyable because

Charlie and I just spent our time laughing at each other getting hit and then laughing more when we sneaked up the other end from a nick or a leg-bye. We even won the match, so it can't have been too bad.

I faced Simon a final time in a first-class game in the Parks. I remember saying a brief hello over coffee before the game and thought that as something of an old acquaintance, I might get some more gentle stuff if I ended up in the wrong place (i.e. batting) again. As usual, we were getting a hiding and the ball was probably no more than 30 or so overs old when I strode to the crease trying to look up for the battle. Jonesy gave me a wink on the way in, which confused me, but which I rightly understood as probably not an encouraging omen.

The thing about Jones is that his approach to the crease was actually pretty slow – he sort of trotted in and then gathered all his energy into the delivery stride before release. When he did let go of it, all I saw was a dark blur somewhere around the middle of the pitch. I was already ducking and turned to see the ball slap into the keeper's gloves above his head. 'The Horse' was still smiling and had not moved an inch back to his mark. It was good-humoured, but I did have to check my trousers to ensure I had not given up my dignity. I did that an over later at the other end, capitulating meekly to Dean Cosker's left-arm spin before telling all the lads how I had been really up for it and how annoying it was to misjudge what was basically a slow, straight ball. All I felt was relief (shame barely entered the equation).

My courage (or lack of it) also came into play when I was fortunate enough to come up against one of the most fearsome Test fast bowlers of recent times – Mr 'White Lightning', Allan Donald himself. Donald was playing for Warwickshire against the boffins of Oxford University as part of a team which boasted no less than nine international players. Quite a challenge to take on in between tutorials and essays, one might say.

As was the accepted tradition, the county pros got first bat on what was actually one of the more lively Parks pitches (thanks for that, Groundie), and after having racked up 356/5 thanks to a hundred from Trevor Penney (Hicks a toothless 0-54 from 13), we were given seven overs to negotiate before the close of play. It was a beautiful sight to behold a master at work as the familiar, jaguar-like litheness of the finely-tuned athlete ran in from the Pavilion End and made 80+ mph look as easy as rolling a hoop down a hill. In fact, it was such a beautiful sight that, as captain, I elected not to strap on the pads as nightwatchman, as had often been my role, but to keep my vital wicket intact for the next day. It was not for lack of opportunity, as we managed to lose three before stumps, with Donald picking up two for no runs and Ed Giddins, being no less threatening with pace and swing from the other end, bagging the other. A score of 10/3 was not looking too clever as we warmed down in the usual way with a courtesy jog and stretch followed by a wander down to the King's Arms for a sportsman's supper.

The majority of the Warwickshire side were there and in good form, too. I was delighted to share a Benson and Hedges with Ashley Giles and have a chat to Neil Smith, who seemed a thoroughly good bloke as we discussed whether there was some potential for some later night refreshment for his troops. A few of us students (led by the three men out who had all earned their golden tickets) felt it would be remiss of us not to escort one of South Africa's finest sportsmen to one of Oxford's finest establishments, and so we headed to the Park End club. Although at first perturbed by the £5 (*'that's 50 Rand, China!'*) cover charge for the entry to what was a student night, the Dutchman (as he was ubiquitously known) happily joined in with the party, safe in the knowledge that some cheap first-class wickets would be coming his way in the morning.

Alas for him, and mercifully for me and the rest of the tail (truth be told, we were mostly tail on that occasion) it was actually snowing when we left the club, and continued to do so for the rest of the next day, leading to the match being abandoned, and although he might not admit it, I think Neil Smith would acknowledge we were good for the draw. Honours even, then.

I actually thought that Simon Jones would always be my answer to the question of who was the quickest I'd faced, but in one of my last appearances for Dorset, I think he was pipped. In recent years, there has developed a pretty good working relationship between the Minor Counties and the major professional counties, with young players getting game time with the minors and young talent from minors being pushed into academies in a pretty clear development pathway. With ECB funding being offered to Minor Counties based on age restrictions, and a three-day rather than two-day format, it has become less the backwater for washed-up old pros fancying a few bob and a bit of hit-and-giggle, and more a development ground. For me, at least, it is a valuable part of the amateur pyramid between Premier League and second-team cricket. It would be a huge shame were we to lose it.

One spin-off from the professional/amateur relationship was an annual Twenty20 match before the T20 Blast, which would give the pros a chance to practise and the amateurs a money-spinning event and a chance for players to pit their wits against full-timers in coloured kit.

My final T20 of this ilk was against Hampshire in a match which for me had a nice sort of ring given that it was the place where my father had first taken me to the cricket and was also where I proposed to my wife; a good place to wind up my own little cricket career.

Although it was May, it was overcast and a bit chilly with a chance of rain. Nonetheless, we took the field against the likes of James Adams, James Vince, Michael Carberry, Sean Ervine and, recently arrived from Barbados, Fidel Edwards.

Now, Fidel Edwards has been clocked at 95mph. Which is fast in anyone's language. Yes, he is small – 5ft 5in – and he may have been jetlagged, and it was cold, but let me tell you, he can still let it go.

Once again, as underdogs, we fielded first and made a reasonable account of ourselves. When you get these mismatches, it is definitely with the bat where the gulf in class tells – batsmen only get that one chance and so you can get skittled cheaply, whilst with a modicum of skill and control, some good fielding and luck, as a fielding unit you can stay in the game. And in fact, our opening batsmen also did OK and we were looking like following their 167 with a 100+ total ourselves, which would not be too embarrassing.

Having passed up the chance years ago to take on Donald, I think I had developed a bit more backbone in my cricketing dotage and was quite up for having a crack in what might be my last bat at this sort of level, and so I cajoled the skipper into letting me strap them on and have a hit in front of a decent crowd, including Dad, as usual, and my uncle, as a misty drizzle started to fall.

What ensued goes down for them as one of the funniest sights on a cricket pitch.

I got away well, knocking Danny Briggs's left-arm spin into the leg side for three – *nice start, good strike rate, happy days*. But it did mean I had kept the strike. And Fidel was making his way in from the boundary. Or was he? He walked in about ten yards and then stopped, at which point I realised that he was actually at the end of his mark. A mark which would have been well outside the boundary on many club pitches. In fact, had it been at Farnham, Edwards would have been setting off from behind the ladies' loos.

Now, it is worth bearing in mind my preparation for this knock, which had been two weeks of teaching English, a bowl against some fifth-formers in the net the previous Tuesday and a handful of throwdowns from the coach on the morning of the match. So when this West Indian Test ace steamed in and assumed his Jeff Thomson-like pose at the point of release, I entered an odd, zen-like state, which I imagine is how you feel when faced with certain death. I had time to assess the reality of what I was actually doing: an out-of-practice teacher just metres away from five-and-a-half ounces of rock, on a skiddy surface in the hands of a trained professional. I was actually going to die. I can even remember the thought process which followed, which was all the right things a coach would say – watch the ball, get in line, if it's short, look to pull (I found that having been hit a few times shaping to hook meant I kept my eyes on the ball better). And I basically gambled that it would be very short, or very full, so I triggered right back on my stumps to give me as much time as possible and waited.

It was short. I saw it, and shaped to hook, as planned. But by the time I was in position to dispatch it confidently over midwicket, the ball was not where it usually was (i.e. four metres away) but was a lot closer than that, and getting closer. It appeared the hook shot was not on after all. Nothing for it then, but to let self-preservation take over and hit the deck. Observed by perhaps the biggest crowd I'd played in front of, certainly at home, I was on my backside in the damp mud, but actually able to laugh. And Edwards was laughing too, as was my dad. Thanks for the sympathy.

All well and good, but that was only the first ball of the over and I had to find a new plan for ball two. This time, he went full, and I managed to get my bat down and smash him for four … right off the inside edge past the keeper. OK, bowler and batsman still laughing, and my strike rate is now seven from three balls. Not bad at all.

Next ball: also full, also quick, but a bit wayward and on to my pads. Too quick, obviously, to hit, but as it whizzed off again to the fine-leg boundary I saw the umpire mistakenly signalling four runs. Outstanding. Four buckshee runs to take me to double figures off four balls. At this point apparently some of my friends were going crazy watching me on Twitter as I 'battered' one of the quickest bowlers ever around the park. And they say, the scorecard never lies.

The fourth ball of the over was a genuine bad ball – short and wide – and of course, I missed it. But by this stage it was dark and getting wetter and the right call was made for us to leave the field. I was welcomed into the pavilion with not quite a hero's return, but more laughter and a tale to tell. Plus, a steady strike rate and red ink. I count that one as a win, and yes, I do reckon he had the edge over Jonesy. Just.

'Hit Him in the Neck'

Although Fidel was fast, I emerged with my body intact, even if my dignity suffered a bit of a blow. There have been times, though, when I have taken one on the lid, and for the uninitiated, let me try to give you a flavour of what that feels like.

Generally, if you are in decent nick, you watch the ball closely and on very rare occasions I remember being able to see the maker's mark on the ball as I nonchalantly swayed away from a bouncer. More often, however, I found myself in less attentive form and this is when problems can arise. I had also developed a bit of a backward trigger movement – rather than getting in line with the ball, I was just edging to the leg side and this actually makes it harder to evade the ball when it comes after you. Too often, instinct tells you to turn away from the ball, and this is exactly the worst thing you can do.

Once you have lost visual contact with the projectile, you are essentially hoping that physics conspires in your favour. Time seems to dilate as you recognise the sheer folly of what you have done and there can appear an elongated pause as you await the worst. It is exactly like when you play and miss at a straight one – the ball seems to take an age before you hear the dreaded death rattle of your stumps being demolished. In the case of a bouncer the result is much less comfortable. After the time lag, if you are hit, in my experience it is the noise which comes first. A sort of tinny clang, followed by the realisation of a serious cranial blow which can send a shock wave through your head and down the nervous system. At worst, your legs give way immediately as the nausea takes hold of the pit of your stomach. There have been times when I genuinely have seen stars – a sort of flash of white light followed by a spectral light-play before the eyes.

Following the initial stunned effect, the brain does something of a rapid scan, *Yes, I am alive, yes, that hurt, can I see? Can I stand up? What the hell do I do next?*

It is a good question, because now you have to accept that, unlike being bowled, the chances are you will have to deal with the cause of all this discombobulation in the next minute or so, as the bowler resumes his assault. You could take the coward's way out, wave the white feather and suffer the ignominy of being entered as 'Retired Hurt' in the scorebook, but no cricketer worth his salt would do this unless in the direst of circumstances. Imagine how the next bloke would feel, entering the fray after his mate has just copped one on the bonce. No, there is an etiquette here, so unless you are literally out cold, you get up, take guard and pretend all is OK.

During your time coming to terms with what might have been a mortal blow (and post-Phillip Hughes this is no exaggeration) the opposition players will largely be pretty sympathetic. There but for the grace of God, and all that. But once you have indicated you are ready and willing to face the music again, the tone will, without fail, turn back to *sotto voce* sledges and a questioning of your manhood from the cordon.

Worst of all, you are now in a position where you really can't get out, as it will be assumed by all and sundry on both sides that you indeed are yellow-bellied and couldn't vacate the crease fast enough. Even if you do get bowled a genuine 'top knacker', you will be at fault for not gritting it out. Oh joy.

I am told there are players who love facing the quicks. The faster, the better, with all the adrenaline pumping. I am not one of those players.

Not that this ever stopped me from trying to wind up our own fast bowlers to deliver some 'chin music' and from offering helpful technical advice to a struggling opposition batsman from first slip. It's an easy game from there.

I do have a scar behind my right ear from being 'sconed' in a first-class game. We were facing Hampshire at the Parks in the early season. In fact, it was so early in April that at the drinks break the twelfth man emerged with a teapot and mugs, rather than squash, and at one point I had to indicate to the skipper that it was actually snowing on me at third man. So it was chilly, but I had somehow managed to burgle a few runs, probably mostly off the edge, and was in danger of looking like an all-rounder when John Stephenson was brought on to bowl.

'Stan' as he is known, on account of his resemblance to Stan Laurel, is definitely a batsman who bowls (indeed, I once saw him open the batting in an Ashes Test), he loves a short ball, and is not especially fast. As such, he would be a good target for what my Dorset team-mates later christened the 'predict-a-pull' – the try-to-smash-anything-remotely-short-over-midwicket shot which was one of my few boundary options.

So in came Stan, and banged it in very short. I obliged by effectively pirouetting on my left foot, swinging so hard that my head was facing the umpire by the time the ball arrived. I told you Stan was military medium, and I had actually got so far through the shot that I was clobbered on the back of the head and tumbled over, dribbling claret in the bowler's footmarks. Stan was so delighted that he insisted on buying me drinks all night as I was the first bloke he had ever floored with the ball. In hindsight, vodka Red Bulls all night was probably not the best response to a potential concussion, but I had my highest first-class score and was still not out – skill and a ticker to match. Well, almost.

I have since got to know John pretty well in his role as head of cricket at the MCC, and his daughters were tutored at school by my dad. He never fails to bring up how he beat me for pace (not true), and when we have played for MCC against some schools, I do chuckle when he tries to repeat the trick. He should know better, at his age.

Although the MCC became a big part of my cricket career later on, whilst I still harboured ambitions of making it on the professional circuit, the MCC remained something of an enigma (which I am sure is true still for many today). At school, we were always told they were the best side we would play, which was sort of true, despite the fact that actually they always seemed to be a load of paunchy, pompous middle-aged has-beens, with two players good enough to outclass us. I realise that now this probably remains the case, and the fact I have captained MCC on many occasions only serves to reinforce the demographic.

We also played a three-day game against MCC for Oxford, an entitled fixture if ever there was one. I only mention it as it was another occasion in which I succumbed to a sickening blow. This time I got it in the neck, and not metaphorically.

One of our players who was gunning for a Blue – Graham 'Butch' (obviously) Butcher – batted like a hero for half a day, scoring 99 on a worn pitch against a line-up including Pakistan leg-spinner Iqbal Sikander and a properly burly Australian paceman called Joe Dawes, who ended up playing for Middlesex. Dawes it was who dismissed the gritty Butcher after a lot of toil in the middle of a hot three days (probably exacerbated by the visitors' choice of rehydration material), opting to come around the wicket and adopt effectively bodyline tactics. Fair enough. Butch had been hard to dislodge and with an old ball, Dawes gets credit for running in hard. What I take issue with, though, is that he continued to stay around the wicket for the new man. One T.C. Hicks.

He was also one of those quicks who push off the sightscreen, so you have plenty of time to consider exactly where you are about to sustain a flesh wound as he runs in. Sure enough, Dawes opted for the more Australian version of the spirit of cricket, and went halfway down for my first ball. I opted to duck, and got as low as possible, watching the ball land and bounce harmlessly over my head as I breathed a sigh of relief. Next ball, and the big Queenslander bangs it in again. Again I duck, watching the ball from my hunched position, only this time I see the ball hit a crack and, rather than ping off the surface, flatten its trajectory and head straight for my jugular. If the sound of leather on helmet is a shock, the dull sound of Dukes on neck sinew is something else altogether. Once again, I found myself prone on the Parks popping crease contemplating whether this really was a better option than that punting trip my college mates were enjoying. You can imagine how sympathetic Dawes was, and given that there was little incentive to battle this one out (i.e. no first-class average to consider, no competition to win), I rather tamely gave up the ghost to a Sikander wrong 'un at the other end. I wonder how many spinners benefit from bowling the other end to someone with a 'bit of wheels'.

Seeing it Early

Farnham CC's greatest son (if you exclude 'Silver' Billy Beldham, who was big news between 1780 and 1810, and who was named in former *Times* correspondent John Woodcock's 100 greatest cricketers), is indisputably Graham Thorpe. Farnham is synonymous with the Thorpe family: mum Toni has scored for decades and, whilst only around 5ft on tiptoes, has the character of an Amazon and you can be sure all the players at the club were scared of Mrs Thorpe – something she relishes. Father Geoffrey – erstwhile club chairman – was renowned on the circuit as an umpire and general commentator on the game. Whilst Geoff's views are most often articulated in frank Anglo-Saxon, and might not pass the political-correctness test of more liberal listeners, you could be in no doubt as to his loyalties, and he would be first to buy you a beer if you'd done well, and first to tear a strip off the team if you'd played poorly. The hours these two put into the club put many others to shame.

Toni and Geoff brought up a trio of boys, and you can be certain that the Thorpe household when Ian, Alan and Graham were growing up would have been no place for the faint-hearted. Ian was captain of the first team when I started at the club, and remained second-team captain for many years afterwards, keeping the club together during some difficult times, and always looking to bring through youngsters. Much like his old man, his team-talks were not known for their finesse, and the young players he was nurturing received a real education in the ways of the world, with opposition players reduced to 'that f****ing p****', and 'that bunch of c****', and tactics kept simple: 'let's just beat the f***ing c***s'. But it seemed to work, and many loved playing under Ian's tutelage.

Alan – the middle brother – had a little more refinement about him, both as a player and character. Alan was still unstinting in his choice of vocabulary, and could seriously lose his rag when he was out, but generally showed more humour on matchdays. He was certainly a class player and unlucky not to have played professional cricket. His body was probably the reason he didn't – by the end of his career it took a whole week for him to walk properly after a match and his back, knees and shoulder seemed to be held together with tape. He wore his younger brother's St George and Dragon England touring helmet and yet he was good enough to carry it off without being sledged for it.

However, no matter how good Alan was, he recognised that it was his younger brother who was the real talent in the family. He recounted to me about a time when he was playing with Graham against a chap called Tony Murphy, who was renowned in Surrey as being slippery. Alan had been ducking and weaving, and wearing a few when his little brother joined him at the crease. The story goes that Graham – only 15, mind – swayed out of the way of the first bumper he received and then clobbered the next one well in front of square, over midwicket for six. As the Thorpe brothers met mid-pitch to review what had just happened, Alan asked, 'When did you pick that up?' To which Graham replied, 'When he was about here,' (indicating the moment the bowler's arm was raised above his head, well before releasing the ball). At which point Alan said he knew that his brother was going to be something special, which he proved with an Ashes century in his first Test, and a long, successful England career during a low period for English cricket.

I don't doubt a word of this story. Sports scientists now know that the top players pick up cues from bowlers so early that it explains why they seem to have so much more time than mere mortals. They actually do. I learnt of an experiment which was done in which a ball was bowled from a machine and then the lights turned out on the point of delivery. Despite being totally in the dark, the top professionals still managed to middle the ball and could gauge the flight and pace through instinct and experience alone, whilst amateurs struggled as they relied too much on their eyes to track the ball.[15]

I thought it a shame that we didn't see much of Graham at Farnham. It would have been a great boost to know he was supporting the club, but that's by-the-by. I did sit next to him during one club annual dinner, and had the awkward experience of explaining that the wine on the table was not on the house but had been bought courtesy of my student loan. On the plus side, I do still have a book signed by him; it just happens to be David Shepherd's autobiography (won in the raffle), which adds a little idiosyncrasy to my cricket library, I suppose.

Pakistan Pace

Regardless of how many times one is hit on the head, or body, and never mind how much you know it hurts, there remains little funnier in the game of cricket than watching your mate take a barrage from an angry fast bowler. I don't know if it is *schadenfreude*, or the laughter of relief that every ball someone else faces is one less chance for you to be killed yourself, but I defy any cricketer to say otherwise. It is the equivalent of the referee being knocked over by a football; it tends to elicit giggles all round when someone else finds themselves at sixes and sevens dealing with the short ball. Even better if they are the one who is the gobbiest in the field.

I could give countless examples of this, but one I especially love is a second-hand story from the NatWest Trophy days when Dorset were drawn to play Surrey at the Oval, at the

---

15 You can read in minute scientific detail about how this works here: https://www.nature.com/articles/nn1200_1340?proof=true

time when Waqar Younis was at the peak of his powers. Those who remember the days when reverse swing first entered the cricket lexicon will remember the aura around Waqar and Wasim Akram when they were able to make the ball 'talk', producing hitherto unheard of late inswing with the shiny side held the other way to orthodox. It was as if there was some sort of shamanistic black magic at work, and the press and the public were in uproar about the fact that these two pace geniuses might have been cheating, with allegations of bottle tops and all sorts of other slander on the back pages for much of the summer. What was never in dispute was their pace, and it was this which the motley crew from Hardy country were to take on in their big day against the big boys.

Of course Dorset struggled, but Waqar had failed to make any inroads into the top order in a wicketless first spell, and was quietly minding his own business, presumably wondering what on earth he was doing against this rabble, when the few hundred West Countrymen who had gone along to support started aiming a few comments in his direction. By this time a few ciders to the wind, it became clear that the visiting faithful were not attempting to abuse or antagonise Waqar, rather they realised that their big mate and Dorset CCC legend – Dorchester policeman Sean Walbridge – was next man in. Although there may have been something of a language barrier, the crowd were able to convey enough to suggest that Walbridge had commented that Waqar 'looked slower than on telly', 'didn't seem to be swinging it off the straight' and that he would 'probably take him to the cleaners'. Of course, Walbridge had said none of this. Equally, a zero in the wickets column would not go down well for a Test legend against these yokels and, as fortune (not Walbridge's) would have it, when the wicket fell, Waqar was recalled to see off the tail.

Just in case the message had not got through, as Walbridge took to the crease, his 'supporters' struck up a chorus of 'Who are ya?' and the ever-droll outburst at the sight of a renowned player: 'Bowler's name?' This, incidentally, is the second least funny line in cricket, just pipped by the 'Owzaaaat' yelled from a passing car at the side of every cricket ground in the world, every Saturday ever.

Safe to say, Walbridge – a future Dorset manager, top bloke and best Alan Green impersonator of the Western Hemisphere – did not last long, but recalls the event with typical self-deprecating humour. Well, he's still alive, isn't he?

The Pakistan pace theme continues on a rather tangential angle now with my wife, Penny. She was a batter of remarkable technique: a top elbow higher than Trumper, and a long barrier sounder than the MCC manual. However, being a lithesome young lass, her power was perhaps less than desired, and this meant that at the time of our courting, she had never once officially registered a boundary. I took the opportunity to question her about this on what must have been something of a memorable date, 'Seriously, you've never hit a four?'

'No.'

'I mean, you've never actually hit the ball over the boundary, off your bat, for a four?'

'No.'

'Seriously?'

'No.'

'But, seriously?'

'No.'

'Not ever hit the ball over the rope, or over the line, or past the little flags with the little eights on them?'

'No.'

'Little white blocks of wood stuck into the ground by a spike? Sawn-up pieces of white guttering?'

'No.' (you get the picture).

Something had to be done. I had actually travelled to Cambridge to watch her and her culotted pals (unsurprisingly traditional, the Oxbridge girls) take on the old enemy on one of the college grounds and witnessed her grind out a match-winning fifty. However, the boundary was never in any real danger as she racked up a series of twos and threes, looking every inch a Rachael Heyhoe Flint fantasy.

We tried again on one of the very few occasions we took the field together, in a friendly Lord-of-the-manor-versus-the-locals type game near her parents' home in Wadhurst, East Sussex. Trying to endear myself to the in-laws, I opted for a steady innings against some rather friendly offerings, picking off boundaries only when the ball was a genuine rank full toss or long hop (unlike my brother who set about attempting to break as many neighbouring windows as he could, whilst curtailing the bowls match over the hedge for the duration of our innings as sixes rained down on scattering pensioners). However, what I took for gentle medium pace was perceived through the eyes of my other half as something akin to Malcolm Marshall bearing down. The chap in question is still talked about in hushed tones chez nous as 'Headband Man'. I suspect he is some property developer or antiques dealer in the Weald of Kent, but he moonlights in the batting nightmares of my beloved, and having notched a couple of twos through the covers, Penny meekly offered up her wicket to this Spofforth-esque demon, leaving her career record of boundary scoring still in zero figures.

Until, that is, she befriended a man who could make the seemingly impossible a reality. England national selector Ed Smith, no less. An influential writer and broadcaster, Ed was also no mean player in his day and probably can count himself unlucky not to have played more than the three Tests he was granted after years of churning them out gracefully for Kent and Middlesex. What is more, as part of the Kent squad in the early 2000s, he was team-mates with one Mohammad Sami, one of the sharpest bowlers in the world.

Ed was living with Alex Loudon (to whom, incidentally, my brother claims to have taught the 'doosra' when they were housemates in Durham – a skill which saw him selected for a tour of the subcontinent with England). The two of them heard of Penny's plight and managed to cajole her down to the St Lawrence Ground in Canterbury to be kitted up with all manner of high-density foam padding and taken out to the middle for a few balls against Sami. The idea was that Sami would start off bowling off-side wides then bring the line in until Penny could dab her bat at the ball, find an edge and watch the ball race gloriously into the advertising boards at third man.

The plan worked. A confused but game Sami took whatever bribe he had been paid to pitch up and bowl at this equally confused young lady, and between them, they contrived to give Penny the experience of hitting a Test player for four. OK, not in a match per se, but there can be few women out there who can claim a similar feat.

Taking it for the Team on a Rugby Pitch

Quiz question: who was once described as, 'The only known example of a rat joining a sinking ship'? Cricket aficionados will no doubt have jumped to the correct answer of poor Martin McCague – the naturalised Aussie-turned-Englishman who was picked – controversially ahead of Angus Fraser – to join a rather ill-fated tour Down Under in 1994/95 having been the top England-qualified seamer in the County Championship averages that year (just behind Courtney Walsh and Curtly Ambrose, who must have been something of a challenge on English green-tops in April). But who would also know that

McCague's later career included a short stint for Herefordshire in the Western Division of the Minor Counties Championship?

Not exactly known as a cricketing hotbed, Herefordshire is a thinly populated, picturesque farming county on the Welsh border, and home to such metropolises as Ross-on-Wye and Hereford. But it was to the town of Leominster (two syllables, not three or four, incidentally) that Dorset travelled in 2002, and where I witnessed probably the best spells of bowling in my career. Sadly for McCague, these came courtesy of Kevin Cooper, late of Nottinghamshire, who took 13 of our wickets in the space of five sessions on two damp and horrible days at the rugby ground of Luctonians.

It was quite an incredible match, actually. We had arrived on the Saturday, and, with the slightest hint of some moisture in the air, had sought out whatever meagre nightlife there was in this rather lonely outpost. It appeared that the home team had come with similar intentions. In that year, Herefordshire seemed to have found an extra slush fund and had acquired the services of several ex-pros – Cooper, McCague, Ismail Dawood of Yorkshire and Glamorgan – and no doubt others were on the payroll, and doing their best to bolster the local economy by putting a few away in the dingiest of loft bars in town. I can't speak for anyone else in my company that evening, but I reckon I was put off my stride by seeing this man-mountain at the bar, who was likely to cause me actual physical pain the next day – he had been picked for England on account of his raw speed, let's not forget, and frankly, that was more worrying for me than anyone who might actually get me out.

In the morning, players arrived in dribs and drabs under drizzly skies and quickly settled into the normal rain routine of idle chat, coffee, cards and changing-room cricket before the entirely predictable early lunch was called by the umpires. Eventually, play did get under way, and we had the dubious privilege of batting first on an awful pitch, not helped by the fact the square goes on almost as far as the eye can see across acres of prime rugby territory. Atmosphere there was none.

Cooper was devastating. No more than just a shade above medium, he swung the ball away late and then would nip it back off the seam in conditions which, had they been any more friendly, would have required a restraining order. We mustered a measly 129 all out.

However, it was doing plenty, and our seamers – Matt Mixer, a left-arm policeman from Poole and Joey Wilson, a Scouser who bowled non-stop, keeper-up, landing it without fail on a proverbial sixpence – took advantage, reducing our hosts to five down overnight. The game was certainly moving forward. No thanks, you will notice, to yours truly, whose loopy off-spin was unlikely to be the best option (was it ever?) in the circumstances.

A further rather late night meant that it was paramount we picked up quick wickets so I could get some shut-eye in the pavilion. We duly did and scores in the first innings were level at 129 apiece. Proper cricket, indeed.

The pitch had not improved one iota from the day before and Cooper was no less a handful. He still had the ball on a string and McCague, who had clearly got over his hangover and was steaming in from around the wicket, made the pitch look incredibly short. Again, I found myself in a Joe Dawes situation – big, burly Aussie opting to stay around the wicket, i.e. the bodyline angle – against me, pathetic but gobby off-spinner/student/first slip. Hell, even I would have wanted to hit me in the head.

I did manage to last over an hour on this occasion, but 13 runs to my name was not exactly taking the game beyond them. When we finally all departed, we had set them only 76 to win. It was always going to be hard to repeat the trick and the greater experience and obvious ability of Herefordshire saw them home pretty easily.

With the game over before stumps on the second day of an allotted three, we got a deserved ticking off from the management. However, there is usually a silver lining to these occasions, in the form of an extra night in the hotel which has already been paid for, with a bit of beer money and expenses in the old brown envelope. It tells you something about Leominster that this was the first, and last, time an entire Dorset side passed up the chance of a paid-for piss-up away from home and all scarpered back down south without sparing the horses. I have not been back to Leominster since, and don't plan to soon.

The Strangest of Places

There are always those names which go around the circuit, especially where raw pace is concerned, and one name which was synonymous with sheer, unadulterated speed and its unsettling second cousin – a wonky radar – was Andre van Troost. Anyone who played cricket in the West Country during the 1990s would know 'Rooster', a Dutchman who would have been a real candidate for international cricket had he been able to control his thunderbolts. As it was, he ended up mainly playing second-team cricket for Somerset (until he went back to university, where he wound up bowling at my best mate, Tom Caines, in the indoor nets: something about which I could barely conceal my mirth).

Rooster was on the team-sheet for a tour game in which my dad was going to play at the beautiful ground of North Perrott, near Yeovil, which was famed as being about as flat a pitch as one could want. It would certainly be a faster pitch than my old man was used to, plying his trade in the village leagues in

Dorset, where you were more likely to get bowled by a pea-roller than take one in the chin (unless you were at the infamous minefield at Wool, or on the coconut matting of Studland).

And being of a certain generation, wearing a helmet was not only not something dad had never done, but it was definitely seen as an admission that your sexuality was in question, and that you were the sort of bloke who probably ordered a lager and lime rather than a 'proper' pint of local real ale. Nonetheless, even dad had heard tales of this madman from the Low Countries who would not pay respect to a lowly Latin teacher from over the county border, and so he asked if he could take mine so he at least had the option.

Incredibly, in the event, he went with just a cap, which must have been like a red rag to a bull, and indeed, history will tell that the first ball (as dad had opened the batting) went close to brushing the peak, before the second one mercifully removed his stumps before any serious damage could be done. I think dad came home with a new-found respect for professional batsmen and no desire to test himself in that arena again.

These outlying pacemen find themselves in the strangest of places from time to time. My uncle Mark, who had also played in dad's village side at Child Okeford as a wily leg-spinner also used to tour with an Essex-based side known as the Two Hopes XI (as everyone knows, the two hopes are 'Bob' and 'No'). In their tour of Cornwall in 2018, their number included one Jofra Archer, the freakish speedster who tore up the World Cup just 12 months later, breaking Ian Botham's England record for wickets in a World Cup.

I have also known of Shaun Tait playing in the lower divisions in Surrey and James Anderson has turned out for Burnley when off England duty – imagine being an accountant or mechanic looking forward to your weekend off to come up against one of these monsters, and having to pay a match fee for the pleasure! I may be wrong, but I doubt Anderson had to stump up a tenner at the end of play like the rest of us.

Stuart Meaker

League cricket has always had its share of fast bowlers and the Surrey Championship was no exception, with the likes of West Indian Ian Bishop playing for Reigate when I was just starting out. Only once, though, have I genuinely felt that a team was out to deliberately hurt me physically and that was against Farnham's local rivals, Normandy. Normandy is a small village near Guildford which boasts a purpose-built complex of two pitches (one apparently the exact dimensions of the Oval), training facilities and has made itself into one of the dominant clubs in the county.

Their success was based on an aggressive brand of cricket which allied a good work ethic with a win-at-all-costs attitude which, to my mind at least, at times overstepped the spirit of cricket. My view is probably not the most balanced one, though, as it became apparent over the years that part of the tactic in our games against them was to try and get under my skin as captain through targeted and personal sledging, taking any opportunity to question my skill and courage verbally. If this sounds like sour grapes, I counter that with the fact that I twice spoke with the captain (two different people) of Normandy after matches to question this tactic, and was told quite clearly on both occasions that yes, it was deliberate, and that our views would have to differ on what was an appropriate way to play cricket – amateur cricket as well, don't let's forget.

And so I was under no illusions as to what might come my way when they were able to field Stuart Meaker in their starting line-up one Saturday. Meaker – who had a pretty good career with Surrey and played a couple of one-day and T20 games for England – was clocked at 94mph and was regularly up around the 90mph mark. I can only imagine the encouragement he was given to make my life uncomfortable, not least as I had been painted as a 'pea-heart' by Normandy and even 'Captain Cry-baby' after my insistence that they were not playing in the spirit of the game.

I doubt that Stuart Meaker knows, or cares, who I am, but when we played Normandy away in 2007, I had made up my mind that I would open the batting, as I wanted to show our rivals that I was not about to shy away from the contest (I also had a wedding to attend, but I wasn't going to let them know that at the time). I knew exactly what his instructions were, as they were made clear and audible from the cordon behind the wicket, and they weren't, 'Bowl it in his half.' And, as predicted, I was on the receiving end of some pretty fast and scary stuff. There is something perversely enjoyable about facing this sort of hostility, especially if you are not getting out, and when you can squirt the odd one away for four through the slips, or off a top edge, always counting down the balls in an over and the overs in a spell, thinking, 'He's surely coming off after this one' (they never do, by the way). I do remember enjoying this particular spell – even the sledging – until I got one wrong, took my eye off it, which is always bad news, and ended up taking it flush on the left side of the grille, near the temple area, knocking me to the ground. What struck me then, and still strikes me today, is that this is the only time in my career that not one of the fielders came to see if I was OK, even in the most cursory of manners. It was very much a case of, 'Leave him there, he's on his own.' Sure, things may have perhaps been different in today's more concussion-conscious climate, but the incident only cemented the antagonism between the sides, or really, between them and me.

Chapter Seventeen

Best Batsmen

IF FACING up to some of the world's fastest bowlers was something of a bittersweet experience, having the opportunity to play against some big names in batting could be equally mixed. One of the great levellers of the game is that the batsman only gets one chance and it only takes one good ball, or one mistake, for them to lose their wicket (or 'just one bit of cricket' as club keepers mindlessly parrot every weekend around the country). This meant that, as a bowler, however hard a day in the field it might have been, there was always the opportunity to add a first-class scalp to your tally, or put a well-known player 'in your pocket', even if they had already sent you to all parts. And if they did score runs – as frequently they did – what better place to witness top-quality skill than from on the pitch?

What struck me most about some of the best players I played against was the ease with which they accumulated runs and rotated the strike. Take Matthew Maynard from Glamorgan for instance. I remember thinking that he was playing within himself and just stroking the ball around the Parks effortlessly whilst never feeling that he was getting on top of us. But looking at the scoreboard, he was on 20 before you'd even felt he'd scored a run, and glided to an easy fifty at a run a ball, barely breaking sweat. His county colleague David Hemp was similar, and county stalwarts like Peter Bowler for Somerset or Kim Barnett for Gloucestershire – all were capable of scoring nearly every ball and putting away the bad ones with the nonchalance of waving away a lazy wasp from a tea-time scone. In this way, it was incredibly hard to exert any sort of pressure or control on the game, even if you did not feel battered in the same way as when the bigger hitters were at the crease.

One of the greatest players to come to Oxford in my time was Robin Smith – the medallioned, moustachioed alpha-male from Durban who England had adopted as their own, and who often was the one player in the Test team's middle order who looked like taking the game to the opposition during that fearsome era of fast bowling. Smith was often devastating. He was renowned as having the most powerful square cut in world cricket and batted with no grille on his helmet, despite once having his jaw broken and continuing to bat on. The flowing locks which curled from the back of his headgear gave him a redolence of the Trojan warrior and his forearms were as thick as the oars from a Viking vessel.

But like all mythical champions, Smith also had his Achilles' heel. Despite fearlessly destroying the world's fastest bowlers, 'The Judge' often came unstuck against spinners, having particular difficulty against Mushtaq Ahmed of Pakistan, whose whirly, windmilly action offered an altogether more unpredictable challenge than having your nose, or toes, broken by Waqar's reverse-swing yorkers. He also had been found out on dusty Indian pitches and against a young Shane Warne.

And so it was, then, that on the eve of the University match against Hampshire in 1999 – my second first-class game – our captain, John Claughton, delivered the masterplan for coping with the Test legend (assuming, of course, that we managed to dismiss a couple of players to get him to the crease). Claughton turned to me, looked me in the eye and said, 'Hicksy, it's well known that Smith struggles against the spinning ball, so as soon as he comes in, you're on.' Now, I loved the skipper's clear-sighted forethought and the way he had pinpointed the best use of our bowling armoury, but I suspect that he had forgotten several things. One – I was not Mushtaq Ahmed nor Shane Warne; two – the Parks in April was not Madras, and was as flat as any pitch around in those days; three – my 'surprise' ball was the one that actually spun, and this was unlikely to be unveiled any time before mid-to-late July on a third-or fourth-day pitch. In all, despite my outward eagerness, I felt that this plan was likely to be as effective as going over the top of the trenches armed with a lemon. I have a feeling my team-mates were equally confident.

Still, we went for the plan, and to his credit, the Hampshire captain showed total professionalism in nudging the good balls around for singles in amassing an unspectacular 45 before retiring 'hurt'. He had clearly had enough batting practice for the day. I did drop one ball a little short in my spell and Smith proved, like all the top batsmen, that he did not miss out on chances to score, and rocked back to hit me for an enormous six over midwicket.

I did learn quickly in those early first-class fixtures the difference between the really top players, and the journeymen, or second-team hopefuls. It was in some ways easier to bowl to the top batsmen, whose modus operandi was to eliminate risk, rather than look to pulverise you. So if you could land the ball on a handkerchief, you would likely meet a respectful defensive shot from the top player, whilst a more aggressive second-tier player might attempt to hit the same ball through the covers for four. A top-player would aim a leg-stump half-volley between mid-on and midwicket with a straight bat, accepting two safe runs, rather than looking to whip it through square leg for four, but risking an lbw or leading edge. Times may have changed with more aggressive play from all players, but those players with an insatiable appetite for runs, like Alastair Cook, Joe Root or, going back a few years, Graeme Hick, Ian Bell and Mark Ramprakash, would sometimes feel less intimidating than blokes with all the shots who could marmalise you if the chances didn't go to hand.

World Cup Winner

There is no doubt that the approach of batsmen changed during my playing career, most probably due to the advent of Twenty20 cricket and a new generation of young players watching their heroes playing shots all around the wicket which hadn't been dreamt up when I was a kid. There was also the expectation for all players to be able to clear the ropes and score at well over a run a ball. Many young players now talk more about strike rate than batting average. I don't intend to appear misty-eyed about the so-called good old days as cricket is so much more multi-faceted nowadays and watching people do what you are incapable of is one of the great joys and brings spectators in.

As an off-spinner, as I have described above, you used to be able to count on even the best players showing some respect for consistent line-and-length bowling, and you could expect to get a couple of early maidens in whilst players took stock of pace and the pitch condition, playing themselves in for a longer knock. Things seemed to change around the 2005 era onwards, when the likes of Kevin Pietersen would suddenly play a switch-hit, or flamingo shot from outside off stump through midwicket. And attitudes changed with these new shots. I came to feel that most batsmen would look to make a statement against a spinner in their first over, and would have no qualms about dancing down the track to loft one over the infield. This now seems totally sensible. Why would you offer the chance to the bowler to get into his stride before attacking? Far better to establish early dominance and make them feel that one more mistake in the over would cost a second boundary.

As quite a slow bowler who aimed to tease batsmen into making mistakes, I used to counter this new aggression by starting with a deep midwicket ('cow corner') and deep long-on, so that players could not get away with a mistimed shot into the wide open areas beyond the infield. What frustrated me was captains insisting that we keep those players up and 'let him have a go', when most players now will not need asking twice. I would end up having to make the seemingly defensive step of sending them back after a couple of easy lofted boundaries, rather than being able perhaps to bring them in once I had settled into my rhythm. Shane Warne adopted something similar with a deep point to cover up for an early 'drag-down', giving away a single rather than a boundary, before bringing fielders closer once he was happy with his ability to hit the right length.

Also, and this is probably more for pitches that offered turn, I felt it was as hard to play a neat push for one down the ground as it was to go through a lofted shot into space. Not quite reaching the pitch of the ball might offer a return catch, or a chip to midwicket or a man on the boundary behind him as the ball grabbed the surface a little.

Bowling maidens became increasingly difficult in all forms of the game. In my early days, I felt that if I could limit the batsman to a drive down the ground or a leg-side sweep shot, I was able to put some dots together. This changed hugely with the development of sweep shots on both sides of the wicket, and very fine deflections and ramp shots also on both sides. Now you had to consider being hit in any one of 360 degrees, which always made me feel one fielder (or more) short. Stick powerplay fielding restrictions on to this and you can see why some felt it became ever more a 'batsman's game'.

One of the most effective proponents of this new explosive combination of incredible power hitting and deft invention is Lancashire and England's Jos Buttler. Buttler's ice-blue eyes and diffident demeanour belie the fact that he is one of the most destructive players of his generation, happily stooping into the line of 90mph deliveries to glance them past the keeper before whipping the next 30 rows back over extra cover with wrists as strong as iron and as flexible as wilting celery.

Buttler it was who played what I consider the best shot off my bowling. I played against him twice – the first a warm-up game for Dorset against Somerset's second XI. We had done well to score around 280 from 50 overs, despite a collapse at the hands of a young lad named Jack Leach who became a team-mate at Dorset. In chasing down the total, we ran into Zander de Bruyn – just off the plane from South Africa but not sufficiently jetlagged to be concerned by our amateur offerings on his way to a century. He was joined by some chap we had never come across – a schoolboy by the name of Buttler, who quickly demonstrated why he was destined for greatness, eclipsing his more experienced partner with a bewildering range of shots to the most outrageous and unorthodox areas. We had no answer then. It is just nice to know we were not the only ones to find him a tad more than tricky to bowl at.

The second time I came across the superstar-in-waiting was again for Dorset in a T20 friendly at Sherborne School when all the talk was of Craig Kieswetter, who had shot to stardom himself with some electric form in the recent T20 World Cup. Kieswetter got a few, as did England's Ashes hero of 2005, Marcus Trescothick, and I even managed to pouch De Bruyn, albeit with the filthiest of full tosses clothed down cow corner's throat (but the scorebook doesn't lie, eh?). I was bowling downhill from the Pavilion End with the wind behind me and a boundary of around 75 metres – fair protection you would think, even when bowling at a proven hitter like Buttler. Following some typically wristy square drives and sweeps, I felt that he was winding up for a big hit, and so I aimed to bowl as full and straight as possible, yorker-length, to restrict his ability to get underneath the ball. As it left my hand, I was relieved to have got it right, landing it around the popping crease on off stump. It was basically the best ball I could have bowled at that moment. To see it land amongst the silver and crockery of the committee marquee at extra cover left me entirely emasculated and under no illusion that I was up against a better player. Not only was my best not good enough, it had been dismissed like an errant dog who had left an unwelcome gift on the outfield.

It's hard to pick a best batsman, as I've been on the receiving end of too many hundreds to mention. I think I've detailed the biggest names I came up against: Strauss, Astle, Buttler, Vince, Shah, Solanki, Smith, Trescothick, and then Hemp and Maynard, who made batting seem the most easy. Watching Chris Jones score two mammoth hundreds for Dorset in the same game was special, and some of Dalrymple's knocks at Oxford were superb against the odds. Cowley was something else on several occasions, and a chanceless 240 by Arul Suppiah for Devon was pretty painful, yet impressive from 22 yards away. On reflection, whilst many still claim it's a 'batsman's game', having been at the other end from some tidy bowlers, I marvel at the skill of the top players, whether it's the shot-making of Morgan, Kohli or Stokes, or the powers of concentration and tight technique of Cook, Gooch or Atherton, I'm most grateful that I can judge them with the benefit of some first-hand experience. Anyone who makes a career as a top batsman, with just one chance per innings and under intense scrutiny of crowd, media and countless replays and research into their flaws, deserves respect.

Chapter Eighteen
Socialising With Some Big Guns

The Best Night Out of My Life – Featuring Allan Lamb

In my mid-thirties and with my dream of captaining England to Ashes glory not quite faded, but fast becoming a less likely occurrence (although I still keep my phone on the day before a squad is announced, just in case), I was working as a housemaster at Wellington College, one of England's leading public schools. At that time, the Wellington College staff could boast a pretty strong eleven.

Second master Robin Dyer had opened the batting several times for Warwickshire, and he could be partnered up top by another housemaster – Iain Sutcliffe – latterly of Leicestershire, Lancashire and Oxford University. Dyer was a remarkable senior master. An old boy of the school, he had a reputation for being the strict disciplinarian, although behind that austere exterior, he was a decent bloke and enjoyed nothing more than a beer in the pavilion and a chat about the game. One of his great skills as a second master was the fact that he was always totally neutral in expression and mood such that when you entered his office, you had no idea what had just come before. He could be dealing with irate parents, expelling kids for bullying, investigating a drugs allegation, listening to a member of staff's worries or all manner of other issues, and yet once the door was shut, he was back to neutral, ready for the next challenge.

I asked him about this gift of his once, and he put it down to cricket. 'It's like facing bouncers, Hicksy,' he explained. 'It can be a bit hairy at times but once it's gone, it's in the past, you take guard again and get ready for whatever is next.' It certainly seemed to stand him in good stead, and is a pretty damn good metaphor for life, in my book. People make a lot of money selling this attitude as mindfulness these days.

Sutcliffe was, in his own way, equally unflappable and could often come across as so chilled-out as to seem horizontal. I do him a disservice here, though, as he is one of those chaps within whom the still waters run deep. However, I bet that phlegmatic attitude helped him in his career. He used to hate talking about cricket – he loved boxing a whole lot more – but when you could collar him for an anecdote or two, he would get misty-eyed about how exhilarating it was to face Wasim Akram in the indoor nets. This is something I could never empathise with. For Sutty, the faster it came, the better. For me, no thanks. He was also really interesting to listen to, talking about Muttiah Muralitharan, for whom he fielded short leg, with apparently no fear at all. Well, I suppose if the batsman is missing it by two foot, you are pretty safe anywhere.

This pretty steady opening pair could boast over 12,000 first-class runs between them, and could be followed up by a group of others who had once had their day in the sun. Tim Head had been a sharp gloveman for Sussex, Jim Dewes had played some decent university cricket at Cambridge, Charles Oliphant-Callum had played second-team cricket as an off-spinner, our head of cricket, Dan Pratt, had been on Surrey's books and Gavin Franklin and I had played British Universities cricket in the same era.

In fact, it was Franklin whom I blamed for several years for scuppering my chances of playing a higher standard. Following my chance to play against New Zealand at the Parks in 1999, Derek Randall passed the reins as coach on to Durham's Graeme 'Foxy' Fowler, who selected Franklin ahead of me for the tour to South Africa which followed the 1999 season. I was livid – I had shown myself capable (I thought) against the Kiwis and had scored fifty at Lord's in the Varsity match. But Franklin was a Durham University lad with a summer contract at Warwickshire, and that seemed to be enough for Foxy, who had seen several lads make it big after his tutelage – Andrew Strauss, Nasser Hussain and James Foster, to name a pretty illustrious three. We Oxbridge types always felt that he had a bit of a bias against us – I guess those who don't get picked often look for excuses.

So Gavin went on tour, and was picked for the Combined University side the following summer against Zimbabwe, which was especially galling because I had taken nine wickets in a first-class match the week before the selection. How could I do any more? In the event, I was even jealously happy when he returned figures of ten overs for 70. I feel even worse thinking back on my bitterness then as this was his one and only first-class game (even though Durham were clearly as good, if not much stronger than we were at the time, they did not merit official first-class status). I had benefited a lot more than him from the vestiges of Victorian hierarchy which kept Oxford and Cambridge elevated above other universities, so who was I to complain if he had taken advantage of his university coach going with what he knew?

Anyway, for some years I would mutter about this useless offie from Durham – Gavin Franklin – who had cost me a tour and maybe a few first-class wickets. We even locked horns on occasion in the Surrey League. It was not until we moved into the housemaster's accommodation at Wellington that we encountered each other properly. He and his wife were the first people to knock on the door, bearing a bunch of flowers and a bottle of champagne, welcoming us into the community. It was then that I realised (and I quote Graeme Swann here) that Gav is 'one of the nicest blokes in the world'. We spent the next eight years in adjacent classrooms teaching English and picking each other's brains about matters of pastoral importance, whose resources to steal and how we would sneak out of school to get to the next Stone Roses gig.

His great cricketing claim to fame (apart from winning the Cricketer Cup with Malvern College) is that, when he did eventually get awarded his county contract by Warwickshire, it had been a toss-up between him and a young lad freshly over from South Africa who bowled offies and could bat a bit. His name was Kevin Pietersen. I wonder if Warwickshire rue that decision.

So we had a decent squad, shall we say. However, the only time we were put together as an eleven we were nowhere near a cricket pitch, but had been invited to dinner by one of the school governors and ex-partner in Goldman Sachs Tim Bunting, who was a such a cricket nut that he had built a two-storey cricket library adjoining his house and had two people working full-time trying to source rare cricketing books and memorabilia. So eleven teachers from Wellington hopped in a minibus on a Friday night and arrived to be served wine which I later Googled to be worth more than £200 per bottle, to be fed (what else?) beef Wellington, and to pore over his incredible book collection. Bunting introduced his collection by telling us that there are around 40,000 books on cricket out there, and that he has 39,000 of them, including three full sets of *Wisden's* – one of which was W.G. Grace's. He also had Grace's cricket 'primer' – the book from which he learnt his own cricket, and several old bats lying around. At one point, Aaron Williams – a former Dorset team-mate of mine – and I pretended to be Wally Hammond and Jack Hobbs, holding actual bats the two great men had used to score Ashes hundreds in the 1920s and 30s. It was quite surreal.

The table we were sitting at was made up of individual leaves, each of which contained full records of each county, including the Minor Counties. So Dyer was sat at the Warwickshire leaf and could flick through old annuals and *Who's Whos* from the permed mullet era, whilst I busied myself leafing through back copies of the Dorset Cricket Yearbook – quite the page-turner. Bunting had even got his researchers to put together an after-dinner quiz to which all the answers were names of people around the table. So they had managed to dredge up some obscure facts from Cricketer Cup matches from days gone by, nondescript second-team fixtures, and the Sussex Premier League from 1982. But of course, each question came with its own anecdote and the evening was just full of bonhomie and laughter as the wine kept coming. Being a proper 'badger', I even managed to win the quiz, and was delighted to be presented with 'The Ian Botham Cricket Game', signed by the big man himself, which I try to keep in pristine condition.

Like that black-tie dinner at Lord's when Mike Gatting christened me Tim, it was another one of those evenings which just got better and better. And the real coup was that we had a twelfth man with us for the evening: one Mr A.J. Lamb. Lamby had forged a connection with Wellington as he was acting as the guardian for Tom, Ben and Sam Curran – sons of his old Northamptonshire team-mate Kevin Curran, who had prematurely lost his life the year before, after Tom had joined the school. And Lamby also came with a reputation as Botham's wing-man – the one (along with perhaps David Gower) who could keep up with Beefy's drinking and carousing. True to expectation, he happily got stuck into the wine that night, and was thoroughly entertaining company, regaling us with what it was like to face the ferocious West Indies on some dodgy pitches in the Caribbean (modestly he let us remember that he had always scored runs in the hardest conditions for England), and my favourite cricket story was his retelling of the famous two-ball trick from Wasim Akram, which turned the World Cup Final of 1992 Pakistan's way and had Lamb and Chris Lewis looking flabbergasted as they lost their stumps in consecutive balls to the wily old wizard. I had to pinch myself on several occasions that night and we left a good two hours after the scheduled departure so our poor driver was not best pleased. It turned out the next day when we all reconvened a bit worse for wear that Lamby and Tim had moved on to the 'expensive' wine after we had gone. How the other half live!

Henry Olonga and the Fig Tart Fiasco

One of the most amazing fringe benefits of working in a top-tier private school is that they tend to attract really interesting individuals to come and speak or present at conferences or for staff training. I have been lucky enough to meet several well-known personalities during my time as a teacher, but for now I'll stick to the cricket side of things and a supper with an extraordinary individual: Henry Olonga.

Most cricket followers will remember Olonga as being the first black man to play for Zimbabwe, and as a cricketer of rare natural talent; a quick bowler with dreadlocked hair and boundless enthusiasm. As it turned out, Olonga had boundless spirit too, and a fierce moral drive which cost him his cricket career, and very nearly his life.

In the 2003 World Cup, Olonga and Andy Flower famously opted to wear black armbands as they took the field. The gesture was meant to represent their mourning for the death of democracy in their beloved country under the increasingly brutal regime of Robert Mugabe. It was a very visible gesture, televised in full view of the cricket-watching world, and both men knew what the repercussions could be. Opponents or critics of the Mugabe regime were known to disappear, never to be seen again: Flower and Olonga knew that they may never be able to return to their homeland.

There was a great deal of fortune involved in the aftermath of the protest, as results went Zimbabwe's way. Infamously, England were knocked out of the tournament having been deducted points for their own protest in refusing to play in Zimbabwe, and had results fallen as the bookies would have predicted, Olonga and Flower would have been due to return to their home country for a Super Six match. Olonga knew that if the team returned to Zimbabwe, there was a good chance that after the match had finished, and the cameras and press dispersed, he may well have 'disappeared' himself. The cricketing gods work in mysterious ways, though, and Zimbabwe ended up playing their Super Six matches not in Zimbabwe, but in the other host nation – South Africa.

Zimbabwe lost their match, but whilst their team-mates returned home, the two rebels went in different directions. Olonga set up home in England and Flower went on to coach England with some success. To date, neither man has ever set foot back in Zimbabwe.

Most of this story I vaguely knew, but was able to hear it from the horse's mouth over dinner at Wellington College, after a chapel service in which Olonga had told his story and met the Christian Forum. I found Henry a captivating, eloquent man – not without a sense of his own importance and the importance of his actions – and we all hung on his words as he repeated his tale. It was – in fact – the final night he was spending in the UK, before emigrating to Australia.

Why am I not more effusive about a man whose action was every bit as radical and brave as those by Jesse Owens at the 1936 Berlin Olympics and Tommie Smith and John Carlos at the 1968 Games? It comes down to my wife's fig tart. Lovingly slaved over as a centrepiece of dessert for a visiting sporting dignitary, Penny's pudding was a work of art, and tasted divine. But would Olonga eat it? Would he hell. Turning his nose up at the sight of figs like a haughty hippo at a waterhole, I felt my better half's pride bruised. So much so, I had to have an extra helping for him.

So, Mr Olonga, I tip my hat at your grand political gesture, but never forget to be polite at pudding.

Walkabout Sundays with Jack Leach

Since I started putting pen to paper to write this, a young left-arm spinner from Somerset has become something of a national cult hero. Jack Leach – whose wiping of steamed-up spectacles and brave rearguard batting displays will stand as some of the enduring, iconic moments of the unparalleled 2019 summer of cricket. Leach's bald-headed, bank-manager appearance offered a down-to-earth contrast to the superhuman heroics of Ben Stokes, the effortless electricity of Jofra Archer and the seemingly ever-present determination and skill of Steve Smith. While these three headline-stealers can be assured of their place in the Pantheon, Leach, I think, realises that his moment in the sun may be more temporary, but his humility is so charming and disarming that the nation's cricket lovers have taken him to their hearts. I hope he keeps his place and goes on to be recognised as a decent Test spinner in his own right, and not just a bloke who almost got his name on the honours board at Lord's (something not even Brian Lara or Sachin Tendulkar managed) by falling agonisingly short in the nineties against Ireland, or the bloke who scored perhaps the most important one not out in the history of Ashes cricket, while Stokes was leading England phoenix-like to victory at Headingley.

Leachy (as he was known in typically creative cricket fashion and before he lost his hair and assumed his Somerset moniker, 'The Nut'), played a key part in Dorset winning the Minor Counties Championship in 2010. Today, I have on the wall of my office a team photo from the final, with a more hirsute Leach and his Somerset spin-twin Max Waller smirking in the back row. Leachy had taken 6-21 in the final against Lincolnshire on a raging Bunsen[16] in Bournemouth to go past 20 wickets in just three matches for us that season. I, on the other hand, had not been give leave to play, and so appeared on the last day and was able to be on the pitch as twelfth man when the final wicket went down. I was also able – as county captain – to pick up the trophy along with vice-captain Chris Park.

It was something of a vision of what was to come for Jack. In the seasons which followed, Somerset made the deliberate decision to move away from what had been acknowledged as one of the flattest, most batsman-friendly pitches on the county circuit, to producing pitches more likely to produce a result, which played into the hands of a young, attacking left-arm spinner. Leachy soon became a vital part of the Somerset machine. Had Somerset not taken this decision, I feel sure that he would have been consigned to being a bit-part player, or second-team and league cricket regular, and England would not have uncovered a genuine rough diamond. Certainly, when Leach was given leave by coach Andy Hurry to play for Dorset, there was no sense that he had great things ahead of him. He became a bit of a cult hero for us, actually, much like Vyv Pike had been in previous years – we knew he was a match-winner, but it was a bit of a well-kept secret for us, and we loved it when

---

16 Rhyming slang: 'Bunsen [burner] = a turner. i.e. a pitch which will take spin.

Leachy ripped through sides, having previously had to rely on my own notoriously toothless off-spin or the unreliable Cowley.

It is perhaps an indication of the sort of merciless ribbing which went on in our side that we started to pick up on the fact that Leachy seemed at one point to be suffering from early-onset 'yips'. Most cricketers will be aware that the time-honoured response to seeing someone 'yip-up' is to shout 'yiiiip-yip-yip-yip' in a very audible, high-pitched way as the stricken bowler reaches the top of his bowling mark. And even though Jack probably did ask us to give it a bit of a rest, I'm not sure anyone paid any attention. I'm not sure why teams behave in this way, but it was definitely part of our dynamic – probably some form of 'tall-poppy syndrome' – much to the disappointment of coach Willows, who wanted an unfailingly supportive dressing room. It's not that we weren't supportive, it's just that humour tended to trump niceness, and I think there was a bit of old-fashioned testing of each other's mettle in there, too, but I'm no psychologist.

Looking back, there probably was a bit of fragility there, which meant that when Leachy was pulled up by the ICC for having a suspect action, it must have been a really tricky time for him. All credit, then, for his remodelling it, and coming back as a real match-winner for county and country.

It's great to see him doing so well now, and his debut in New Zealand kept my spirits up during an all-night vigil at our home in Cornwall where we had sprung a leak one Easter Sunday and spent the whole night baling water out of the bathroom with *Test Match Special* and Sky Sports offering succour to our labours. I caught up with him on the first day of the Lord's Test in 2019 in the pavilion where he remarked to me that life was a bit different from 'Walkabout Sundays' – boozy Bournemouth nights drinking snakebite from plastic pint pots. Although Leachy is definitely a Somerset lad, Dorset is very happy to claim him as their own and I know that all the Leopard lads are rooting for him every time he pulls on an England shirt. You've come a long way, Leachy lad, and deserve all the success (and free specs).

Courtney and the Duchess

Ten years after the tour to Croatia, and having roomed with Darren Bicknell for our MCC game against the Minor Counties at Lord's in 2012, I was fortunate to be able to persuade him to select me for the annual match between the Duchess of Rutland's XI and the MCC at Belvoir CC – a stunning rural ground in the lee of Belvoir Castle in Leicestershire, where he works for the foundation, delivering countryside education to underprivileged children from the surrounding area.

I was delighted to join forces for a game which not only promised the best of quintessential English summertime, but also brought together some pretty good cricketers, if not, perhaps, all in their pomp. The biggest draw of the day was undoubtedly the West Indian legend and former captain Courtney Walsh, who had just finished coaching Bangladesh in the World Cup (New Zealand were in the throes of completing their surprise victory over India in the semi-final as we played). Although now in his mid-fifties, the sight of that unmistakeable Walsh action, which had led him to be the first man to take 500 Test wickets, was still a real treat for the players and spectators, and a good couple of hundred had turned out to enjoy a picnic and see the great man in action.

And having been offered the chance to bat at No.3, I soon had the chance to experience what it is like at the other end from a man who had been part of one of the most feared new-ball partnerships in history. OK, so he was carrying a bit of a paunch and the shoulders may have been creaking a bit, but with the pitch reasonably 'sporting' (not Sabina Park in 1998, or indeed Vis, Croatia 2009, but a bit lively off a length), and a not-so-helpfully placed copper beech blocking the sightscreen, this would still be a test for me, having barely picked up a bat in the preceding months. And you could tell there was still a bit of the old warrior spirit in Courtney; the eyes had that old familiar glazed expression and the way the ball came out of his hand you knew he was still thinking about exactly where he wanted it to land, and what he wanted it to do, hitting the seam at will and making some firm indentations into my fingers and inner thigh as souvenirs of the occasion. Cheeky git even tried to 'Mankad' me at the non-striker's end!

On this occasion, I managed to see off the new ball and even take a few runs off the Jamaican hero, but imagining what he must have been like 20 years previously, with an extra 15 miles-per-hour and with only Curtly Ambrose to look forward to at the other end, it was just about possible to get a feel for why they call it 'Test' cricket. Happily for me, the end of Walsh's spell brought some more run-of-the-mill MCC bowling and rather than having to deal with a baying crowd, all out for blood, I was able to enjoy the luxury of dinner in the castle as guests of the Duke and Duchess. Now, that's the sort of cricket I can certainly enjoy, and just another amazing occasion which I have been lucky to have been afforded, thanks to this great game and the friends you make.

Walsh was one of three Test cricketers playing that day, with MCC head of cricket John Stephenson also taking the opportunity to enjoy the day, and Neil Johnson, of Zimbabwe, who scored a century against Australia at Lord's in the 1999 World Cup, also in the Duchess's side. Johnson gave me a lift and has become a good friend as he is a colleague of my wife's at Oakham School, where he is head of cricket. Remarkably for an ex-Test player, he turned up with no kit and was a little dismayed when he realised he had not seen anyone batting left-handed and he might be forced to borrow kit from a righty! When he did bat and bowl, though, the skill was still very much in evidence, as was the competitive streak. I guess it never leaves you.

Scott Boswell, Keith Medlycott and the Yips

Thinking of Jack Leach and his battles with the yips, it was also fascinating in that same game as I faced Courtney Walsh to watch Scott Boswell in action with the new ball. Boswell is now head of cricket at Trent College in Nottingham, but became infamous in cricketing circles for an excruciating over at Lord's in the final of the 2001 Cheltenham & Gloucester Trophy, in which he bowled eight wides and 14 balls in total, leading effectively to the end of his professional career and a ten-year recovery from the trauma of getting 'the yips' on the biggest occasion of his life. He has since become something of an internet sensation, with a YouTube video entitled 'Is this the worst over ever?' having over a million hits, but more importantly, Boswell has become an advocate for mental health and psychology in sportspeople. He was certainly an interesting and friendly chap to meet, and what was even more fascinating was that whilst he took a brisk four-fer, he was still unable to bowl with his fingers down the seam in conventional fashion for fear of 'yipping-up' again. He just bowled cross-seam deliveries, which happened to be perfect for the pitch we were using.

It's a horrendous thing to happen to any bowler – the yips – the inability to do what had come so naturally, out of nowhere, and in such a public way. Many will remember the same thing happening to Simon Kerrigan on his Test debut at the Oval in 2013, when an Ashes call-up – the dream come true for any English or Australian player – turned sour as his usually impeccable left-arm spin deserted him. Whilst it may appear funny at the outset, especially if you are on the batting side, I

wouldn't wish the yips on my worst enemy and it is really hard
to come back from.

I do feel it personally, as my brother lost the ability to bowl
having been one of the best off-spinners of his year group in the
country. Guy went from an England Under-15 cap and then
five wickets for Hampshire (a team including the likes of Jimmy
Adams and Chris Tremlett) in the under-19 county final, to no
longer being able to land the ball on the cut strip, often bowling
over the head of the batsman or dropping it at his own feet.
And many years on, he can't bowl spin with any fluidity as the
old demons arrive just as his arm is about to come over. He –
and others – have also articulated how something often goes
so wrong in the neurological pathway between brain and hand
that you can forget even how to release the ball, and the arm
comes over with the ball still stuck between the fingers. It all
sounds utterly bizarre, but sadly it is clearly a real phenomenon
which has plagued even some of the very best.

Another who really suffered from the yips was Keith
Medlycott, who toured the West Indies with England in
1989/90 as a highly promising left-arm spinner, and whose
career also burnt out on the pyre of the yips. Like Boswell,
Medlycott has remained in the game as a schoolboy coach – at
Reed's School in Surrey – and worked for the county for many
years as a coach. I came across Medders several times in club
cricket and he struck me as one of the game's real theorisers,
often having an off-the-wall plan, like when he made me bowl
to a 6-3 off-side field in an inter-league final at Saffron Walden
– an experiment which did not last long and made me wonder
if you could match-fix at club level. But Medders was most
interesting to face, as he chose not to run up, but to bowl 'from
the coil'. Which literally meant that he would stand with his feet
already in position, the ball between two hands at this chest,
so that all he had to do was roll his arm over and let go. It was

quite remarkable to see someone still unable to let go from that position, and at times, he would appear to be ready to start and then stop and apologise, as if some invisible lightning bolt had struck him on the point of release. One felt huge sympathy for him, but then of course he would let one go and then it would land, spin, catch your outside edge and you were on your way back to the pavilion, cursing his very existence and wondering if it was all a big trick.

The yips only threatened me once, at the end of the 2000 season when after a long and successful year with Oxford University I tried to come back to Dorset and put so much pressure on myself to perform, I lost all rhythm and eventually was dropped for the Minor Counties Championship final. This, of course, hurt my pride enormously, but was the right decision for the team. One thing which helped me get back my form was running up in the nets with my eyes closed, just to feel what was natural again. I don't know anything about the psychology of this, but it worked for me, as did a good rest, and I was able to recover and avoid the affliction that others have had to suffer.

Mental Health

If anything, this book has been about the lighter side of cricketing life. As it should be. Cricket is a game, a pastime, and should be played for fun, even if you do become a professional. Ed Smith writes eloquently about how players ought to be more amateur, in the true meaning of the word. That is, to be 'lovers' of the game; and those who seem to find the enjoyment seem to perform the best. The sheer joy of a Tendulkar, Richards or Pietersen in full flow is what cricket is all about. And the laughs, the jokes, the friendship, on and off the field. But for too many people, cricket becomes a chore. Or worse, it becomes a source of crippling self-doubt and anxiety, leading to addiction, depression and, in too many cases, to suicide. I don't intend to go over ground which is far better covered elsewhere, and I have to say that I have been extremely lucky to be generally well mentally. Sure, I have had some difficult times, not least when my daughter was born, and I would certainly argue against anyone who claims that post-natal depression does not affect men, but I've happily avoided falling into those deep dark places from which it is extremely difficult to escape.

I've been struck as I enter my 40s by the amount of men around my age who have taken to social media to open up about their own mental-health struggles. On the one hand, I'm glad that the taboos around mental health have been lifted and more men now feel able to voice the troubles they are facing. But on the other, it worries me that these feelings seem to be all too common, and often seem to afflict cricketers particularly.

For those who have made it to professional level and signed with counties, even for a short time, they will find themselves automatically registered with the Professional Cricketers' Association (PCA). The PCA does incredible work in supporting professional and ex-professional players with all manner of issues, not least mental health. It seems an incredibly important and effective operation and I am glad it exists. However, I worry that there are also many cricketers, like me, who have given heart, soul and a whole lot of time to the game yet haven't quite made the grade and therefore fall by the wayside, not qualifying for the support the PCA offers. I'm not talking about guys who play the odd club game, but those who have had the dream of becoming professional and spend summers desperately trialling, being told 'no' time and again, their confidence being knocked as they spend their meagre expenses on another tank of petrol and head off to the next outground or budget hotel, sacrificing the chance of a regular job and probably a relationship at the same time. Or those for whom the shared experience of the team offers a sense of security lacking in their 'real life', and who come to the end of their career with few prospects and their reason for existing a thing of the past.

Because for many, cricket really is what they live for. I certainly did for two decades; spending my working week counting the days until the next game, checking the averages obsessively and turning over selection problems and tactics whilst others were more interested in their family or football team. I longed for the dressing room, the banter and mateship, as well as the rush of success. Footballers say that scoring a goal is better than sex, and I can say the same for a spectacular slip catch; that moment as an off-spinner when the ball drifts, lands and spins through the gate of the approaching batsman; the feeling of timing a cover drive so sweetly you hardly feel the ball on the bat; or seeing a seamer knock the poles out of the ground. How can you expect someone suddenly to do without that sort of adrenaline rush? It's no surprise that some ex-players, or even those just in rough nick, look and feel like junkies going cold turkey. They literally are; they are no longer experiencing that natural chemical high which comes with perfect sporting moments. And it's no surprise that so many sportsmen therefore turn to drink, drugs and gambling as a substitute.

And so finding a way to support all those who do find themselves in some sort of mental difficulty is going to be an ambition of mine now I've hung up my boots. Ex-players like Patrick Foster, who visits schools and cricket centres around the country telling his own cautionary tale of gambling and the links to suicide, are doing a great job raising awareness[17], but we could do so much more so no one feels alone. Cricket may be God's greatest gift to man, but it's not worth losing your life over.

---

17 You can find out more about Patrick Foster's work at https:// www.epicriskmanagement.com/

Chapter Nineteen

Broken Bones and Bowing Out

Why Cricketers are not Doctors

During the course of a career you can expect a few injuries, and I was luckier than most, missing very few games. This was probably mostly due to my being a twirly spinner and not putting my body through the sort of horrific pounding fast bowlers do (some estimate it as being up to eight times your own body weight going through the leg joints, and slow motion footage of the likes of Flintoff or Brett Lee hitting the crease, with ankles and knees jarring, is enough to bring a tear to the eye).

Growing up, I did have some issues with my back – growing pains most likely – and had to play in the tournament in Jersey where Simon Jones was a fearsome 16-year-old tearaway without bowling, such was the pain. My future captain at Oxford, John Claughton, refused me a runner when Dorset Under-16s took on Hampshire in that festival, showing the hard-nosed qualities which had earned him the England captaincy for our age group, and also shows just how competitive youth sport was even in those days, and how seriously we took ourselves.

I had ongoing shin splints during my time at Oxford, although never officially diagnosed; I never was one for going to the doctor with these things, thinking a bit of ice and plenty of paracetamol and Ibuprofen would always do the trick, not to mention a bit of self-medication at the King's Arms after a day's play. In hindsight, walking everywhere in town probably didn't help, although of the two occasions I did try to join the bicycle brigade, I was run over once – a hit-rate I felt was not in my best interests. I think I generally just shifted injury around my lower half: the back gave way to the shins, and then to the knees and a right ankle which now feels as if it is held together more with tagliatelle than tendon.

By the age of 36, I found myself with chronic foot problems – a bony lump on my right big-toe joint which means shoes are almost always painful, but for which an operation would mean fusing the joint, meaning no flexion at all. I did have an operation to remove bone fragments in my ankle in order to allow more flexibility there and take pressure off the toe joint. But this just made the ankle weaker, and so now I limp around, one day opting to avoid pain in the toe, the next choosing to ease the ache in the ankle. For now, and the foreseeable future, football, squash, and even cricket, really, is out of the question. I limit myself to static gym exercises and running occasionally, and that in straight lines on roads, not cross-country. Ironically, the loss of all those things which I used to love as a younger man has developed in me a tougher mentality and a sense of patience, rather than despair. I could have done with some of that resilience a few years ago.

At the last count, I reckon I have broken seven of my ten digits on the cricket field. The stone-cold certainty of arthritis in the winters of my dotage looms like unwelcome rainclouds on the morning of a match day. Even during the last years of winter netting I could barely feel the ball in my hand and settled for tossing down spineless grenades as fodder for the batsmen. (Thanks to those wags who are thinking 'no change there', then. You know who you are.)

You'd think that once you'd broken a finger, that would be you out for the next few weeks, but cricketers are a strange lot. They'd do anything for a bit of rain to stay off the field, but when it comes to a slightly bruised finger, the old warrior spirit kicks in and you continue in the face of all reason. Two particular breakages spring to mind for me.

The first happened in an innocuous end-of-season affair against Wiltshire at Dean Park. I don't think either team was in any danger of silverware, but as a local derby, it was one we wanted to win. I found myself at backward point, which implies less that I was there for my lithe athleticism and quick reflexes, and more that the slip cordon had been disbanded and we had gone to plan D or E, which usually meant scouts out to the four corners for damage limitation. What I do remember is a regulation square cut coming my way. Not a Robin Smith piledriver by any means, but one which I just caught wrongly on my left thumb. Instantly, I knew it was trouble. As did everyone watching, who would have heard me squeal like a porker in the slaughterhouse, including Penny, who went straight for the car keys to take me to Bournemouth General. Now, bearing in mind it was the final game of the season, the last place I wanted to be that evening was sat in a miserable waiting room to be told my season was over. Certainly not when a mates-rates curry had been lined up, with the regulation several lagers that would accompany a dead-rubber match.

'It could be just bruised,' proffered one hopeful team-mate (whose medical expertise extended only as far as dressing up as a nurse during the last fancy-dress team night out).

'Yeah, stick some ice on it and see how you go,' was the considered second opinion.

The first aid kit – if you could call it that – was so poorly stocked (some out-of-date plasters, a roll of bandage but no pins, a cigarette lighter and two sheets of toilet paper) that poor

Penny had to nip to the corner shop for more painkillers, as the ones from the start of the game had been popped like smarties by the bowlers and, ironically, by me and Cowley following the previous night's exertions.

'You can't do anything for fingers and thumbs. They just sort themselves.' This last judgement, from one of the coaching staff, was enough to persuade me to tough it out and see how it was in the morning.

Pretty f***ing painful was the answer, especially once the Kingfisher and Nurofen cocktail had passed through the system. I vowed to get it seen to.

But not before the end of the following week, as I had the small matter of an inter-league cup final to consider. This was a pretty rogue competition which pitched a 'select' XI from each county's Premier League (and second tier) against each other in a limited-overs, national format. In reality, teams tended to comprise those who could afford a day off every fortnight – so the same bunch of the self-employed, teachers, students or utter cricket badgers which tended to comprise Minor County teams. On this occasion, my brother and I fitted the bill for the Surrey Championship team to take on the East Anglia Premier League at Saffron Walden, taking in a night out in Cambridge. On expenses. Definitely one not to miss before the school term started again.

So without confessing to my injury, which in the cold light of day saw my thumb bent at an angle of around 30 degrees, I went into the match, which we lost. Nonetheless, spirits were not dampened and I enjoyed a decent night out on old enemy territory.

With the thumb still at an angle more unorthodox than Medlycott's batting stance, and still offering me constant pain, I thought it might just be worth seeing what an actual medical professional might have to say about it. When questioned as to why it had taken me so long to seek assistance, I brazenly offered the undisputed fact of the pavilion, that 'there's nothing you can do with digits'. This was met with the incredulous reply of, 'Who told you that?' (The *'you f***ing dumbass'* was implied.) 'You need to come straight in and get it sorted. That is, unless it has already fused itself.'

'OK. No problem,' I replied. 'You're probably right.' I'm sure the doctor was delighted with my vote of confidence. 'If it's OK, I'll come in after the weekend as I have a match on Saturday I'd like to play in.'

'You can play on Saturday,' said the doctor, reassuringly.

'But it'll be the last game you ever play …'

I went in the next day. And was in plaster for the rest of the season after the doctor rebroke and reset the digit.

It could have been worse, mind; when I was asked to sign the papers for the operation, the notes clearly said 'Thumb, *right hand*.' Imagine going in with one broken thumb and coming out with two.

A few weeks later, I received a follow-up letter from the surgeon. 'There had been a minor complication,' it read, 'and it appears the screw may be loose.'

Never a truer word spoken.

The Quickest Fitness Test Ever

The second nasty break I had was in my penultimate season for Dorset. Farnham were playing a Saturday match at Esher, down by Kempton Park racecourse, in amongst some of Britain's most expensive homes. Like us, Esher were a yo-yo club, bouncing between the top three divisions as fortunes – literal and metaphorical – shifted year on year. This time, we were well on top, with our openers unplayable on a bit of a seamers' paradise. The ball was following me everywhere and I was grabbing slip catches for fun. That is, until I got a bit giddy and tried to dive across from second slip with my left hand. Once again, that familiar feeling of sharp, localised pain, mixed with the horror of impending hours of boredom stuck in a hospital waiting room with all Kingston upon Thames could offer up on a Saturday night. Lord, no.

My immediate diagnosis was that the ring finger on my left hand was – to use the correct medical term – 'utterly f***ed', and that I would on this occasion deign to put myself at the mercy of actual doctors, since they could, apparently, do something about broken bones. The complication for me this time was that this was my last year representing the county, and I was not going to let that slip away with a whimper. I was due in Herefordshire the following day and had every intention of being in the side there. We also had a match to win right now, so I offered to open the batting and do what I could before excusing myself to get to hospital.

'What I could' amounted to three balls, the third of which I edged behind off an ex-pupil of mine who was happy to send me on my way with some choice advice about packing up the game there and then. Probably not bad advice, to be fair.

After a couple of hours, I was scanned and told exactly what I knew already: that the finger was broken, that I should do no activity with it, and should report to my local hospital the next day to get it properly set and a sling put on. Thanking the doctors for their time and expertise, ten minutes after discharge we were driving down the M4 looking for a McDonald's on the way to Hereford.

I'm not totally stupid. I was going to have a fitness test the following morning at the beautiful ground of Eastnor, just near the Malvern Hills and overlooked by Eastnor Castle. Maybe my finger would have miraculously healed itself overnight.

As it was, the 'fitness test' consisted of me walking out to the middle to see a pitch which was underprepared and would definitely spin from ball one. I declared myself ready for duty. And for once, it was one of those glorious occasions where folly is unjustly rewarded with spectacular results. I took five wickets on the first morning of the match, six overall in the first innings. This was followed up with three in the second (not four, agonisingly!) and then in a tense afternoon where we collapsed during the chase, I held firm and was able to smash the winning runs with consecutive pull shots, my smashed-up hand punching the air with glee for the first three-day victory we'd had that season. I was officially man of the match and whilst I was barred by the family from joining the lads on a celebratory night out in Gloucester, a couple of pints of 'Shropshire Lad' with my old man in one of the weirdest pubs I've ever entered (the sinisterly named Yew Tree Tavern) was reward enough.

Heading to Frimley Park Hospital the next day for some more scans revealed that I had managed to add to the single fracture from the Saturday with four extra bonus breaks to the top knuckle, presumably from an ill-advised attempt at a caught-and-bowled. NHS hell ensued as I was transferred to Wexham Park in Slough on one of the hottest days of the summer, to be shunted down the list time and again until the ward closed, leaving me with the choice of coming back the following day, or putting up with the injury and letting it sort itself out. I've not had it looked at since.

Well, you can't do anything for fingers and thumbs, can you?

Packing It In

By the end of the 2015 season, something had changed. I'd always heard cricketers say that you just know when it's time to retire; I just never thought it would happen to me. But as the season went on, the drives to games felt longer, as did the days in the field, the banter had moved on and I got used to seeing old team-mates turning up in shorts and flip-flops to watch whilst I was still chasing a small ball around a big field. Above all, though, the body was telling me that my time was nearly up. I'd been told that things can go downhill rapidly in the fourth decade, and although I thought 35 sounded young, the morning after a game it felt anything but.

What was most frustrating about this was that I was in serious nick with bat and ball. I'd worked out my game as a batsman and felt I could read situations well and bat accordingly. I didn't net often, but when I did it was often against the Curran brothers at Wellington College (until Sam got a bit slippery and started to find the ridge in the school nets with alarming regularity, threatening the three fingers I hadn't already broken in my career). Also, with the ball, I could have it 'on a string' for a short spell, but after around eight or nine overs, my shoulder would refuse to reach the vertical, and then the ball would just slide out and be easy meat for the batsmen. Not to mention that nagging toe inflammation which had been diagnosed as gout several years before, but which was now re-diagnosed as a *hallux valgus* – a type of bunion which made it very hard to run or walk.

I'd also stopped playing regular league cricket as the goodwill had run out at school and I was expected now to coach and umpire on Saturdays. This was OK, but I still got frustrated having to watch schoolboys fail to light up some incredible grounds at places like Eton, Tonbridge, Marlborough and Radley when I felt I could be playing my own competitive cricket. And so I got out of match practice, too. By the time Dorset reached their penultimate fixture away to Devon at Exmouth, I had to travel on my own by train, and catching sight of myself alone in the fading light, drinking from a can of cider in an empty carriage whist my wife and kids were at home, I realised that perhaps there was more to life than this game I loved.

But like a birdie on the last hole which makes up for a round of hacking about the golf course, I bowled one of my best spells ever on the first morning to go into lunch with two for spit and our arch-rivals on the rack. Someone put the kiss of death on me and said I should clean up in the afternoon. And I ought to have done, but rather than tuck into the shepherd's pie, I spent the interval having my rotator cuff pummelled by our weightlifter-cum-physio just so I could get my arm over in the next session. I didn't get another wicket and was like a different bowler.

The next morning was when I knew I had to call it quits. Waking up on my back, I tried to roll over and felt like I'd been pinned to the bed. My right shoulder would not budge and there was just an amorphous achy lump where my arm had once been. No amount of stretching, showering, massaging or Deep Heat balm seemed to work and I was happy to watch as younger, more flexible athletes took their opportunity. In the end, we won the game, which was in fact the only time I'd played for a Dorset side to beat Devon in a three-day game, which felt sweet, but also like another omen.

The chairman at the time – Barry Lewis – still the record run-scorer for the county, urged me not to be rash, saying 'You're a long time retired' and nice things like I could still do a job and the team needed me as they rebuilt. And, of course, there was always the voice in my head which didn't want to give up (it wasn't my wife's voice, that much I do remember...)

Our last game was at home, back at Dean Park, which had now been sold and was looking likely to be made into a school playground or sold for housing. I can't tell you how sad this move was for so many people involved in Dorset and Hampshire cricket, and anyone just interested in English cultural history and heritage. But hey, that's 'progress', I guess. What it did mean was that Dorset would not play at the old ground again, and so there was something that just seemed fitting, a sort of poetic ring composition, for this to be my last game for Dorset too. I left it late to decide but I remember the exact moment I made my mind up. No one would have noticed, but finding myself at deep long-off (why?), I looked around at the place and made peace with the decision in the final overs of the second day.

Later that evening, I made a few calls to tell people that the next day I'd be retiring, and it was lovely to see that a number of people made the effort to turn out. My family all came – dad in the same spot as ever – and quite a number of ex-team-mates, some supporters I recognised and even, would you believe, some press. It wasn't quite the standing ovation at the Oval at the end of an Ashes series I'd dreamed about in my youth, but in its own way, it was lovely. Although I didn't make many runs, being caught by sheer fluke at short leg, all the Dorset players formed a guard of honour with their bats as I made my way off and everyone in the ground was on their feet. Not everyone gets to retire on their terms, so to walk off to this reception on a ground I'd made my home, where I'd watched my first game, where I'd picked up the championship trophy and where my wife had agreed to marry me was pretty special indeed.

To receive a letter from the Dorset committee some weeks later informing me that I'd been made a life member in recognition of my service to the club was the icing on the cake.

What Next?

Well, it turns out that cricket takes a bloody long time. Who knew? (Well, only every cricketer's wife or girlfriend ever.) I thought I'd miss the game terribly, but once I'd made the decision, it actually felt pretty good. I started to really enjoy umpiring those school games now I was not bitter that I was missing my own. Coaching was more fun and when I wasn't coaching, my family and I could plan to do all sorts of things.

We found out what actual people do if they don't play cricket. Such outlandish experiences as going to the park, having a picnic, heading to the beach, realising you still had friends who didn't hang around musty old pavilions week in, week out during the best months of the year. And holidays. Proper summer holidays in places like France, Spain and Cornwall (yes, there's apparently more to Cornwall and Devon than Redruth or Bovey Tracy CC).

I got into running and ran two marathons – one in Rome and one in Salisbury – and would have run more had it not been for the bunion. And I could even contemplate a career move not just away from the south coast, but away from England entirely.

It's not an exaggeration to say that for almost 30 years, cricket was my life. And I wouldn't give any of that back. But now cricket is behind me, apart from the odd MCC game and friendly, I feel like I've been given a second life and I can choose what to do with it. Hell, I may even become a writer.

Postscript

AFTER RETIRING from what one might consider 'serious cricket' in 2015, I feared I would miss it hugely. I always thought I'd play on forever, still winkling out league batsmen, even in perhaps the second team or a lower league, well into my fifties and sixties. But I gave myself the first year virtually completely off, playing maybe a couple of low-key MCC fixtures, and I didn't miss it at all. But like a virus, or addiction even, the game remained dormant deep under my skin, waiting for the chance to pounce.

In 2020, we took the decision to move the family to Hong Kong, to an international boarding school. Yes, right in the middle of the Covid pandemic and when the UK headlines were full of protests and unrest in the former British territory, we decided to opt for the biggest upheaval of our lives. That's a whole other story, but wouldn't you know, within two months of the move, and still recovering from a fortnight's quarantine, I found myself in the nets at Hong Kong Cricket Club and committing to the next four seasons. Granted, the fringe benefits of family membership, with a swimming pool, bowling alley, golf simulator and no fewer than six bars and restaurants did sway the decision (truly, if Carlsberg made cricket clubs, this would be it). But say it quietly, and don't let on to the other half, the biggest draw for me was getting those whites on and that ball back in my hand. Three balls into my debut, my arm-ball found the edge and was pouched by slip. After a punch of the air and some high-fives in the huddle, it felt like I'd never been away.

Also available at all good book stores

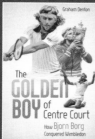

9781785317774

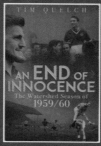

9781785317583

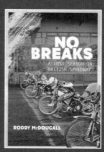

9781785317729

9781785317576

9781785318238

9781785317859

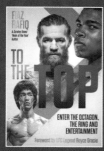

9781785318856

9781785317811

9781785317767

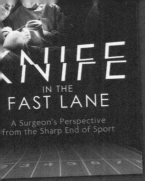
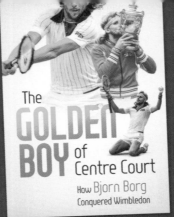
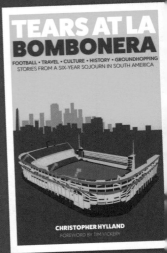